THE HOPI SURVIVAL KIT

Thomas E. Mails is the author of ten books on Native American individuals and cultures including *Mystic Warriors of the Plains* (which served as the primary sourcebook for the epic film, *Dances With Wolves*), *The Pueblo Children of Earth Mother, Fools Crow—Wisdom and Power, The Cherokee People,* and *Hotevilla, Hopi Shrine of the Covenant, Microcosm of the World.*

THE HOPI SURVIVAL KIT

THOMAS E. MAILS

PENGUIN COMPASS

PENGUIN BOOKS
Published by the Penguin Group
Penguin Group (USA) Inc., 375 Hudson Street, New York, New York 10014, U.S.A.
Penguin Books Ltd, 80 Strand, London WC2R 0RL, England
Penguin Books Australia Ltd, 250 Camberwell Road, Camberwell, Victoria 3124, Australia
Penguin Books Canada Ltd, 10 Alcorn Avenue, Toronto, Ontario, Canada M4V 3B2
Penguin Books India (P) Ltd, 11 Community Centre, Panchsheel Park, New Delhi – 110 017, India
Penguin Books (N.Z.) Ltd, Cnr Rosedale and Airborne Roads, Albany, Auckland, New Zealand
Penguin Books (South Africa) (Pty) Ltd, 24 Sturdee Avenue,
Rosebank, Johannesburg 2196, South Africa

Penguin Books Ltd, Registered Offices: 80 Strand, London WC2R 0RL, England

First published in the United States of America by Welcome Rain 1997
Published in Arkana 1997

20 19 18 17 16 15 14 13 12

Library of Congress Catalog Card Number: 96-61237
ISBN 0 14 01.9545 9

Printed in the United States of America
Set in Times Roman

Dedication

To all of the Traditionalists who for nearly a thousand years preserved the message from the Creator that will enable the planet and us to survive

Table of Contents

THE HOPI SURVIVAL KIT

CHAPTER 1

The Secret of Land and Life

Techqua Ikachi! is the creed of the Hopi Traditionalists. In its English translation, what it means is "blending with the land and celebrating life." The traditionalists' aim has always been to achieve this for themselves and everyone else in the world. About A. D. 1100 the way to accomplish it was given to them by Maasaw, the awesome Guardian of the Earth. For the next 750 years, the people blended and celebrated, living in peace and happiness through a Spanish intrusion that lasted for 140 years, through constant depredations by Apaches and Navajos, and through most of the normal problems human beings face in life. With this impressive reputation, the Hopi are broadly known today as the peaceful people, and outsiders living in a world beset with turmoil have often wondered how they achieved it. It was only as this present century began that the Hopi situation changed. As the White government steadfastly turned the people away from Maasaw's teachings, peace and happiness was turned away with it, and doing what was necessary to achieve the Hopi aim for the rest of the world was frustrated as well. We find that human acts and choices have a powerful effect on the direction, pace, and intensity of what happens on the grand stage of life. They also affect the timing. Even little-noticed things can do this. In testimony to this truth, the following incident in Hopi history is one of several that has delayed, by nearly a century, the delivery of an urgent secret of survival to a world that has been recklessly endangering itself.

In the year 1921, gentle, stoic Yukiuma, chief of the Hopi village of Hotevilla, was in prison for the eighth time in fourteen years. Sometimes he was locked up in cells with murderers, robbers, and child molesters—individuals who had committed the most appalling crimes in America. He even spent a year on infamous Alcatraz Island. His offense in each instance was his refusal to sign a United States Government "paper" giving it permission to remove village children from their homes and educate them in distant boarding schools. All Hotevilla Village fathers rejected the demand and were similarly imprisoned. Only old people, mothers, and a few older children were left behind to continue as best they could.

There were no trials concerning these actions and consequences. Parents were not asked why they objected. Justice was simple and direct. Over a period of years, Hotevilla fathers were at intervals herded forty miles to the agency jail in Keams Canyon, where they were chained in pairs and then sent out to work on reservation roads in the hottest and the coldest weather. Burdened in this way, they labored with picks, hammers, and explosives. At night they were chained in groups of six so that, if one had to go to the bathroom, the others had to come with him. Soap was mixed into their food to make them sick. All they needed to do to end their misery was to sign a copy of "that paper."

Each time they were freed and returned home, they were arrested again and imprisoned. It was a vicious process that went on for more than two decades. Why the Hotevilla men never gave in is both a miracle and a question demanding an answer. Since U.S. soldiers and Navajo policemen took the children by armed force anyway, nothing justified the imprisonments. But what the United States Government really wanted was to break the last of the Hopi spirit and resistance to conversion. From the year 1906, Hotevilla was at the top of the administration's most-wanted list, and its steadfastness in refusal was an embarrassment to the Government. Long before this day in 1921, the other Hopi villages had capitulated—even the mother village, Oraibi, had lowered its flag. Only Hotevilla stood firm, and Yukiuma was its backbone. Vengeful school principals lashed out by entering Hotevilla homes uninvited, verbally abusing parents, smashing pottery used for cooking and eating, and cutting blankets needed for winter warmth into shreds. They made surprise winter raids so fleeing children could be tracked in the snow. Even though Hopi children received no physical discipline at home, the White teachers whipped the children in class whenever they felt an example needed to be set. When schools were placed near a village, even little and poorly clothed children were forced to walk to classes in mid-winter across rocky mesa terrain that was covered with snow and ice.

Yukiuma was a little man. Like most Hopi people in those days, he stood no taller than five feet and weighed at most ninety pounds. He was never a physical threat and, except for hunting, never carried a weapon. Mahogany-skinned, naked except for a breechclout, and looking half-starved, he sat this day in the Government Agent's swivel chair, his knees doubled under his chin and his skinny arms folded around them. His position was like that of a child in its mother's womb, and it was symbolic, since as an adult he lived, heart and soul, in the womb of Mother Earth.

Only three years before, the United States and its European allies had won a great war against Germany. It was one in which Hopi men, even though they could not vote, were forced to fight. Yukiuma thought about that while he smiled pleasantly at two White men—an army colonel named Scott, and the agency superintendent named Crane, who stood to one side and talked about him. Any Traditionalist who knew the Hopi prophecies could have told them years before that the great war was coming, and even who it would be fought against. Their ancestors learned about the earth-shaking engagement from Maasaw 800 years before it started, and handed down from generation to generation an astonishing amount of even more important information having to do with the Hopis and the world. They were ready to tell all of these things to the first Whites to come to Hopi country in the 1800s, but when they experienced how the Whites behaved toward them, they decided against it. In consequence, information that was not intended to be a secret became one.

The Agent made reference to the wrinkled and stained sheet of paper he held in one hand, extending it toward Yukiuma. But the chief shook his head and turned away. While he did not understand their English words, he knew what they were saying about him. Translators had told him that his captors thought he was "a filthy, dried-up chimpanzee," and a "mild lunatic" who would rather wear a g-string than accept the comforts of modern life. Since whoever got Yukiuma to sign that paper would have a feather in his cap, the Government employees kept trying. But his inflexibility, and that of his usually gentle followers, was frustrating, and it comforted the officials little to know that even when the chief was taken a decade before to Washington, D.C. he was not persuaded in the slightest. White missionaries had sought again and again to sway him and accomplished nothing. How, the two men wondered aloud now, had this "little spider" developed such an impenetrable shell, and why in fourteen years of trying had no one been able to crack it?

Part of their problem lay in the fact that they let what they saw affect their judgment. They believed that no people who lived as simply and poorly as the Hopi could possibly offer anything worthwhile to the burgeoning outside world, let alone a message of greatest magnitude. In particular, they asked themselves, how could a dirty, unkempt, unschooled beggar, the leader of a pacifist people who had accomplished nothing of significance, know anything that was vital to world survival? It was plain to these officials that the only hope the Hopi had was to learn to live as Whites.

So they had not come to the chief or to any Hopi to listen. And, as a result, they failed to learn the secret of living in peace. They never discovered that Yukiuma's ancestors had made a solemn vow that they would always follow the pattern of life their Creator had given them. And they never discovered that included in the vow was the promise that, when certain warning signs indicated that the close of the Fourth Cycle of the world had begun, the Hopis would pass on specific warnings and a way of survival. But again for Whites, the idea that such information could come from the Hopis was an impossibility. The Creator would never choose such a "primitive" people for so vital a role in history.

Understandably then, when highly educated White anthropologists forced their way into the Hopi worship chambers at the turn of the century, it was to photograph and write about their enchanting, "primitive" rituals. They were certain that, in capturing these picturesque and esoteric ceremonies, they were recording the only thing that was really important about the

Hopis. When the natives saw that the intruders' minds were closed to anything else, they withheld information of utmost value to the earth and its inhabitants. Silence became the standard response to any questions about Hopi understandings.

Here in the Agency jail two decades later we see the response in operation again, as the scorn of Whites for Hopi understandings and ways continues. Yukiuma concludes that, like the scientists, the colonel and the Agent do not deserve to hear the secret of blending with the land and celebrating life. He intuitively knows the time still has not come to tell the outside world what it desperately needs to know.

The scrawny chief did hint at it one day when he said to the Agent, "You see, I am doing this as much for you as for my own people. Suppose I should not protest your orders. Suppose I should willingly accept the ways of the Bahannas. Immediately, the great snake would turn over, and the sea would rush in, and we would all be drowned. You too. I am therefore protecting you." But the agent made no attempt to understand. He was too well educated to believe in awesome floods and giant snakes, and recognizing this, Yukiuma did not pursue the matter.

So this quiet day in history ended and time moved on. A second world war that was also predicted came and went. In truth, prophecies of all kinds were being fulfilled regularly, and the Traditionalist Hopis knew it. Even seeing that the countries of the world were moving ever deeper into trouble didn't move them to reveal what they knew. They kept the greater part of their secret to themselves. After Yukiuma died, his son, Dan Katchongva wrote a little book in 1972 that outlined some of the principal thoughts of the secret, but that was all. Writers Frank Waters and Micha Titiev gathered small bits of information about the secret during their years with the Hopis. After they wrote what they knew about it, it was a tantalizing mystery known to exist, but whose details were still hidden. Hopi delegations went four times to the United Nations headquarters in New York City, where they tried without success to tell the secret to its members. Over an eleven year period, five of the elder Traditionalists wrote a newsletter to warn other Hopis about the consequences of abandoning the secret, but so many of the people had embraced White beliefs and ways that the effort fell on deaf ears. The Tribal Council controlled the schools, money and the jobs now, and that was all that mattered.

Seventy-five years of silence flowed slowly by like a meandering river. One by one the keepers of the secret left this world, taking what they knew about the secret with them, and went to live with the Kachina spirits. Meanwhile, the more fortunate areas of the outside world prospered richly, but at the cost of mistakes, the consequences of which accumulated in time to the point of threatening its very life. In reaction to this, some people in the outside world began to look and to work for solutions. They also became listeners. The Creator and Maasaw observed this, and set certain wheels in motion at Hopi Land.

Then one day in May, 1993, I answered an invitation to come to the remote Hopi reservation and meet the man who would turn out to be the last remaining keeper of the secret—the only person still alive who knew everything about it and was able to pass it on.

One-hundred years old at the time, he was so like Yukiuma in size and attitude it was amazing, and the second day after we met, he chose to give me the secret to give to you. On hearing it, I knew immediately that it stands with the most important revelations ever given by the Creator, for among other things, it tells us why certain events are happening in the world today, what is coming soon, and how we can influence and survive it. This secret includes awesome prophecies, sublime instructions, and dire warnings, that together make up a unique survival kit. In the midst of what is happening now and is certain to occur in the near future, it can enrich and save your life, rescue the earth, and is quite probably the only thing that can deliver the world from extinction.

Hopi Land, situated in the northeastern corner of Arizona, is so old and so infused with spiritual life that it is hallowed ground. It is bathed in an aura of the sacred, and carries with it an ever present possibility of the unexpected. Visiting there does strange things to your senses, and the minute you cross the reservation border something unusual begins to happen to you. It is as though you have moved into a different time frame and are in touch with a myriad of new senses and deities. As my friend Katherine Cheshire and I traveled toward it from Flagstaff, Arizona, in her 4x4 truck on an afternoon in May, 1993, my mind was a jumble of thoughts, most of which appeared to me at that time to have little to do with the Hopis. I knew nothing about Yukiuma, and nothing of consequence about the secret. Most of my meandering thoughts were what most people would, had they been there to hear them, believe to be far fetched. Among other things, I reflected on the fact that in numerous countries the world is in its most serious trouble ever today. Facing this global emergency is a first priority for everyone. And without asking myself why I should even have any such ideas at this particular time, I found myself wondering whether my visit to this ancient, remote and honored place might have anything to do with that.

Before long, the first of the flat-topped red and brown mesas that identify the Reservation area began to loom in the distance, and overhead in the deep blue sky a few white clouds followed us as though there were Hopi Kachinas in them who were watching us. The highway was flat, the asphalt paving was in good condition, and the curves were broad. The truck did not sway, yet I shifted around in my seat like an anxious child and clung tightly to the padded handle bolted to the roof. I sensed that I was on the verge of something important, yet hadn't the remotest idea what it was or why I should even think about it.

A half-hour later we rounded a bend and headed northwest, not going far before Katherine slowed the truck down. I noted that we were just across from the place where the village of Kykotsmovi's main street meets the highway. As she deftly turned the truck off of the highway and in the opposite direction, I looked back at the village. Except for the somewhat imposing box-like and rust-colored tribal headquarters building, Kykotsmovi was in no way impressive. Judging by its architecture, you would never know that Hopis even lived there.

As we bumped along at five miles an hour over as rough and jarring a dirt road as anyone is ever going to experience, I found myself wondering again whether or not the invitation was a coincidence or fated. I have mixed feelings about such things as fate, but in light of all that has happened since that time, I see nothing accidental in it, including the timing. If the trip had waited until now, none of the things that have been accomplished since then could have been done. And, the future of the world would have been for you and me a far worse one than it will be.

"Come and help us," Manuel Hoyungowa's letter had pleaded as a follow-up to two lengthy telephone conversations.

Help these particular Hopis with what, I found myself asking. What could I do for them that they couldn't do for themselves? If there were serious problems, I hadn't learned anything about them during the time when, ten years earlier, I had visited the Reservation on numerous occasions while I was researching what became my two-volume series on the Pueblo Indians. The dangers of being only an outside observer can be seen here! The festering problems and searing divisions at Hopi escaped me entirely. More importantly, I did not learn anything at all about the Sacred Covenant and the critical need to proclaim its message to the world.

This time though the situation would be different. I would be visiting Covenant Land itself, the western end of the Reservation where Hopis live on the third of three mesas that contain the twelve Hopi villages.

Here, out in the quiet farming lands of the village and under a pale summer moon, I would on this very night meet the man who above all I had come to see. Although he is an exceptional individual, he is much too humble to think of himself in this way. Since most of you will probably never meet in person an ancient gladiator whose only armor is that of Maasaw, and whose only weapon is peace, I want to describe this one to you.

His name is Dan Evehema. Born in Old Oraibi in 1893, he has a deeply etched and mahogany-colored face that is topped by a thick and unruly mane of silver-colored hair. He stands amazingly straight and, as a result of a century of hard work, squares his broad shoulders like a marine standing at attention. But he speaks of himself and other Elderly Elders as "gnarled old roots." In appearance and

toughness he surely is that. Yet he is a root filled with remarkable energy for his venerable age, having a quick mind, a ready smile, and dark eyes that sparkle whenever he laughs—which is often. Like the Hopis of old, Dan Evehema is a peaceful and a happy man—qualities which defy the fact that he has been honed by adversity. His entire life has been plagued by unfair intrusions of the worst possible kind.

I was astounded to learn that he still works in his fields every day, either alone or side by side with White friends and Hopi relatives who plant, cultivate, and harvest corn and other crops. He is also a well known medicine person and healer. And when he is not farming or healing, he is actively engaged at Hotevilla Village with the other members of his Roadrunner and Greasewood Clans in ceremonial or political activities. In these he is always a leader, and undoubtedly the most knowledgeable man present—an irreplaceable repository of ancient lore. This much is certain. However he has lived, and whatever he has practiced over the past hundred years, has sustained him in Fountain-of-Youth fashion, remarkably well, and it is worth looking into. I do that under the heading, "The Ark's Instructions," and what we learn there has everything to do with survival.

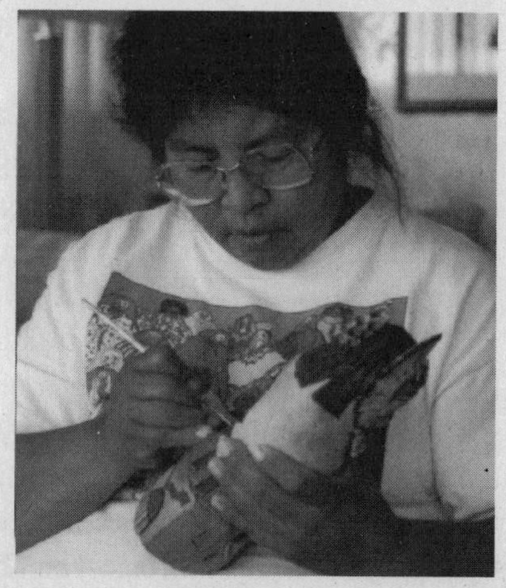

Dan is cared for by his sister's daughter, Susie Lomatska, who is herself an exceptional person, a wonderful carver of kachina dolls, and among the staunchest of the younger Traditionalists. Dan lives on his ancestral property with Susie, her two children, and her Navajo husband, just six or so miles—a trip made infinitely longer by the roughness of the road—from Kykotsmovi.

Their flat-roofed house is small by most outside-world standards. It is a patched-together building made in its oldest part of mortared sandstones. In its youngest part it consists of plywood, tarpaper and any other material that has been conveniently at hand. None of it is painted, and none is finished off. Except for a propane stove and a gasoline driven generator that provides small amounts of electricity for short periods of time, there are none of the conveniences the modern world takes for granted—no running water, no lights except in the kitchen, no air conditioning, and no indoor plumbing facilities. No one in the family has their own bedroom. Winter heat comes from a single pot-bellied stove located in the living room. The furniture has seen better days, and the upholstered pieces are covered by blankets. Despite the limitations, everyone is happy at Dan's home, and it is a warm place to visit. Many people do—both Hopis and outsiders. Whatever food is available is freely shared, and there is seldom a time when someone has not come from near or far to visit with Dan and Susie.

If there are no guests present, Dan goes out alone in the late afternoon to pray to Maasaw, asking him to watch over the family through the night. In the chapters ahead, you will learn who exactly this important deity is, and how he goes about this "watching."

If the generator has fuel, Dan and the family might watch a little television to see what is going on in the world. Otherwise, he goes to bed shortly after sundown. He is up at sunrise and goes out to pray to the Creator to guide him through the day. He does this at the foot of the mesa, where Evehema family members have prayed for generations. Then he has breakfast.

Dan has an excellent appetite that is kindled by Susie's expertly cooked food. Susie has a robust son whose craving for food is as ravenous as that of most growing boys. While we were eating one morning, I noticed that he had his eye on several links of sausage that still sat on a plate that was in the middle of the table. But he wanted to be polite, and bided his time before making his move. When he did, he was chagrined to find that Dan had already wolfed them down.

Dan's farming fields are across the road from the house and readily accessible. He can walk to them in a few minutes. They lie in a broad and flat wash that collects the rain water as it comes rushing down from the plateau above. The rich and fertile sandy soil, so fine a handful of it feels like silk, absorbs the water like a sponge. Once the corn has been planted, the moisture that has already settled in the wash gives it its first boost toward the surface.

There is a separate ranch extension where livestock is raised. Courtesy of the Peabody Coal Mine which is exhausting the underground water as it uses it to transport the coal to a processing plant in Nevada, the watering basin has gone dry, and with hand-watering the only alternative, this part of Dan's work has diminished considerably.

Except for moderate dress clothing and a limited amount of silver jewelry donned on festive days, he wears the plain work outfits of ranch hands or farmers everywhere—checkered woolen shirts with long sleeves, belted Levi pants with rolled up cuffs, and heavy work shoes. Now and then he uses a colorful bandanna or a cap to hold his hair in place. In the winter he adds a hip-length, black woolen coat with a rolled collar, and a knitted wool hat.

For a century, Dan has lived off this land and been self-sufficient. Money is of little consequence to him. If any comes his way, he uses it to purchase things that, because of Reservation changes, he is no longer able to produce. Most of it goes to the family. Until we began our work together, he had never possessed more than one hundred dollars at any given time. That was a gift some White person had given him years ago in return for information about Hopi farming practices.

As you would expect, there have been other outstanding male Hopis among the Elderly Elders, but all except one of these have put on the "cloud mask" and gone to live with the Kachina spirits. I introduce you to some of the most notable in Chapter 5. Through long years of personal experience, each of them, along with some Traditionalist Hopi women, became an eloquent Keeper and source of information about Traditionalist Hopi feelings and history.

To say what I do about Dan is one thing. To be with him is another, for he has an aura of profound spirituality about him, and when his eyes capture yours, they look so deeply into you that you feel nothing is hidden from him. When in the 1970s I was with my friend Fools Crow, the last Ceremonial Chief of the Teton Sioux—and at Pine Ridge, South Dakota, wrote the story of his remarkable life—I thought I would never again meet a Native American equal to him. But Dan Evehema is. He and Fools Crow have to be counted among the greatest of the Native American leaders to live during this 20th century. Although Fools Crow died in 1989, he is steadily gaining this reputation both at home and in the outside world. Dan is not looking for honors, but his will nevertheless come in due time. I just want you to have the sense of him before we move on, and to be able to see him in your mind's eye when you reflect on the material that follows.

Katherine and I met late that evening with Dan, Susie, and two other Hopi men Dan had invited. It was a smaller group than

I expected, but I learned later that Dan wanted the meeting to be private. One of these men was Manuel Hoyungowa. The other one, whom I will not name, was to my surprise overbearing and dominated the conversation from the minute we started. Most of all he made it painfully clear that he considered himself to be the spokesman for the Traditionalists, and that any outsider who helped them would be of his choosing and subject to his authority. Since I was not one of these, he concluded that this meeting would be the end of it. I was puzzled, because I had read about his efforts on behalf of the Traditionalists, and assumed he was as concerned about the situation as anyone. When he finished and the others said nothing, Katherine and Susie were plainly upset, and I concluded that I had wasted my time coming. So I said very little in reply, and resolved that I would return to California the next day. By then, and in spite of my wondering about so many things on the way in, I was in a "who-needs-them" mood, and ready to bail out.

Dan was quiet also, and seemed to be dozing much of the time. That didn't help me either. But once the two men had left, and before we parted company, Dan roused himself, laid his hand on my arm in a comforting way, and said in a very friendly manner that he would talk with me in the morning. Encouraged by that promise, I had a good night's sleep in the trailer home Katherine keeps on his property.

I was up early. The air was crisp and there was no wind. It was one of those clear and sparkling days that are so typical of the high mesa country. As I walked around the property, the rich smell of sage, juniper and cedar hung on my shoulders like a heavy and pungent cloak. I was followed by two short-haired mongrel dogs—one black and one brown—who were decidedly curious as to who I was. I ignored their sniffing as best I could, while I paused to look at the ruins of ancient stone houses on the mesa side and top above. Coming as I do from an urban area, I was particularly aware of how silent it was. I had forgotten how much I enjoyed this tranquility when I was at the First and Second Mesa villages a decade earlier. We city dwellers grow so accustomed to noise that we are puzzled when there isn't any. But silence is still a pervading characteristic of Hopi Land. It is something that comes from Soyal, when they begin their ceremonial cycle. In all but the most modernized villages, the people walk softly and talk in muted tones. A feeling of overwhelming reverence permeates the air. There is the uncanny sensation that the spirits of generations past are hovering around and influencing what the people think and do. Perhaps it is the antiquity of the aging villages. I'm not certain what it is. But I do know that when no one is looking, you have a powerful urge to touch the stone walls that in themselves testify to eternal things. In old Oraibi itself, you can touch walls nearly a thousand years old. Where else, other than in the pueblo ruins, can you do this in America today?

The dogs followed me to the house, and sat down to wait while I went in. After a Bahanna-type, family-style breakfast Susie prepared in her cluttered kitchen, which is really the center of the house, we stayed at the kitchen table and talked. I was pleased to learn that Dan had not been dozing at all at the meeting the night before and admired my restraint. In fact he thought it was an admirable quality, very Hopi-like, and the best thing I could have done under the circumstances. It seems that the unnamed gentleman who spoke was not representing Dan at all. He was only representing himself.

I understood though why he had been invited to the meeting. He lives in Kykotsmovi and is a much-traveled, flamboyant individual. Other than as a spectator, however, he does not participate in the ceremonial life at Hotevilla, and does not provoke adverse relationships with the Tribal Council. He is, therefore, sort of a cross-section of what is going on. Nevertheless, Dan considers him a friend, and wanted to gauge his reaction to the meeting with me. As you will see, Dan had already made up his mind about what needed to be done. He was just measuring things to see how it might all fit together. His status is such that no one else is in a position to tell him what he will or will not do or say. He has, we outsiders might say, "paid his dues," and "earned his spurs." That is why other Traditionalists refer to him as "a high priest," and why any film maker or writer who comes to Hopi Land would give most anything to woo Dan's participation in whatever they hope to do. Even Leigh Jenkins, the assertive Director of the Hopi Office of Cultural Preservation, knows that where Hopi religion is concerned there is no one else who can compare with him.

Manuel was invited because he had issued the formal invitation to me, is a leader-in-training, and because he has become one of the official spokesmen for the Traditionalists. Dan wanted him to at least sense what was about to happen. He was, and is, hoping that Manuel will measure up to his potential as a leader of the Traditionalists who will need to carry on the Traditional ways after Dan departs.

At this point I learned from Dan the true magnitude of the problems faced by the Traditionalists at Hotevilla, and what type of help they needed. The village had begun as the place where the Covenant was preserved, and, among other things, the cycle of yearly activities kept the world in balance with enough harmony to survive. It became a Mother Village, a shrine, a microcosm of the world, and the home of the last of the Keepers of this Covenant of greatest magnitude. But powerful forces led by the Hopi Tribal Council and the Office of Cultural Preservation were, as the Whites had done in Yukiuma's time, not only obstructing the keeping of the Covenant, they were also impeding the issuance of the secret but urgent message to the world. Because of this, once peaceful Hotevilla had become a battleground where two worlds clashed, in a war of differing desires and opinions.

Long before Dan and Susie finished telling me about these astonishing developments, any thought of leaving had evaporated and I sat spellbound. I learned also that he had seen some of my books, including *The Pueblo Children of the Earth Mother*, and liked them. In truth, my books had stimulated him to ask me to do the Traditionalist Hopis a special and vital favor. Being more qualified than any other Hopi to make the request, he told me how very much he wanted me to write a book that would deliver the secret message to the world. In his mind, the decision to make this request came even before I arrived, for he knew something incredible about himself that made it necessary. He believed my book would be an answer to years of the Traditionalists' prayers—that it was part of the Creator's plan. The book would accomplish the one thing the Elders themselves had not been able to do

Since he did not say so at the time, this "something incredible" Dan knew about himself only later became clear to me. Of the more than 100 amazing Hopi prophecies given to the Hopis in A.D. 1100, one of them points directly to Dan Evehema. That may seem to be a far-fetched claim, but when you have read *The Hopi Survival Kit* you will agree that the prophecies include this last of the ancient gladiators. In the final chapter, I tell you which prophecy it is and why Dan is the one who is designated there. The reason I mention it now is that he recognized this himself, and it was why he knew the Hotevilla book had to be written. When I visited him just a few weeks ago to deliver the first printed copy of the book, he said as he leafed through its pages, "This is good! I am the last one, all of the rest are gone." Perhaps you can imagine what it would be like to be singled out for such an honor, and then bear the weight of fulfilling it.

As we talked that first time, it became apparent that if we did not dodge issues, such a book as we were considering could stir up a hornet's nest of responses on the reservation—particularly from those who do not want the public to know that there is controversy and skullduggery. Specifically, these would be the Hopi Tribal Council and the Office of Cultural Preservation—who are described by the Traditionalists as two-hearteds who seek to live in two worlds at once, as opposed to one-hearteds who follow the single Covenant path. Two-hearteds include the Council's most avid supporters, together with the officials of several U.S. Government agencies, and those Whites, called "Bahannas" by the Traditionalists, who still seek to take advantage of the Hopis. Considering the opponents involved, I believed that if what we were doing became known, Dan and Susie surely would be harassed and threatened. They agreed that this would happen. So Dan, Susie, Katherine, and I made a pact of secrecy. We would say nothing to anyone else about the book until we were ready to print it. If the Council moved to do anything drastic then, a whole lot of people in the world would know why, and the Council would face their wrath.

I wish you could have seen the four of us there in that quiet, remote place, clasping hands like a group of conniving conspirators as we made our vow—cultures miles apart, a solemn old Hopi root, his equally determined niece, and two somber Whites who knew how privileged they were to be a part of what was going on. However melodramatic that moment was, it was a bargain we kept until the book Dan and I co-authored, *Hotevilla, Hopi Shrine of the Covenant, Microcosm of the World,* was printed in November of 1995.

Most valuable of the things Dan gave me to work with were copies of newsletters entitled *Techqua Ikachi, Land and Life*. Two were all he had in his home, but there were more. He told me they were part of forty-four issues that four other Elders and he had put together during the years 1975–1986. One of their purposes was to answer allegations made against the Elder Traditionalist leaders by the Tribal Council. Another was to remind every Progressive and on-the-fence Hopi on the Reservation of their proud heritage and solemn responsibilities. So many of them had foolishly exchanged their traditional way of life for the White man's ways that a major crisis of culture and responsibility was brewing. Above all, the newsletters retold the ancient message Maasaw gave to the Hopis at Oraibi in A.D. 1100. In Chapter 4, I describe the delightful way in which these newsletters were clandestinely assembled. The heading on each of them expressed the magnificent Hopi creed I began this chapter with—magnificent because it is the essence of the secret.

He watched me carefully as I started to read the first one, and his face glowed when he saw my excitement. Why so? There was information here that was absolutely rare, and he saw that I recognized it.

Previous books written about the Hopis, including my own, contained little of this kind of information, for this was deeply personal, encompassing to an amazing degree, and in places as sharp in its wisdom as the blade of a freshly honed knife. While less than professional in terms of modern literary standards, the newsletters are filled with astonishing information of a kind no one outside the Traditionalist Hopi family itself—the people who had lived it—could ever have put together. Along with the broader information, there were intimate things about the Hopis that we need to know. Think of it! What was missing here comprised nearly eleven years of personal and honest insights into the Traditionalist Hopi mind and teachings by five of the wisest Hopi leaders from Hotevilla. It is a treasury of information compiled by men whose life-long goal was to carry on a superb heritage. Among information having to do with thoughts and events at Hopi Land, it contained PROPHECIES, INSTRUCTIONS and WARNINGS that were to be revealed to the entire world when it became apparent to the Elders—as it ought to be to us as we look at what is happening in the world today—that the closing of the Fourth Cycle of the world is underway. By "closing," the Hopis do not mean that the end of the closing will be as though a final door has slammed. But what the prophecies do say is that this cycle of the world will so effectively close that future historians will be able to say it was a time of making a clean transition from one cycle to the next.

When we consider these newsletters, we are in a sense stepping onto holy ground. As a Lutheran pastor, I have always been impressed by the Apostle Paul's statement to the Ephesians that, even while we are alive, we are taken up to sit at the right hand of God so that we can look at the world through His eyes. It is not difficult to appreciate the difference this perspective offers us. In the same way the newsletters lift us up to give us a position from which we can view through infinite eyes both the Hopi and our own world of the past, present, and future. What gift could be more special!

Yet when they were first distributed within Hopi Land itself, few of the newsletters were kept. Anglicized Hopis thought they were outmoded and not worth keeping. But someone else kept them, and let me propose for you a possibility for their surprising preservation. When I received these first copies, only ten years had passed since the last issue had been published, yet it was as though all of them for some mysterious reason had quickly vanished from sight, covering themselves over like a ground beetle does when it retreats into its earthen borough. Since the material was so vital, I asked myself why this should be, and why just the opposite had not happened. And then as I pondered the question in bed one night, the answer came to me. While the Elders believed that the greatest need for the newsletters was when they were written, they were in fact destined for another time. That time is today, when deteriorating circumstances at both Hopi Land and in the rest of the world finally have gotten our attention. We see at last what is going on everywhere and are ready to listen. So Maasaw, who knew this would happen, did it. He covered them over and shielded them from view in the home of a White woman who lives in Sedona, Arizona, where we found them. Maasaw did it so that they could show themselves at the propitious time, and not be irretrievably lost. Why else would they only be discovered and broadly published now?

The day I left the ranch that first time, the last Gladiator signed a letter authorizing me to write the book. He also made for me a special prayer feather through which the Creator would guide me as I wrote. As you would expect, I prize it greatly, and I include photographs of it at the end of the chapter. Each time I have been stymied as I worked, I have contemplated and touched the feather for a few minutes. Through it the Creator has given me some very special insights to pass on to you.

I also keep next to the feather an actual lump of Peabody Mine coal which was sent to me by a special friend named Sierra. I like to think that the feather is putting a curse on the coal. When I was with Dan recently, he said that Peabody is supposed to "stop in December of 1995," but he did not know the exact meaning of this news he had heard—whether the mining was to stop completely, or whether an alternative method for transporting the coal to Nevada would be used.

Beside my desk, too, is an ear of Hopi blue corn, an ear of

white corn, some white cornmeal from Dan's own supply, and some sacred tobacco from a batch used by the Hotevilla Traditionalists in their Kiva rituals. All of these things keep me in a mood to produce something worthwhile for the Traditionalists of Hotevilla.

As soon as I had all of the newsletters, I spread them out on the floor of my living room to get an overview. At this point I saw they exceeded my fondest hopes. They were an absolute treasure. As I reorganized and pieced together all of the information I had, and added Dan's personal comments and answers to my questions, I continued to be amazed. It included not just a few, but all of the Hopi prophecies. It was loaded with insights into the Traditionalist Hopi mind and Pattern of Life. Even paragraphs that at first glance appeared to duplicate other material included candid new insights to help our understanding. When I appended the great and urgent message to this, I knew that what I had was in no way ordinary. It was a serendipitous find of greatest magnitude, and if everything it claims proves to be true, it can take its rightful place as one of the greatest finds in world history.

It does not matter whether anyone out here in the world believes this great secret the moment they first hear it. As Dan explains, the prophecies will prove themselves by their continued fulfillment. "Your own experience," he said, meaning everyone's, "will tell you." The principal point to bear in mind is that we do not have long to wait for proofs that can neither be denied nor ignored. Hopi prophecy indicates that within our lifetimes—yours and mine—most, if not all, of the predicted "chickens" will come home to roost.

Recognize that this amazing Hopi secret I am about to tell you is not fantasy or fiction. It deals with real people in real life situations, and it deals with real events. It will provoke considerable thought, and, more than that, it offers you something that has for nearly a thousand years proven itself in actual life. As such, we don't want to make bad judgments and miss it as others have in the past—for example the colonel, the Agent, other Government officials, the missionaries, the White schoolteachers and tourists, and, above all, the White scientists.

Many of those who have gone to Hopi Land in past years have been archaeologists, anthropologists, and ethnologists such as Frank Waters, Mischa Titiev, the Rev. Henry Voth, G. A. Dorsey, and Walter Fewkes. Others were Indian buffs whose interests lay in unearthing all of the esoteric secrets they could about Hopi religious life. Finding a primal culture still thriving in the midst of an industrialized and expanding America left all of these people giddy and enthralled. Imagine! For over 200 years of America's emerging industrial life, these natives had been nothing more than a rumor untouched. It was as though people living for millennia in a jungle suddenly had the trees torn away and stood there near-naked for the outside world to ogle.

The fascinated intruders simply had to dig into it and then tell the world about it. And they accomplished this with surprising success. Although the Hopis hated what the trespassers were doing and did everything they could to prevent the exposures, books abound today with descriptions of sacred Kiva paraphernalia and rites, and museum collections everywhere have large displays of Hopi religious materials. Yet right before the noses of the researchers was something vastly more important than ritual details and artifacts. It may be poetic justice that in their passionate efforts to expose sacred practices, the researchers shut themselves off from this greatest treasure of all—the Hopi and world survival kit. I think we can easily understand why resentful Hopis did not see fit to share this great secret with such insensitive people. The Kiva ceremonies that so entranced the intruders are indeed fascinating, but in the Hopi mind their performance is only a natural part of fulfilling a greater call by far.

The Hopi, for example, understand the matter of, and need for, "cycles of human existence." When the Mayans and the Hopis speak of the Four Cycles of the world, they normally illustrate this as a circle that is divided like a pie chart into four equal parts. Dan Evehema, in an intriguing departure from this norm, described the Four Cycles as "four layers of the wheel." He did not explain what he meant by this, and it took awhile for me to understand it. Finally, it became clear he was pointing out that the four cycles are not equal in length and turn at different speeds, for in Hopi understanding the pace and duration of each cycle is determined by the behavior and choices of human beings.

"Man's behavior," the Elders say, "is reflected in space and time."

Therefore, it is more accurate to portray the cycles as individual wheels, one above the other, mounted on an axle, or spindle. Then each wheel is free to turn at its own speed, and for as long as it endures. When each wheel, or cycle stops, after some unknown interval has taken place the next wheel begins to turn.

Three of these cycles have already opened and closed. The Fourth Cycle is in the closing process now. The unanswered question here is how the Fifth Cycle, or wheel, fits in. Does it stand alone on a new spindle, or is it the first of four more layers? The Hopi have no answer for this. Apparently, Maasaw did not tell them, although his statement that He would take over control of the world at the end of the Fourth Cycle makes it clear that there will be a Fifth Cycle. It is my guess that since decisions such as this actually rest with the Creator, additional cycles will depend on how people behave during the Fifth Cycle.

There were several reasons why we were anxious to get the *Hotevilla* book into print. One was, and still is, that despite Traditionalist objections, the Tribal Council and the U.S. Department of Health and Human Services are in the process of moving utilities into and modernizing Hotevilla, the Shrine of the Covenant. The Council has moved enough of its employees into the village to get the numbers they need to authorize the work. They have the money to do it, and they have the police to back them up. They have even paved the road from the highway to the edge of the village.

Possessing these utilities would not seem to be a problem for those of us who would not know how to live without such conveniences, but it is a problem for the Traditionalists of Hotevilla. The following chapters explain why it is a move that will undermine the spiritual energy that, although it is endangered, still exists today in the village, and which is needed for world balance and survival. Beyond this, if the buried Hotevilla mother-village marker, which you will soon read about, is destroyed by utility-ditch diggers, it will guarantee that an Armageddon-like war of the worst possible kind will occur soon, and that the end of the cycle will be a disastrous one. These are truths that need to be brought to world attention as soon as possible, so that people everywhere can react, and any other intrusions hosted by the Tribal Council can be undone. There are ways that global calamities—you will see what these are in the prophecies given in Chapter 7—can be both softened and pushed back in time.

Crisis! Because of delays caused by self-centered Whites and Hopi two-hearteds, the message the Traditionalists have wanted to reveal to the world has taken on a sense of urgency. It is long past the time when the world should have received it. Since the Fourth Cycle of the world is closing down, we must do everything we can as quickly as we can to influence its outcome. Time is short, very short. The secret revealed in this book tells us how we can influence the world's course by making right choices and changing our pattern of life.

While the secret is not religious, it is nevertheless something that is essential to survival, for it is a supplement that every religion needs. The world's religions have done and do everything possible to preserve themselves, but they have provided nothing to preserve the planet and its non-human forms of life. For example, even the Bible tells us nothing about how we can do this, or even that it needs to be done. Thus, in its quest to save itself, the church has ignored something vital, and unwittingly joined with unbelievers in undercutting the soil it needs to stand on, the water it needs to drink, and the air it needs to breathe, until the final salvation arrives. In other words, there are two halves to the ultimate salvation whole, and the millions of believers have, until recently, paid virtually no attention to one of the halves.

A second thing to consider is that Dan has dreamed about and prayed about this opportunity since the day we made our pact of secrecy. He has done so much and asked so little in return that I wanted very much to place a printed book in his hands before he passed on. He needed to know for certain that the Covenant message is going out to the world. Our publisher, John Weber, shared this desire. In the middle of the first conversation we had on the telephone, he said that he was having a vision in which he placed a printed copy in the venerable old root's hands. You would be amazed if I told you about the lengths he went to in order to get the Hotevilla book into print. Without his help we might not have had it for you until late in 1996.

Serendipitous? It certainly is! Dan has his copy now, and because UNESCO is underwriting the book's translation into French, the secret will soon be spreading around the world. In the final chapter, I tell you how this fortunate development with UNESCO came to pass.

THE NEED FOR THE HOPI SURVIVAL KIT

Hotevilla turned out to be a large and profusely illustrated book that yields its insights best when it is read, re-read, and studied carefully. Its paragraphs are filled with sentences that reveal the Traditionalist mind. They tell us what has been survived and must be survived. They also start us on the way to survival. But there are several involved stories, or threads, that run simultaneously through *Hotevilla* and weave themselves into a seamless blanket. Taken together, they cover all of Hopi history, placing ever increasing emphasis upon the last millennium and century. For concentrated examination the threads must, as is done in this book, be taken apart. The *Survival* book lets us see what for us is the most important of these threads in action, and presents its information in such a way that we can immediately put what we learn to work. The reason for doing this becomes plain when we recognize that at the core of everything lies the Covenant. And the Spiritual Ark that floats at the center of the core itself is the place where we make use of amazing PROPHECIES, INSTRUCTIONS, and WARNINGS. With these, everyone in the world can find answers to life and its continuance.

It is not surprising that even when the *Hotevilla* book was finished, I had the nagging feeling that everything I had been called by Dan Evehema to do was not done. The solutions to the world's accumulating problems were not identified cleanly enough, and not in a simple enough form to be easily followed. While Dan and I were doing the *Hotevilla* book, I did of course see that the Creator had placed in our hands the opportunity to influence the pace, intensity, and nature of prophetic fulfillments, as well as our day to day existence. And I write about that, and about what the Hopis and we must do to accomplish these things. The truth is that this central understanding regarding the survival kit itself only came to me as the entire story soaked in. It was during the months that followed, and I contemplated everything that is given there, that the mist cleared and I began to see what the prophetic information was all about. Only then did I understand why I had felt it did not make sense for the Creator to lead people into a maze of prophetic material that ends in frightening scenarios without giving them hope and opportunity to find a way out. At the same time that I recognized this, a prolonged illness gave me additional time to think. It was in this painful crucible that *The Hopi Survival Kit* was born. It could be that the Creator himself needed some time with me to help my understanding, and to allow things at Hotevilla Village to develop to where they are today. Therefore, if He did not cause my illness, He at least took advantage of it to help me think through the Traditionalist and our situations and see how they actually end. If I had been able to complete *The Survival Kit* when I first wanted to, I would certainly not have known what I know today, and my work would have been misdirected and incomplete.

Everyone who has known about the mentioned bits of Hopi prophecy has waited anxiously for the whole of it to be revealed. Some, I fear, have given up hoping it would happen. If they had known about the Spiritual Ark, their anticipation would have been much greater. Even without this information, those who have held on to the hope want passionately to compare what the Hopi tell us with the Bible prophecies and with prophets such as Nostradamus or Edgar Cayce. The reason for their passion is found in Traditionalist Hopi characteristics that prove them to be exceptionally perceptive, as well as unyielding in their vows and faith. As previously stated, over the centuries the Hopis have endured countless trials and tribulations, yet remain happy and fulfilled—thereby conveying the idea that what they think and say carries a tested, balanced, and reliable view.

In the newsletters there are scattered paragraphs that when pieced together—not because they say it but because of how I see it—tell the heroic story of the struggle by the Traditionalists to keep their Covenant vow. They do this by standing against a series of foes whose devious and even malicious methods make one wonder whether or not they are serving some prodigiously evil force. From all that has happened in this struggle, it does seem clear that there is "something out there" which does not want the world to hear the Hopi message of survival—more expressly, which does not want *you* to know about it. Their goal is to see that no one will be equipped to adequately deal with what is happening now, and will surely happen in worse measure in the near future. Evil does that kind of thing. I will be surprised if, as you read this book, you do not get the uncanny feeling that they are after you, knowing something you don't know yet, and believing that you are as involved in what happens from here on out as the Traditionalist Elders are.

The two-hearteds know that nothing can hurt the Creator more than the eradication of believers. And the way they seek to accomplish this parallels what the Devil does in the Biblical account as he tempts people. He never tells outright lies. He ever so slyly twists the truth just enough to keep the poorly informed from discovering what he is doing until they have followed him too far and become lost. As we who live in the space age know, if something is just a couple of degrees off course when it starts out, by the end of its long journey it can miss the target by thousands of miles.

The two-hearteds want to silence the Traditionalists, and even though they know it has to be done carefully, they are compelled to try. The forces assaulting the Hopi world know how successful the Pattern of Life given in the INSTRUCTIONS can be for anyone who chooses to embrace it to survive and to remain close to the Creator. If the evil ones fail to defeat our use of this Creator-given gift, they lose everything.

In the Genesis account the Serpent prefaces his question to Eve about the forbidden fruit with, "Did God really say?" Eve doesn't know whether He did or not. You see, her husband, Adam, has been too busy enjoying the pleasures of life to tell her that the fruit of the Tree of the Knowledge of Good and Evil, placed next to the Tree of Life in the middle of the Garden of Eden, is off limits for food. The Serpent observes this, and sensing her vulnerability slithers in closer to play upon her vanity. Then we learn that her pleasure-loving husband joins her in eating the fruit. Whether or not this story is a myth is beside the point. Its consequences are all too well known.

In terms of what has happened to the Hopis, and especially to the youth, the Bible story provides a chilling parallel. When temptation comes in the guise of the rich Maasaw, whom you will learn about later, they don't know what to say. White education has steered nearly all of them so thoroughly into the Anglo culture they no longer know what the true Maasaw said.

It is natural to ask how it happens that the Creator does not arrange for the Traditionalists to easily persuade everyone and win all of the battles of life? It is because each of us has freedom of choice, and in exercising it joins in determining how the contests will go. In the end the Creator and his followers do win the war. The *Hotevilla* and this book are testimonies to that ultimate victory. They show us how to make it through the minefields of life and on to the other side.

Having read the small bits of prophecy that have leaked out to writers who have stayed for a time with the Hopi and written about it, I knew, of course, that it was very special. But in researching the newsletters I discovered that their issues included the entire range of Hopi PROPHECY, along with INSTRUCTIONS and WARNINGS that have never before received their proper place and credit. This is probably because it has not been recognized that Maasaw's main reason for giving the prophecies is to point up the fact that, even before they are fulfilled, the gracious Creator has given us a way to survive them. This is the key to the secret, for it reveals that, while the Creator tells us what is richly deserved and so is coming, He also shows us how to defeat it. Moreover, the way of survival that is offered to us satisfies all of our needs. It enables us to be calm and serene in the midst of any crises, and especially during the record kinds of crises that are occurring at home and abroad today. It gives us something to keep us actively focused while the storms rage within and around us. And, the instructions give us ways to survive the cataclysmic events it appears will attend the close of the age. I explain in the introduction to the prophecies in Chapter 6 that the term "probably" is applicable here. For the moment, however, please accept that, while most other prophets are rigid in what they predict, the Hopi prophecies are surprisingly flexible and unique.

To put this relatedness of Maasaw gifts in graphic form, the prophecies were placed in a basket containing not one, but three items, and these are intertwined. They serve together, and not independently. The operation of any one of them is dependent on the operation of the others. The prophecies are related to the instructions, and the instructions are related to the warnings. Moreover, because of this intertwining, the now urgent secret of the Elders becomes, instead of the usual doomsday prophecies of other prophets, a well-rounded message of magnificent assurance and hope. Once this far reaching truth dawned on me after I had finished the *Hotevilla* book, my exhilaration soared and I had to tell you about it!

While all of this information is there in the newsletters, Dan did not mention the relationship of the three items to me. Perhaps he had not recognized it as such, for the Hopi do not question, analyze, and organize their religious practices. Instead, they follow a Pattern of Life that turns out to be organized, and involves a rational succession of repetitious experiences. So the Hopis have learned through the carrying out of daily activities how these three aspects of the kit work together. In this method, inner peace and understanding come as specified duties are performed. This is because Maasaw gave his INSTRUCTIONS to the Hopis in functional form. In other words, he gave them something to do—a way to live—that has helped their thinking process and let their problems work out or be eliminated while they performed daily tasks. In this approach, no one sits helpless and defenseless. What they do every day takes care of everything that needs to be done. This achieves its desired end for the Hopi Traditionalists, because they believe in obedient fulfillment with the fewest questions possible. But it is a way that will also work for us, which is why the Creator told them to pass the secret on.

The curriculum in Hopi schools does not include the kind of Hopi history that it should. Even in what little is taught there the Traditionalists are expunged from the literature as though they have never existed. Since, however, the secret is encompassed in a historical format, we need to know Hopi history from the Traditionalist point of view. Without this, we are not able to understand it. We need to know about the Underworld, the Anasazi ancestors, the sagas of Oraibi and Hotevilla, and especially about this past century that has seen such a dramatic change in the Hopi culture. Most of all, we need to know about the historical fulfillments of prophecy and the feelings of the people as they have lived the way Maasaw directed them to. Among other things, we need to know that time really began for the Hopis on a particular day when, about a thousand years ago, they came upon Maasaw while he was tapping with a small stone on a large rock.

From a Traditionalist point of view, Hopi history is absolutely fascinating. Among other things, it explains why the Creator and Maasaw chose them of all peoples to be their channels to the world. We learn that Hopi qualities make them the ideal people to carry the urgent message. Hopi history also gives us valuable insights into human nature. We are shown in it the course of prophetic fulfillment. Traditionalist history helps us understand why the cycles of the world follow the patterns they do, and are necessary.

Once we have learned these things, we easily understand why Hotevilla Village has for the past century occupied such a special place among the Hopis, and how, in an extraordinary way, it has come to hold in its hands the fate of the entire world. Therefore, it remains a shrine of great consequence, and we can expect that, as this becomes better known, more people than ever will want to make pilgrimages to it. Despite the untoward things that are happening there today, Hotevilla has made its place in the Sun. That truth will never be erased. The Tribal Council ought to be thinking hard about this fact, instead of laying utility lines into the Village.

Until now, most Kachina dances at Hotevilla have remained open to the public—an interesting fact considering that all of the other villages that have become Bahanna in their orientation have closed theirs to outsiders. Until now, the summer Home

Going Dance that ends the open Kachina season at Hotevilla has drawn large crowds of non-Hopi spectators who come to show their profound respect for a superb culture that has, until now, always had the world's best interests in mind. They have watched with reverence as the Hopis, with their splendidly painted bodies and dramatic costumes, dance the dances of a thousand years to keep the world in balance.

But visitors may no longer be able to do this. The Hopi Office of Cultural Preservation, which has no personal involvement with Hopi ritual, has moved in and is attempting to close even the Hotevilla dances to outsiders. As chapters ahead will tell you, the situation at the village is beginning to change dramatically, and has become a perilous one.

Somewhere along the way as this story continues, you are going to wonder whether or not I personally believe these amazing things the Hopi Elders tell us. The revelations are so astounding that I couldn't blame anyone for doubting it. During the time I have worked with the material, I have asked myself the same question many times. What I can tell you is that I am already following the INSTRUCTIONS, and that as soon as *The Survival Kit* is published, our family will continue with our preparations for what the Hopi tell us is certain to come. We are on the Spiritual Ark—the great Ark of the Secret—that you will learn about shortly, and which you will discover is available for everyone's life—wherever you are or whatever you do.

It may interest you to learn that, including the moment when he first asked me to write the *Hotevilla* book, Dan has not once inquired as to whether or not I believe The Elders' accounts or his personal disclosures. If this surprises you, recognize that he simply assumes these astounding revelations will stand on their own, and that once they are received by anyone who, unlike the two-hearteds, is open to them, they will validate themselves. His innocent acceptance of this fact is a more eloquent and powerful testimony than any other form of persuasion.

Although nothing would be more desirable, the *Hotevilla* and *Survival* books are not aimed at transforming the world overnight. We envision miracles, but not that kind. On the contrary, the books are aimed at getting one reader at a time—you—to weigh their merits, and then to decide whether or not you want to do what we suggest. The Creator, Maasaw, the Elderly Elders, and I are convinced that you will do this, that the number of conversions will expand regularly, and that the world's situation will change accordingly.

In the meantime, it appears that the Creator hopes humanity will continue to look at what has been going on in the world and move on its own to redirect its course. To encourage this, He has even asked Mother Earth to do things that should get our attention. People who live where volcanoes are erupting, and where earthquakes, storms, floods and fires are regularly happening, say they have never before seen anything like these that are occurring now. Thus far her efforts have, however, only reached and shaken us for short periods of time. We human beings are such a stubborn and willful lot that even record natural disasters have not been sufficient to do the trick. So I am expecting the Creator to, in the near future, unleash a major prophetic fulfillment—something that will at last get us to stop living our lives as usual, and begin searching fervently for ways to handle the other prophecies whose fulfillments are standing in the wings and ready to come on stage. When you look at what this book describes, you will see that there is a whole line of them out there. Which of them do you think it might be?

As you might expect I don't actually want these terrible things to happen. Their nature is such that I do not want anyone to have to face them. I don't want my family to face them or to face them myself. There are so many joyful things and so many wonderful people in this still beautiful world of ours it would be marvelous if all of the tragic problems would just solve themselves. Then a blissful life-ever-after, or at least something close to it, could go on forever. But prophecy suggests that this is not likely to happen.

It is also a fact that the prophecies, instructions, and warnings were programmed in at Oraibi and etched in stone. This tells us that while we continue to dicker over "whethers," the clock will continue to move. Much of what you will learn herein has already happened. More is even now taking place. I have mentioned that things are happening at Hotevilla that will severely impact the village and us. It is fresh news today. But by the time you have it in your hands, some of it will already be "old hat." All you will be able to do is look at what it portended, and then look to see what has happened in the world as a result. In this sense our secret story will always be an ongoing one, and something we must keep up with for years to come in order to know what to expect and do.

Bear in mind that I write about a living, pulsating situation. It may often seem like fantasy and fiction, but it is not. The amazing story marches on. It gathers increased urgency with every passing day, and it beckons constantly with its great challenges and opportunities. There is some comfort in the knowledge that Hopi prophecy does not tell us that the world will collapse tomorrow. But it does warn us that the way we spend our time will affect things that are of great consequence. If we are wise, we will accept the responsibility of doing what is necessary to influence the outcome and be prepared. Part of the secret is that we must continue to move with it until the Creator decides when the Fourth Cycle should close and the Fifth Cycle should begin.

Even during the months I have been writing the *Survival Kit,* the picture at Hotevilla has changed considerably. And, so far as the current situation regarding the Traditionalists is concerned, the book has not gone the way that I originally thought it would. Part of my problem has been that I let what I hoped would happen color my judgment. I have wanted the Traditionalists to win an overwhelming victory, yet they have not. What has taken place, however, does work perfectly with the prophetic picture. You will learn, as I have, that there is an "if" condition that attends every prophecy, so that its pace, intensity, and force is not really known until it occurs. The present situation is not what I would have preferred. But preferences do not determine prophetic outcomes. Choices do. In future chapters you will see what I mean by this.

As you begin to read their story and to identify with the Traditionalist Elders, you too will develop strong feelings about the way you would like their story to end. But it will probably not end as you want it to either. Eventually, however, you will understand as I do that, circumstances being what they are, the Creator is handling His creation in the best possible way. Do me a favor though. Don't skip to the last chapter to uncover in advance the present state of this supernatural secret. If you do, you will spoil everything for yourself, since you will not know what led up to what has finally happened.

Thanks to the last little gladiator, Dan Evehema, to Susie Lomatska, to all of the other Traditionalist Elders, at this point the secret of blending and celebrating, cloistered for so long up on the mesas, opens itself to us as naturally as a flower to the morning sun. If Yukiuma were still with us today, he would be pleased to see it happening. He would come to each of us, take our hand in his and say, "This is good!" Then he would ask us to sit with him in the shade while he would tell us an amazing story, a story about the keepers of the secret, of which he was very proud to be one, and about ourselves.

We pick it up far back in time and in an unusual location. It is a mysterious place where we will begin to merge our thoughts with those of a culture far different from our own, yet one which speaks to us of wondrous things that concern and involve us more profoundly than we have ever imagined.

June 1, 1993

Chief Dan Evehema

I, Dan Evehema, being the eldest of our tribal leaders, hearby grant to author Thomas E. Mails exclusive rights to publish and write a book telling the history of the traditional Hopi people of the village of Hotevilla Arizona. Including general events, and especialy the prophecy given to us in ancient times regarding the end of the world's fourth cycle and the beginning of the 5th cycle, including the vital roll the traditional Hopi people are playing in this crucial time.

We have been looking for many years for someone with a true heart to come to help us tell this story. It is my belief that Thomas E. Mails is this person. He will help us share our message of prophecy, peace and harmony with all the peoples of the world.

Dan Evehema
Chief Dan Evehema

Title

Roadrunner + Greaswood
Clans

6-1-93
Date

Susie Lomatska
Witnessed / Susie Lomatska

Chapter 2

The Amazing Story

In spite of their small population that numbers 10,000 members today, the Hopi are one of the best known Indian tribes in the world. Their peaceful manner of life and dramatic ceremonial performances have captured the attention of people the world over. Therefore, historical sketches of their customs, together with illustrated books of their crafts and Kachina dancers, abound. But you will never read another Hopi history quite like this one, for it is the first to be told by the Traditionalists themselves.

Traditionalists, as opposed to Progressives and on-the-fence Hopis, are the only Hopis who for their entire lives have fought against the most dramatic assaults ever made against their culture. And, through it all, they have attempted to keep their sacred vow to serve the Creator and to follow the ancient ways. Traditionalists are the only remaining Hopis who grew up in Traditional families where they received word for word from their parents and grandparents the history of their people as it has been handed down from one generation to the next for thousands of years. They speak from a unique vantage point and give us insights that are enormously valuable.

Scholars who have written Hopi histories from the conventional point of view may wish to protect what they have said by contesting some of what is related here. But they cannot dispute the fact that this is the way the Traditionalist sources have both seen it and lived it. In other words, what we are about to share now is neither an outsider's view nor the discernment of a Hopi who is attempting to please everyone by walking simultaneously in both the Hopi and the White worlds. It is generally accepted that accounts vary according to their sources, but what is given here is the product of unanimous agreement, and it has one goal in mind—that of conveying an urgent message to a world that is more in need of it than it knows.

Of special interest in this historical account are the references to the fulfillments of prophecies as they take place in Hopi history. Histories written by others make only passing and cursory mention of these instances where the Creator is active in history to advise, warn, and redeem—as if to say it is not scientific to believe that matters of faith such as these have a place in legitimate accounts. One could maintain such an argument if it were not for the fact that the giving of the prophecies, and their associated instructions and warnings, is amply documented, as are their fulfillments in history. To put this plainly, it has been stated that these things would happen and be done, and they have. We cannot ignore this fact.

People frequently question whether or not the ancient and imaginative Hopi legends, such as this one we are about to consider regarding their Underworld beginning, are entirely fantasy, or contain one or more historical truths. As a rule, outsiders think they are just stories. But from observing what has occurred in Hopi history, Dan Evehema accepts that there are historical truths in the legends. More importantly, he believes that the legends help us to understand the makeup of human nature, and why life proceeds in its various ways. An analysis of this engaging story as it is set forth in the newsletter accounts supports his view.

For example, in the Underworld legend told by the Traditionalists, we learn how human nature has both its good and its bad sides, and that the sides vie constantly for control. We learn also that there are forces—call them forces of good and evil if you wish—that employ temptation to draw these individual sides into their fold, forcing us to make choices. In the legend, we see this situation in action in the Underworld, and learn that the two sides of our character remain to vex us human beings throughout all of our generations. A look at the human situation in the world today amply sustains the truth of this assertion.

Strangely enough, we find that where choices are concerned it is the bad side that dominates—perhaps because it is more self-serving and contentious. From a global point of view, this leads finally to consequences that require a thorough cleansing of humankind. The Hopi Elders use the word "Purification" to describe this cleansing, and explain that the culmination of the process necessitates an ending, or closing, of each world cycle as a prelude to the opening of the next. "There is," they say, "a continual beginning, and then an ending, and then a beginning again." It is fascinating to see what their prophecies demonstrate about this transitional truth.

THE UNDERWORLD

The Hopi story of the Fourth Cycle of the world begins long, long ago in the Underworld, in the mysterious and shadowy abode of the spirits. The Creator Himself does not live in this place, but he is always in touch with its residents, and with the Spirit deities He has appointed to watch over them. The human spirits who live here represent only those who believed in Him during the Third Cycle. We are not told in the legend where the spirits of unbelievers went when they died.

As time passed, many, although not all of the spirits, used their freedom of choice to follow the path of materialism and pleasure. The storytellers inform us that being creative individuals, the Underworld residents have produced several of the pleasurable things we focus our lives on today, and continue making the most of them. In doing this they have turned their backs upon the Creator and His Spirit assistants, and live debauched and worldly lives.

But other human spirits, along with the Kachina spirits who lived with them, were exceedingly unhappy about this kind of conduct, and wanted to separate themselves from the spirits who engaged in it. So they sought a way out. Having heard someone walking on the surface of the earth above, and being curious as to who this was, they sent three birds in succession up to find out. When the third bird discovered it was Maasaw, the Guardian Spirit of the Earth, he asked for permission for the spirits to come up, and received it. After several failed attempts, the group succeeded by climbing up the inside of a large reed and emerged onto the surface of the earth. They exited through a hole known as the Sip-pa-pu, that is located to this day in the floor of the Grand Canyon. No date is attached to this historic moment, but it was a very long time ago.

THE EMERGENCE

When the Underworld people and the Kachina spirits who were escaping with them reached the top of the reed and climbed out, they were delighted to find they were in a beautiful place. In Hopi lore, this experience is known as "the Emergence." According to Hopi prophecy, when the Fifth Cycle of the world begins, the survivors from this world will join those who are already in the Underworld or on the San Francisco Peaks as the first of its inhabitants.

As the ceremonial cycle gets underway in Hopi villages each year, the emergence story is reenacted in the Kivas. In further annual testimony to this dramatic escape, the dozens of magnificently painted and costumed Kachinas who dance at the annual Home Going Dance carry in their arms huge loads of green corn stalks, cattail rushes, and reeds. Tied to these are woven plaques, packets of piki bread, and carved and painted kachina dolls and little bows and arrows that are given as gifts to Hopi children who are in the audience. Each time this is done, the old Hopis who watch and who have not forgotten the story are reminded of the Emergence, and in their hearts celebrate it once again.

The residents of the Underworld who remained behind at the time of the Emergence were still corrupted in their behavior, although as time has passed it appears that their conduct has improved, since the faithful, who have since then died and returned to the Underworld, apparently live contentedly with them. The inhabitants carry out there, in a reverse order, the cycle of life followed by Hopi people who are living on the surface of the earth. In the Underworld, there is a spirit counterpart for every Hopi thing that exists on earth. And when the major performance of each ceremony is being done here on earth, the minor form of that same ceremony is being performed in the Underworld. On these occasions, communion between the inhabitants of the two worlds is carried on through small sip-papu holes that are cut in the floors of each subterranean ceremonial chamber, called a "Kiva." How much of a Kiva is actually underground is determined by its location; by how difficult it is to make the excavation. Most Rio Grande pueblo Kivas are round. Zuni Kivas are rectangular. Most Hopi Kivas are rectangular. Each Kiva is considered to be "the womb of Mother Earth," so that when ceremonies are performed there, the performers are within her and in constant communion with her.

As a rule, the spirits of the Hopi dead return to the Underworld, the exception being that of Hopi leaders who have held important positions, and who have made significant contributions to their people. They go instead in their spirit form to the San Francisco Peaks, north of Flagstaff. At a sacred site there they join with other spirits who have preceded them. They then return each year to Hopi Land during the Kachina season as bearers of rain, riding inside fluffy white clouds. When dances are held, the performers and the spectators usually look up and see them drifting past in the cerulean sky. They come in response to the prayers and powers generated by the ceremonies. This rain the Kachinas bring is essential to the growth of Hopi crops in that it augments the only other water supply the Hopi have—ground water, itself a shrinking source today. Together, they make existence in Hopi Land possible. Without both sources of water the people suffer greatly. Having learned from personal experience that a drought can happen at any time, they remain acutely conscious of the fact that their conduct has a direct bearing on the amount of rain that comes. If the people behave badly, the Kachinas may be displeased and refuse to bring rain. In 1994, when the Progressives and on-the-fence villagers at Hotevilla turned against the Traditionalists and permitted the Tribal Council and the U.S. Department of Health and Human Services to begin the installation of sewer and water utilities, Dan predicted that this would happen, and it did. The Kachinas refused to come and there was no rain for the crops. The corn was planted, but it did not grow, and in the fall there was nothing to harvest.

The total body of people present at the Emergence was not small, for the Pueblo peoples themselves were numerous enough to be divided into tribes that were further divided into clans. Present also, though, were people of other races, a fact made clear by the mention in Hopi prophecy of a certain "White brother" who will one day fill an important role in Hopi history.

Shortly after the Emergence, the people met the Creator Himself, and also Maasaw, who divided them into groups, and then, for a special reason in the case of the Pueblos, required each of their leaders to choose an ear from a pile of corn. While the rest of them chose the handsomest ears, the last one to choose found that all that was left was the smallest and most miserable-looking ear. So he did not really choose it. The little ear was all that was left. But he did take it without complaining, indicating that he and his followers were humble people. So Maasaw gave them the name, Hopi, which in its rudimentary definition means peaceful.

As we contemplate the acceptance of the pitiful ear of corn, we obtain our second Hopi characteristic. They are a people who do not put themselves forward, and who are satisfied with being less than supreme. When we add this quality to their first characteristic, which is their abhorrence of materialistic living, we can begin to envision them as servants to whom the Creator will entrust His sacred mission.

THE MIGRATIONS

Once divided and named, the Pueblo peoples were directed to migrate to all parts of the North American continent, using corn as their staple food, and sinking their spiritual roots into Mother Earth as they went. They were to do this in several ways, but the primary one was that of building small prayer shrines at which they would deposit prayer feathers, called "pahos." They were also directed to leave their etched and painted symbols on cliffs and rocks. This was to record their journeys and accomplishments, and to mark the land they travel over as theirs. The Hopi did not mean in terms of ownership—since the Creator is the owner of all land, but as the abode of those who have accepted the privilege of relating in one-ness with it, and the responsibility for its preservation. Above all, they were to search for Maasaw, who they had been told would be waiting for them in an unknown place. Meanwhile, the shrines would become channels for two-way communion with Mother Earth. As the Hopi have revisited these over the years, She has assisted them in meeting the challenges of life, and has told them how She feels about humans who mistreat Her. On top of this, She has told them what She plans to do about it.

No one can contest that the Pueblo people did *covenant* with the Creator to migrate and do as He asked, for they kept at it for an incredibly long period of time, and left behind them as they travelled more than 15,000 villages of varying sizes that have been discovered so far by archaeologists.

By the year one on our calendars—as long ago as the time of Jesus Christ—the first Pueblo Indians had become a cohesive group of roaming "basketmakers" who lived in brush shelters and caves. Later on, they graduated to living in expertly constructed wooden pithouses. After this, they developed stone structures, some of which are splendid cliff dwellings whose impressive ruins we still marvel at today. Cliff Palace at Mesa Verde, Colorado, and Chaco Canyon in New Mexico, are among the finest examples of this kind of Pueblo craftsmanship and design. If you visit either of these ruins after you have read *The Survival Kit,* you will have a spiritual experience that is unique.

They will come alive for you, and you will identify with them and the ancient people who dwelt there in a way that is beyond anything you expect.

Always though, the Hopi bore in mind the command that they were to continue migrating until one of their groups found Maasaw. Those who did would be specially blessed and challenged. At the Emergence, the people made their First Covenant with the Creator, which was to carry out this search, no matter how difficult the assignment should be, or how long it took. And so it went on, for how long exactly we do not know, but there is artifact and architectural proof that it continued for thousands of years. Consequently, we see here another Hopi characteristic that the Creator would surely have recorded in his book of desirable qualities—that of keeping promises in the face of every kind of situation, and for however long as is necessary.

Nevertheless, it should be remembered that as the successive generations migrated, they carried with them the divided natures that they had inherited from those who escaped from the Underworld. This fact is made clear in the legend which tells about the daughter of a chief who misbehaved in the manner that witches do, and as punishment was returned to the Underworld. On another occasion, the legend describes how the chief of the Bow Clan left his people for awhile to return to a place where he could participate in some of the "pleasures" of life. As we will see, this was an act his descendants would pay dearly for at a future time.

Except for the scattered ruins that cover a large part of the southwestern area we now call the four corners region, and which today consists of portions of the present-day states of Arizona, Colorado, Utah and New Mexico, we can only guess at the life-way that was followed during the migration period. By comparing artifacts and structures that are found with those made by living Pueblo descendants, a few assumptions can be made, but that is all. We know something about their religious practices, their building techniques, their crafts and clothing, that corn was their staple food, and that they were involved in trading practices that brought the pueblos into contact with one another, and with other tribes. From these, we know enough to tell us that they were extremely talented people.

It is clear, too, that the basketmakers and their descendants, popularly known today as the "Anasazi," were deeply religious people. In truth, religion infused the whole of their lives. An abundance of carefully crafted religious objects has been found in caves, pithouses, and in the subterranean Kivas that came into being in the stone-dwelling period. Yet religious developments remained pliant until Maasaw finally was located and a whole new era in Hopi history began.

Another important thing learned from Dan Evehema was that whenever the people left a village to move on to a new place they were to break their pottery. Like everyone else, I had assumed that the broken pottery shards found in the trash heaps of the ruins were nothing more than the result of accidents. Instead, at least some of these broken shards represent Traditionalists who were remaining faithful to Maasaw and the Covenant, along with individuals who are designated to fill a special role as the Fourth Cycle of the world closes. In this light, Dan Evehema and the other Elderly Elders are living pieces of broken pottery who stand in a long and continuous line of broken shards.

It is also important to know that, during the migration period, the spiritual roots, that were sunk at shrines and while planting into Mother Earth, entwined their fingers into hers in a kind of love relationship that was considered "fluid." This appears to indicate that the life-way, while it was building toward what it has become today in the pueblos, was not fixed during this time. It was continually undergoing a process of evolution that did not end until the people found Maasaw.

Nevertheless, the shrines left behind occupy an important place in the Hopi spiritual scheme. Until the land they were placed on was taken over by intruders, certain of them were visited regularly by spiritual leaders. At these times they performed rituals during which they communed with Earth Mother, expressing their gratitude for the annual blessings she so consistently sent them. In return, she expressed her love to them, and up-to-date information about the condition of the world. At these holy places the Hopi priests also received further guidance for carrying on the Hopi Pattern of Life.

Our next Hopi characteristics are found in the migration period. We see that they are a faithful, obedient and talented group who are maintaining communication with Mother Earth, and are learning the lessons they will need to live in harmony with the whole of creation and the universe. Recent discoveries in the principal ruins show they have already achieved a high degree of sophistication. Even solar calendars by which the Hopi and other Pueblo peoples regulated the seasons for farming and ceremonial observances have been found.

During the tenth to twelfth centuries, the Pueblo peoples who lived in the northern areas of their land individually began to abandon their dwelling places and move south to the new locations in present-day Arizona and New Mexico, where they still reside. No one knows for certain which of the groups went where. That is, we know what villages the different Pueblo peoples live in today, but we are not able to say with certainty which of the ancient northern villages they came from. Some settled in the Rio Grande region of New Mexico, where they are known as the Eastern Pueblos. Others settled in Zuni, Acoma and Laguna.

The Hopi migrated to the Black Mesa country of Arizona, with one of their groups moving to a place there named Oraibi, which means "the place where the roots solidify."

MAASAW

Here, sometime around the year A.D. 1100, they found Maasaw, being drawn to him by a noise he made each day by tapping on a rock that magnified and projected the sound. As it turned out, this tapping was the first of many tests he would apply to measure the group's sensitivity to the Creator's wishes. Only those who really listened instead of just wanting to hear themselves talk had any chance of finding Maasaw, and as such were deserving of the blessings he was ready to bestow. Persistence was also a characteristic he prized, for he knew it was something they would need to survive the years ahead and to fulfill the challenges he was ready to present to them.

Since it marked such an historic turning point in their lives, we can understand how Maasaw's sounding rock became a shrine for the Hopi. Yet in a typical example of Bahanna insensitivity to the sacred things of the Hopi, a few years ago a Government highway crew needlessly bulldozed this rock and destroyed it. Until that time the Traditionalist leaders made annual pilgrimages to it, just as they once did to their territorial shrines.

For reasons explained in Chapter 5, Maasaw was as macabre a visaged individual as anyone could imagine. I doubt that any description of consequence had been handed down to the Hopi from their ancestors, and it must have shocked them to see his menacing figure and face. His huge staring eyes were like sunken black holes, and his gaping black mouth bristled with sharp white teeth. He had no nose. His entire head was covered with caked blood, bunches of feathers, and different colored blotches of paint. He wore a long cloak made of black and grey rabbitskins. Hung on a neck thong was a buckskin pouch containing corn seeds, and secured to a belt cord was a gourd filled with spring water. In one hand was a planting stick, and in the other hand was a blazing torch.

Considering Maasaw's frightening appearance, we would assume that the Hopi were tempted to run and hide. Instead, it excited their curiosity and drew them close. Still, they must have wondered why the Creator would appoint as Guardian of the Earth an apparition like this. The private discussions must have been something else! But once they came to know Maasaw, his appearance made perfect sense. His hideous image matched what he had to tell them, for both of these were contrary to anything they might have expected. It taught them that the ways of the Creator are not man's ways; that He begins by using the unexpected to capture people's attention while He glues what He has to say in their minds. And, this disparity was an aspect of His being that kept them listening raptly to His every word and carefully watching His every move. In this manner they discovered the fullness of His nature, remembered it vividly, and in consequence their descendants are able to relate it to us today. This is the way oral tradition is instilled in those who do not write books. It follows then that having all of this take place in such a remote location as Oraibi, and with such an unassuming group as the Hopi, is no less surprising than God's choosing to have Jesus' birth happen in so obscure a place as Bethlehem.

When things had settled down, the Hopi asked if they could stay at Oraibi with him. He answered that all he had was his digging stick, his seeds, his cloak, and his gourd of water. Then he added, "**If you are willing to live as I do, and follow my instructions, the life plan which I shall give you,** you may live here with me, and take care of the land. Then you shall have a long, happy, fruitful life." Since they already lived simple lives, it was not a difficult decision to make. So the people agreed to Maasaw's terms. Later on, when Bahanna arrived with his conveniences and choices could be made, we find that many of the Hopi changed their minds.

If the writers of the newsletters learned the full details of the meeting with Maasaw, they did not include them in the articles. Nevertheless, they could reconstruct what did take place by seeing what happened in the years that followed. From the amount of teaching he did, it is apparent that he stayed with the Hopi for some time, and that when he was done, the awed people asked if he would watch over them and be their leader. Quoting the Elders, His answer was, "No, the one who led you here will be the leader until you fulfill your Pattern of Life," for he saw into their hearts and knew they still had many selfish desires. While he was not going to abandon them, it would be their own responsibility to work out their day-to-day problems. Maasaw did give them instructions in how to do this, and added that, when the end of the Fourth Cycle came, he would take over, for "he was the first and would also be the last."

During his teaching period, Maasaw laid out for the Hopi a Pattern of Life they were to follow as they lived there at Oraibi. In considering its value, we must not forget that where survival is concerned, the Creator Himself is the instigator of the Traditional way of life the Hopi have followed from its inception until today. While Maasaw delivered all of this information to the Hopi, he was not its originator. He has been described as a deity, and now and then in a slip of the tongue has been called the Great Spirit. But the Hopi Elders do not confuse him with the Creator. Instead, they know he serves the Creator, and that his assigned task is to be Guardian of the Earth. We must never forget that the information he gave at Oraibi came directly from the Creator, or as we outsiders might choose to say, from God Himself.

In general, the teachings received at Oraibi fell under the headings of PROPHECIES, INSTRUCTIONS, and WARNINGS. The PROPHECIES are awesome in their scope, and where the last stages of the Fourth Cycle are concerned, sharply pointed and frightening. They deal with both individual human lives and with world events. There are several reasons for this, and it is vital that we understand what these were. We also need to understand how the Hopi PROPHECIES work, for they are unique in this regard. It is the prophecies, for example, that point us toward the instructions and warnings, which are our way of surviving what the prophecies will bring to pass. In other words, the Creator told the Hopis what would happen, but at the same time told them how they could survive these things. The WARNINGS are stern and uncompromising, yet they are also meant to rescue us in times of peril. But the INSTRUCTIONS, which teach the Hopi to do certain things in both ceremonial and daily life, hold a special place. They show the people a whole new way of deliverance from catastrophes and evil forces. Since each of these three topics is considered in detail in the following chapters, more is not said about them here. But remember that the three of them work together, and in their sum bear a significance that is worldwide in its scope, for they reach beyond the Hopi and out to everyone. They are the ingredients of *The Hopi Survival Kit* that can serve us so well today.

Above all, what Maasaw gave the Hopi at Oraibi was the secret that would enable them to blend with the land and celebrate life. Among other things, it was a way to become natural environmentalists who simply grew up being people who through their manner of life would became one with Mother Earth, and would neither waste nor abuse her. As a natural result of the life-way, they would also live in warm fellowship with one another, and with other human beings and creatures. It was a gentle way for a gentle people, a way to deal effectively with the things that so frequently cause pain in life, and a way to counteract the fulfillments of prophecy. As they repeated day by day, month by month, and year by year, the cycle of things Maasaw taught them to do, peace ruled their hearts. This peace would achieve its greatest value when the closing of the Fourth Cycle of the world came to pass. This was a secret for happiness that was not intended to be a secret, for it was a secret to be shared with all people who truly deserved to hear it.

It is reasonable to ask how the Hopi people who met with Maasaw there at Oraibi could possibly remember as much of this information as is claimed. Part of the answer lies in the magnitude of the meeting. It was a monumental moment in time, and its impact alone would have caused anyone connected with it to retain a vivid impression of everything that was said and done. The lessons were also committed to memory, and for further retention were to be repeated in an annual review. Equally important is the fact that the instructions were put immediately to work, so that as the people followed their life-way the teachings were being reviewed and their benefits were being received on a daily basis.

There was an element of profound mystery about the prophecies. How could it have been otherwise? They included all sorts of information having to do with people of other races and worlds, and with times, events and things about which the Hopi had no knowledge and nothing to compare them to. The Hopi must have been greatly puzzled by it. They could not have avoided wondering why the Creator had chosen to give it to them at that time and in that place.

The answer to this question lies in a further acknowledgment of why the Hopi were chosen for their task as bearers of the news. A survey of their history reveals that throughout their successive generations the Traditionalist Hopi have accepted the Creator's challenge. They have kept the Covenant and preserved the message until now. The Hopi people of that time and their descendants have been individuals who measured up to the task. Once we add up their qualities, we easily understand why they were selected.

Once again, just as the Hopi agreed to live simply as Maasaw himself lived, they agreed also to preserve and pass on his great teachings. The fact that time and oppression have worn many of their ancestors down does not diminish what was begun there, and has been carried on for almost a millennium. Lesser people would not have held fast to their promises for anywhere near as long as these generations have.

Remember that there are two Covenants: a first one made at the Emergence, and a second one made at Oraibi. Both are vows the Hopi swore they would not relinquish, and are promises that reverberate throughout history. Since those who kept these would become known as the followers of tradition, or Traditionalists, it is most unfortunate that the Christian missionaries who came to Hopi Land did not understand this distinction. If they had, they would have known why these natives would prove to be the most obstinate of all Native Americans where conversion was concerned. It was never simply a matter of converting from one religion to another. To relinquish these vows would be an unconscionable thing for the Traditionalists to even consider, and for the missionaries to expect. I would like to believe that had the evangelicals been better informed, they never would have asked this of people whose preceding generations had faithfully kept their promises for nearly a thousand years.

If you or I had been keeping such vows, would we have been inclined to renounce our faith and accept the religion of a foreign group who ignored entirely what we believed and how this belief had served us? And would we passively have submitted to conversion if, on top of this, we knew that the survival of the world depended upon our passing on a message of survival at the most critical point in its history? I trust that we would not—at least if we were made of the right stuff!

We are told that as the Hopi do all of these things asked of them by Maasaw, they will have still another responsibility, which is that of keeping the earth and universe in balance and harmony.

These two entities are interrelated, and balance has its own way of functioning, for it is not a juggling act wherein all of the aspects of the world and universe are to be kept in balance at once.

Balance and the Hopi's manner of life are related. As people live each day according to the Pattern of Life given to them, balance is maintained. That is, despite what anyone anywhere in the world might be doing that could throw the earth and human spirit off balance, the Hopi provide enough balance to keep the world turning on its axis, and to keep life in harmonious synchronization. Thus the globe spins in measured control on its axis and the universe continues to function in its normal and harmonious way. I know as well as you do that this is not acceptable science. But I doubt that the Creator allows Himself to be controlled by what science concludes, and He likes to show us now and then that He is still in charge.

The Elders say that in ancient times there were chosen tribes in every part of the globe who shared in this responsibility. But as the various cultures have succumbed to foreign intrusion, the Hopi Traditionalists have assumed the entire burden of world balance. If so, present and future balance rests in Hopi hands, and expressly in the hands of the Elders at Hotevilla. However absurd it may seem for the Creator to place the fate of the world in the hands of this remote, politically and militarily impotent people, this is, according to teachings given to the Hopi at Oraibi, the way it is, for the kind of balance I am referring to is something that is spiritually achieved. No one can manufacture it. Would we rather have this responsibility placed in the hands of the powerful people who are boastful and serve only their own interests? What might their response be when the Creator really needs them? Where, in fact, are they when all of them are needed now?

Remarkably, this assertion regarding the Hopi Traditionalists and balance—be it scientific or not—is a verifiable claim. We can test it. When we come to the end of this historical sketch, we will see how a common development presently taking place in Hotevilla Village will factor into the equation of the great Road Plan of life. We will see how it has already set in motion certain actions having to do with the closing of the Fourth Cycle of the world. In other words, while in the Hopi prophetic scheme there are no set dates for prophecies to be fulfilled, since Hotevilla Village is a microcosm of the world, what takes place there causes these same things to happen at the same time to a greater degree in other parts of the world. This aspect of fulfillment narrows down speculation regarding time periods considerably. As soon as something begins to happen at Hotevilla, the microcosm clock begins to tick. The Elders see this, and can tell us that we have now moved into a certain predicted phase of prophetic fulfillment. All we need to do is look at what is happening in the world to find the verification. I can see this in the news every passing week. You can too. If it happens at Hotevilla, it will happen elsewhere. Considering the value of such revelations to those of us who want to prepare in advance, we need to be concerned about two things: how we can support the Traditionalists and keep them going, and how we will obtain this kind of information regarding Hotevilla when the last of the Elderly Elders has moved beyond this world.

To indelibly mark this vital meeting at Oraibi, Maasaw made several small stone tablets for the Hopi to keep, both as a record and a reminder. They are also a testimony to the fact of the Oraibi encounter and what transpired there, and until recently, when the most important of them was taken from its rightful Traditionalist caretakers, they were reviewed annually at the time each cycle of ceremonies got underway, and more often if necessary.

One of the tablets was given to the Bear Clan, and the symbols Maasaw inscribed on it concerned ownership of Hopi Land. To this day it is still used as evidence when land disputes occur between the Hopi and other tribes or outsiders. A second one is one of far reaching significance, in that the symbols pecked on its two sides follow a time line that tells in a simplified way the entire prophetic story. It is called the "Pathway stone." Although it is nearly a thousand years old, looking at it from our present-day perspective, the accuracy of what it portrays is absolutely startling. Much of what it predicts will happen to the Hopi and the rest of the world has already happened, suggesting that the rest will happen too. We will look at this remarkable stone as our historical sketch continues, but it is illustrated and examined in depth in Chapter 10, where we look through Hopi Traditionalist eyes at the present and future global situation.

Maasaw also gave the Hopi a "Road Plan" in which he spelled out in graphic fashion the straight path the Hopis must follow if they hope to survive, and the comparative path Bahanna follows that leads to chaos. To memorialize this plan, and to have it where it could be reviewed on a regular basis, the Hopi leaders drew a pictograph of it on the side of a rock wall that is not far from Oraibi. It too is referred to in our historical sketch, and final references are made to it in Chapter 10.

Whenever we consider these valuable stone works, we should recognize that to the Hopi they are more than just drawings on a rock. Each of them is an entire package of information, for as the symbols are studied, the people are transported in memory back to the historic meeting at Oraibi, and everything said and done there is called to mind and reviewed. Just one little symbol can kindle hours of discussion.

According to the account of the Oraibi meeting given in the newsletters, "After having left all of the instructions with them, he [Maasaw] disappeared." This does not mean that he went far, for we discover that he took and still takes an active part in Hopi life, both at Hotevilla and other Hopi villages. He also assumes the form of a fireball and circles each night around the entire world. In Chapter 5 you will learn why he does this, and it is just one more amazing thing in this already amazing Hopi story.

Under the leadership of the chief of the Bow Clan, who was, because of what his ancestor had done earlier in seeking pleasure, soon deposed and replaced by the chief of the Bear Clan, the Hopi set to work gathering the stones needed to build the walls of the houses and Kivas that would make up their village. Nearby trees provided most of the roof beams, and larger ones came from the mountains to the west. A large dance plaza was created by locating the buildings around it. Once the plaza was completely enclosed, they christened the village "Oraibi," and having allocated farming plots to each family, the people began to follow Maasaw's INSTRUCTIONS.

Word of the meeting with Maasaw and of what was happening at Oraibi spread quickly to all of the Pueblo peoples, and shortly after that other Hopi groups began to arrive. When they asked to be accepted into the new community, some were and some weren't. Since the aim of Oraibi was to promote the harmony and unity needed to keep their Covenant vow, boastful people concerned with their own interests were turned away and told to settle in other locations on the three mesas. Finally there were nine or more sovereign villages, each independent from the others in that it governed itself and conducted its own ceremonies, and yet united in common causes that had to do with the well-being of the tribe.

Over the years that followed, Oraibi continued to grow and prosper, taking its place as a mother village that served as a spiritual center for the other villages. Year by year it followed the instructions—the cycle of ceremonies and farming practices that Maasaw had taught the people. In time, the population of the village became as large as the combined populations of all of the other villages. Life was untroubled, and the citizens of Oraibi were united in all that they did. Most years the springs ran free and the Kachinas brought the rain, so that crops flourished. Now and then there was a drought to remind the people not to take the Creator for granted. But they always laid aside sufficient supplies to get through, and life went on. In a couple of rare instances, there was not enough food, and some died of starvation.

Always too, the annual review of leadership responsibilities, prophecies, sacred tablets, and Road Plan, reminded them that one day a strange people from another country would come to their land. There were also the prophecies of divisions and terrible wars to come. In their Kivas the leaders talked about these things, and wondered what would happen when they did occur. And then there were those prophetic "ifs" that would be determined by the choices people made. One of these prophecies said that "if" the Hopi were fortunate, the foreigners who came would not be a problem, but that "if" the Hopi were unfortunate, the situation would not be good. Should people become too complacent and, if the bad side of enough Hopis began to assert itself as it had with some of their ancestors in the Underworld, the leaders knew that the meeting with the strangers would not go well. It was obvious that choices played a major role in what would happen. We can assume that the leaders never rested entirely easy, and were fortunate to have the instructions to calm their fears.

Even while the Hopi were considering this, and wondering when it would all take place, haughty men wearing glistening armor and bearing superior weapons were boarding ships in

Spain and heading for the shores of this new world that had already been discovered. Bearers of the cross were coming with them, but conquest and gold was what was on their minds. The ships landed. By 1438 the Incas had been crushed and by 1520 the Aztecs had been subdued. All too soon the same Spaniards would arrive to terminate the 400-year lull in Hopi Land.

As predicted, Spanish soldiers and priests bearing the Cross entered Pueblo Indian country, and came to Hopi Land in A.D. 1540. With the arrogance that was common to them in those years, the militant invaders moved swiftly to take control of both secular and religious affairs. The peaceful Hopi were soon in turmoil because they did not know how to handle this kind of predicament. So they compromised by submitting themselves to Spanish wishes in matters having to do with daily life, but sought to continue their cycle of religious ceremonies, practicing them in secret when they had to. The Spanish priests bided their time by using Hopi laborers to build their churches, and then launched campaigns to obtain conversions. When they achieved only limited success, they used the soldiers to employ pressure and then military force. Even with that kind of intimidation, most of the instructions were never followed, and conversions were few.

The Hopi did not fight back and give the Spanish an excuse to kill them. But it has been reported that one Hopi was burned alive, and any Hopi whose obstinacy was sufficient to cause a priest a particular problem might have a hand or a foot cut off, thus making it impossible for him to be self-sufficient. Such practices, and worse, became common throughout Pueblo country, until at last the Pueblo people began to seethe with anger. After one hundred and forty years of continual abuse, in 1680, the Pueblo Indian tribes joined together and rebelled, driving the Spaniards off their land. The Hopi also killed several of the priests by throwing them off of the mesa tops onto sharp rocks below. Then in 1700, when the Roman Catholic priests attempted to reestablish a mission in a Hopi village named Awatovi, angry Traditionalists, including some from Oraibi, burned a number of converts to death in an Awatovi Kiva. As quickly as possible thereafter, the stunned and fearful priests gathered up their sacramental items and fled south.

Both of these actions were uncharacteristic and abhorrent things for the Hopi to do. Compared to the records of other nations, these don't amount to much, and are the only black marks on their entire history. Unfortunately, they were necessary actions if the Covenant was to be preserved. The Spanish gave them no choice. Throughout the occupation, they had appealed regularly to the Spanish leaders to leave them alone. But they had no success. If the Covenants were to be preserved, there was no alternative to making a statement the Spanish would clearly understand. As indicated, the Spanish did get the point, and while later on they returned with an improved and conciliatory attitude to the eastern Pueblo villages, they did not return to Hopi Land.

Spanish occupation was, however, such a bitter experience for the Hopi that it left its mark on them. Life would never again be quite the same, but at least it settled down. The routine of following all of the INSTRUCTIONS resumed, and for the next one hundred and fifty years the only serious problems arose in connection with marauding Apaches and Navajos. Both of these tribes, who are cousins, had come from the north in the 1400s. In time, the Apaches left and established themselves in other parts of the southwest, but many of the Navajo chose to remain on Hopi Land, providing a contentious problem that still exists today.

The Hopi had come to know and trade with most of the tribes of the southwest, and perhaps others in the east and west.

Relationships with all but a few were amicable. But prophecy had forewarned the Hopi that there were acquisitive and dictatorial kinds of peoples in the outside world, and with the arrival of the Spanish, Apaches, and Navajos they had been introduced to some of these. Worse still, they were told that one day another group of White people would arrive, and that these were people whose ways and goals did not bode well for the Hopi. The Hopi had ample cause to wonder about what this promised. The Spanish had taught them enough to let them know what kinds of things they could expect, and prophecies clarified the picture even more.

So once again the Hopi leaders studied the stone pictographs, watched and waited. They knew by now that whatever was prophesied was going to happen. But they had their calming INSTRUCTIONS to follow, and the word passed down to the Elderly Elders who live today was that life during that time was beautiful. The people were united in all that they did, and especially in keeping their Covenant vow. The days were long, rich, and warmly remembered. The Hopi had earned the right to this period of peace, and no one else had the right to take it away from them. But they were soon to meet people other than the Spanish who did not care about rights other than their own.

The one-hundred-and-fifty-year hiatus ended about 1826, when the first of the next wave of Whites appeared, coming as hunters, trappers, and explorers. These were uneventful meetings, but the Hopi knew that more Whites would follow, and were certain they would fit the expectations. Now it was just a matter of time for other prophecies to fulfill themselves. As word about the existence of the Hopi and their "enchanting and primitive" way of life spread, missionaries came to transform the heathens into Christians and save their souls. As I suggested earlier, the authoritarian missionaries simply assumed that from a religious point of view anything the Hopis believed would not be worth listening to, and needed to be eradicated and replaced with Christianity. They were convinced that this was Jesus' mandate, and in evangelical minds their own faith, conduct, and devotion were so exemplary and right that it justified whatever they chose to do. Surely, they told themselves, the simple Hopi would see and understand this, and realize that conversion was the best thing that could happen to them. The missionaries did not know anything about Hopi resistance during the Spanish occupation. Nothing could possibly have happened in the past lives of the Hopi to alter this need for conversion in any way. And so the missionaries never, even in their remotest thoughts, imagined they would encounter such resistance to conversion as they did. So they were absolutely bewildered by it. They did not then, and because they still don't listen today, know anything about the imperative Covenant vow, OR ABOUT THE SECRET.

The United States Government was not far behind the missionaries, for it too was always looking for new territories and new peoples to conquer and control. There were about 2,000 Hopi at this time. With half of them residing in Oraibi, it had become a good-sized village. And the land the Hopi were on, essentially arid and barren though it was, nevertheless was a large territory begging to be explored for whatever underground riches it might contain.

In 1881, the Government sank its teeth into Hopi Land when it established its Agency near First Mesa, at the opposite end of Hopi Land from Oraibi. Then in 1882 a Hopi Reservation was established by executive order. Once the boundaries were drawn, its size was less than a tenth of the actual land area claimed by the Hopi. The Hopi were not consulted in the matter. The reservation boundaries would be redrawn again in 1934, 1943, and 1977, the land becoming smaller with each new draft. Before long, with tacit Government approval, Navajo settlements completely surrounded the Hopi, and today the Hopi Reservation sits in the middle of the Navajo Reservation.

Considering the difficulties the missionaries were having with conversions, the Government agent quickly realized that Hopi culture was the major obstacle to control. He knew that to gain this the first thing he had to do was to break the back of that culture and replace it with the White culture. As prophecy foretold, these newcomers, referred to now by the Traditionalists as "Bahannas," would be "people who liked to carve others into their own image." The best place to start, the Bahannas realized, would be with education. This is the primary image changer. In the Hopi way, education was something that was pursued from the cradle to the grave. The child was brought up in it and remained immersed in it for life. It included close personal experience as well as intellectual knowledge. This meant that children must remain in their community where they could be a regular part of everything that went on. One does not embrace Hopi religion, it embraces you.

So the Government decided to remove the children from the nest, opting to place them in boarding schools so far from home as to make it impossible for them to participate in daily village activities, and particularly in the ceremonial life. The Traditionalists saw immediately what the cost of this would be to the Hopi. In the end it would lead to the eradication of the ancient culture. And if anyone else did not see this for themselves, prophecy pointed it out to them. So, short of taking up weapons in a situation where they were outmatched, the Hopi people folded their arms, set their feet, and refused to let their children be taken away. When the Government had enough of this stubbornness, they sent soldiers to force the Hopi to comply.

One by one, the villages gave in, although Oraibi, the major plum, was the last to fall. Even then education was the issue that began to divide the community, and as other factors crept in, the situation grew steadily worse. By 1890, there was already an open wound that gave no sign of healing. Then the Agent, having made certain that as many Hopi as possible were shown the amenities of White life, lured the residents with offers of reservation jobs funded by the Government. This technique had worked well with the other villages, and it was expected to work here. It did. Those at Oraibi who accepted the offers were dubbed the "friendlies," and those who rejected them were called the "hostiles." Meanwhile the schools, most of which were run by missionaries, were indoctrinating the children with White language and ways while they derided the customs of the Hopi. When children were finally allowed to come home, their attitudes and behavior reflected this.

The Traditionalist leaders, led by the indomitable Yukiuma, saw the danger flags and warned the people that accepting what the Bahannas offered would lead to disastrous consequences—not the least of which would be the failure to keep the Covenant vows. But the seeds of dissention were so successfully sown at Oraibi that many of the people were not listening anymore. Money was bringing them new things and opening new doors. By comparison, the simple life that Maasaw advocated no longer looked so good to them. Who wanted to hand carry spring water when he could have a pump and a well? Who, they asked themselves, wanted to plant with a stick when he could have a tractor? Who wanted to settle for a corn crop when he could get an abundance of things at a market? Who wanted to wear only a single outfit when he and his family members could have several? Who wanted to pursue a religion that was not strong enough to overcome White people? Besides, maybe the missionaries were right in what they taught in the schools. Could it be that the

Hopi religion was a false one that was a product of archaic superstition and legends?

Understandably, ceremonies were disrupted, and family, friend, and clan relationships were torn apart for the first time in 800 years. The Government and the missionaries were elated. So they increased the temptations, and in 1906, the dissention at Oraibi erupted into an open battle. Foreign diseases had already cut the population somewhat, and some residents who couldn't stand the bickering moved away to other villages, so that Oraibi had only about 700 residents left. Finally, on September 7 of that year the two sides engaged by mutual consent in a traditional kind of pushing contest, with the loser to be banished from the village. Even though the numbers were evenly divided, with approximately 350 people on each side, the Friendlies, who the Elders say were astonishingly enraged, won the contest. The Hostiles bent their heads in sorrow, and taking with them only the clothing they were wearing and the sacred Pathway Stone, walked away. There were still a few Traditionalists in the other villages, but the Government was just getting started. They had done some exploring of the land by now, and the possibilities for exploitation looked very good. The only question left was how the Government could take possession of some, if not most of it. Prophecy had told the Hopi how the Whites would do this, and so it was just a matter of seeing it come to pass. Delaying tactics would be the only option open to the Traditionalist Elders, and this became a full-time occupation for them.

The hostiles spent their first night out of Oraibi in a makeshift camp, and the next day moved to a spring named "Hotevilla," where they decided they would build their own village. The stones needed for the walls of the houses were readily available, and it went up quickly. Farming lands were allocated to each family, and in no time at all the Pattern of Life resumed. Thanks

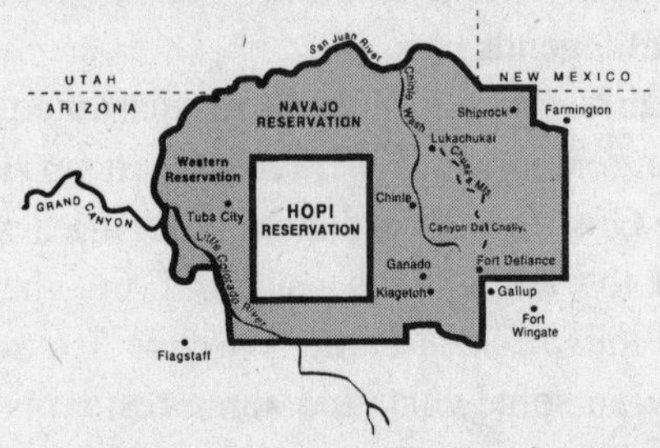

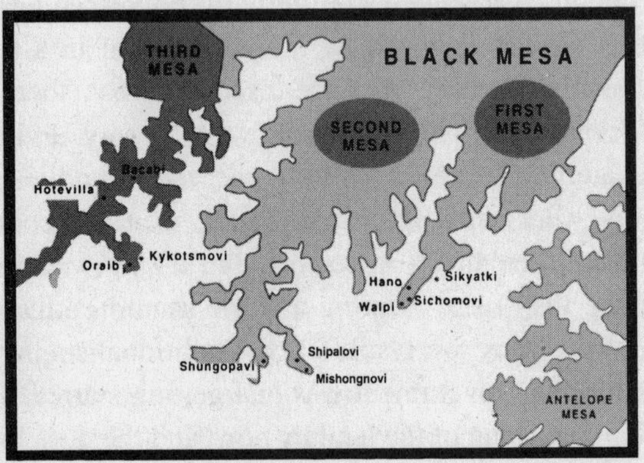

The Hopi Villages

to their following of the INSTRUCTIONS, the Traditionalists had become resilient people. Remember this when you are encouraged to follow the instructions in the chapters ahead.

In regard to this, the Elders tell us that, "After his death, Chief Yukiuma's clansman Pongyayouma was appointed to take over the leadership, and thus became the keeper of the sacred stone tablet. He quickly became very active in carrying out his task in accordance with his uncle Yukiuma's teachings. However, like Chiefs Lololma and Tewaquaptewa of the Friendlies, he did not surrender his stone tablet to the Spider Clan, which was still waiting to receive it, in accordance with their commitments to the leadership structure. "Therefore," the Elders continue, "we are now awaiting our White brother who traveled eastward across the big waters long ago, who was to return when he hears of our difficulties. He will then deliver the sacred Hopi stone tablets into proper hands."

As the statement indicates, the sacred Pathway Stone tablet rests in unknown hands today, although some Traditionalists believe that someone in the Tribal Council has it. We can understand why they look forward to the time when it is returned to them.

Irrespective of how the new village was getting along, the Government was not about to leave things alone. It moved swiftly to capture the Hotevilla children and cart them off to boarding schools. Parents tried everything they could to avoid this, even hiding the children when agency people came. The Government's reply to this was to imprison the fathers, putting them in chains at the Agency jail and even sending a few, such as Yukiuma, to notorious places like Alcatraz Prison. At times, there was not a single father left in Hotevilla Village to help with the work. The women, the old folks, and whatever older children were left had to do everything without them. Dan Evehema experienced all of this. He was a teen-ager in 1906, and since they had to fill the places of the absent fathers, some of the other boys and he formed what they called "The Men's Society." It became a group whose brotherhood lasted until they became known as "the Elderly Elders," with Dan and one other man being the only members of the group who are still alive.

As we might expect, the pain of the split at Oraibi was deeply felt and lasting, and both communities have suffered greatly for it. Interestingly, even though the Friendlies had the support of the affluent Agency and all of their Kivas intact, enough clans were divided to affect the Oraibi ceremonials in a negative way, and almost immediately the village began to decline in stature and energy. On the other hand, once Hotevilla got past the imprisonment phase and the men returned home, it began to prosper and grow strong. The bitterness of the break with Oraibi remained, so Hotevilla's number of residents increased slowly. But it became a stronghold for the Traditionalists and soon was known as "the shrine of the Covenant." They built their own Kivas, and made their own religious paraphernalia. In no time Maasaw's INSTRUCTIONS were being followed again. The full cycle of rituals was underway, and the farmlands of each family bloomed with corn, other vegetables, and fruit. Sheep and cattle, first brought into Hopi country by the Spanish, were obtained, and a number of small ranches were established. Dan's family somehow retained the land they had when they were at Oraibi, and they have continued to farm it ever since. Some of the ancestral ruins on its mesa top are very old.

"So," the Elders say as they put this in their own words, "the new village of Hotevilla was settled with hardship and grief. In spite of the problems, the foundations were laid, rooted deep into the earth and enshrined as the heart of the community. All paths within the village are linked to all the directions, and to sacred places of spiritual power, for the delivery and receiving of prayers. Therefore, the village is a shrine itself, a special holy place, identical to the Bahanna's church. This includes the layout of the village, clan duties, and the Kivas where the chief important deities and symbols are placed and planted, and then blessed with certain powers to maintain the balance and directions for humans in relationship between heavenly and earthly forces of nature complete with ceremonials and the ritual cycle. All shrines grew deep in all directions, weaving their roots into the earth like fabric, and thus maintaining the balance and harmony with all life. They are endowed with powers of self-protection, a weapon of mysterious power. *Those who defy and disturb their roots without respect suffer great misfortune which can extend to the whole of mankind."*

"Our elders are right," the authors of the newsletters say. "Education in foreign concepts is wrong for all Native people. The foreign education cannot blend with our culture and traditions into which we have been molded since ancient times. This education will pollute our minds and do great harm to our culture and tradition. Our spiritual values, identity, and language will be lost. Most important, all our land will be lost."

A step of great significance was taken when the Hotevilla leaders decided that, since they were the true Traditionalists, they needed to transfer the former power of Oraibi as a mother village to Hotevilla. To do this, as soon as the main dance plaza and the six Kivas of the village were completed, they gathered one night to prepare a special object whose nature identifies the mother village, then wrapped and buried it in a shallow pit in the ground. I have been told what it is and how it was made, but am sworn not to divulge its nature to anyone. Only Dan knows its location today, but it is the primary source of spiritual power needed to keep all life, the earth, and the universe in balance. As is seen from the Elders' words above, power is also planted in and drawn from many places. When they dance in their sacred paint and costumes, the dancers—even those who do not know that the object is there—draw upon this primary power first and then all of the other power sources, and it passes through them and out to the world. *So sacred is this object that if it is wantonly harmed or destroyed, it will cause the end of the village, the end of the energy of the people who occupy the village, and serious harm to the individuals who injured the object.*

Yukiuma

The village will not collapse immediately, but it will disintegrate over the years, while the energy and power produced by the dances will wane until none is left. In this regard, you should know that the Elderly Elders believe that the moment the hostiles turned their backs and walked away from Oraibi on September 7, 1906, the object that marked it as the mother village was torn in half by an unseen but displeased spirit, and that is why Oraibi has steadily deteriorated and become today only a sparsely inhabited ghost of its former self. Soon you will learn that Hotevilla's object is itself in jeopardy today, and that what happens to it will affect us all.

"So in 1906," the Elderly Elders say, "they left. They were the true believers in the words of the Great Spirit, the Creator, carrying with them their most sacred possession, the stone tablet which was their title to the land and power of authority. Thus Hotevilla Village was founded. *There they planted the spiritual power to keep all life and land and heavenly bodies in balance.* The sacred pipe was passed and an oath of commitment was made to uphold the purpose upon which the village was based, to protect and defend them from harm . . . The oath of commitment is not written in words, but it is as good as the written constitution of the Bahanna."

It is time you are told that the Tribal Council, together with the U.S. Department of Health and Human Services, is presently attempting for the fifth time to lay sewer pipes, water pipes, and telephone lines into Hotevilla Village. Those who doubt the story of the buried object need only wait to see what happens if any one of the ditches required for these utilities destroys it. For if it does, the dreadful results will speed up. As you will learn shortly, the Tribal Council is still Hopi enough to believe in evil curses. I am anxious to see whether they or the Progressives who support them have the courage to test this curse. Having revealed this, I know that whenever you go to visit the village you will wonder where the sacred object is buried, and whether one of the ditches has destroyed it. You will look around and with some anxiety see if you can figure out where it is, or was. And, you will pray that it hasn't been touched. For if it has it won't be long before the mystery resolves itself. Hotevilla and the world will be taking a distinct turn for the worse, and a savage Armageddon will be guaranteed.

In the early 1880s, anthropologists and other scientists were making their way to Hopi Land to discover what they could about the intriguing Hopi culture, and especially its entrancing religious ceremonies. As previously mentioned in Chapter 1, they had remarkable success, and proceeded to publish their findings so that the whole world could know about it. The Hopi resented these intrusions, but sometimes cooperated because they didn't know what else to do. They realized that if they pressed the matter too far they might incite the Government, and they had already had an impressive sampling of what it could accomplish when it was offended. In their resentment, they did not, however, choose to tell these intruders much about the Covenant. A few favored writers did learn something about the prophecies and their connection with the end of the world's Fourth Cycle, but that was all. They were told nothing about how the instructions and the warnings fitted into the equation. What was not intended to be a secret became one, even though the Hopi knew the world would shortly begin to move into serious trouble. If any outsider wondered how the Hopi were managing to hold up as well as they did under all that was happening to them, there is no record of it.

As outsiders salivated over these fascinating accounts of what they concluded was a primitive civilization still alive, they were flabbergasted by reports of a particular dance being done by the Hopi. It was called "the Snake Dance" because the performers danced in public with live snakes held in their mouths, some of which were poisonous rattlesnakes with their venom sacs still intact. They had to see with their own eyes this "death-defying act," as they called it, and in the summers began to flock by the dozens to the Hopi villages when the dances were held. They also wanted to photograph these "bizarre" performances, for without seeing them, no one on the outside would believe the snake dances were actually done. So they came parading in with their bulky photographic equipment and their rude manners, and with a boldness that turned the dances and the villages into a circus. There was no respect whatsoever for their sacredness or the privacy of the people. Only a few visitors came who were profoundly affected by what they saw, and then did their best to persuade others to understand the dances better and to feel the same way. But decades passed before that was achieved to any significant degree, and in the meantime the Hopi paid a tremendous price for Bahanna insensitivity. The Bahannas were paying a price too, but they didn't know it.

No one asked the Hopi how they felt about all of this, and the Bahannas did not seem to think that Hopi feelings or shattered families mattered. Over the years though we see the insensitiveness take its toll on the tribe, and nowadays very few snake dances are performed. Dan Evehema was once a snake dancer, but today none are done at Hotevilla. They don't even have a snake priest, and there is only one revered horned priest, who is quite old. For the most part we can thank Bahanna disrespect for causing this, but it also has something to do with altered Hopi attitudes. Many of the Hopi have been so well educated in White schools that they no longer believe in the efficacy of such archaic performances—even though the sky is usually clear when the snake dance begins, then it often clouds over and pours down rain as soon as the dance ends.

While all of this was going on with the tourists, Government officials were hard at work polishing a program they would steadfastly pursue to accomplish Hopi cultural termination and land control. Since there are few accounts elsewhere of how this has been done, it is something of a phenomenon to actually be able to see the formula in action at Hopi Land. It is one that was used to destroy the culture of one Native American tribe after another, until, as the prophecies say will happen, we have come to the last of them, the Hopi.

At this very moment we are witnesses to the final act in the cultural death of Native America. And it is not at all a proud time in our history. When Dan Evehema, the last of the Hopi Traditionalist Elders of Hotevilla, is gone, there will not be one tribe left that has leaders who are schooled enough in the traditional ways to be capable of leading in the practice of the full culture that gave it its identity in ancient times. We know that the cost to Native Americans is obvious. But we fail to recognize what it has cost the outside world, not only in terms of human relationships, but also in terms of what these great cultures have to offer in the way of insights and wisdom. The vital Hopi information presented here is only one example of that. Think of what all of the Native American tribes could be offering us if they had been allowed to mature naturally until today.

You will see in future chapters that Bahanna conduct and Government invasion techniques were foretold in detail in the Hopi prophecies. This gives us another reason to pay special attention to the prophecies. They offer us the advantage of being able to prepare for their fulfillment in advance, so that we are not caught unprepared when they occur. And time is a factor here. Agreeing with outside specialists, the Elders say the sequence of world events is accelerating at such a pace that prophetic fulfillments that are yet to come will from this day forward follow closely upon one another. Since what we will be dealing with in each of these instances is cataclysmic, when each event strikes, it will be with such magnitude and force that, if we are not already prepared, nothing we can do then will make any difference.

Chapter 3

The Amazing Story
Part Two

By reading between the lines as we are taught from a Traditionalist perspective, we learn a number of lessons we would otherwise miss, for Progressive Hopi and standard historians would never tell us about these things. One of the most valuable of them is that we see exactly how the two-hearteds work to undo and frustrate every good thing that the Creator attempts to accomplish.

If our interest in these "hidden" lessons is sufficiently aroused, we also want to know how the two-hearteds go about their work; and what techniques they use. This is a protective desire that springs up within us naturally, for we intuitively know that, as soon as we take advantage of what the Creator offers us, the two-hearteds will come after us as well. It is obvious that our relationship with the Creator does not take place inside high walls that provide splendid isolation, and that we do not receive His gifts without their being contested. Nor do they fall into our laps because we are so deserving of them.

With His permission, the two-hearted forces simply take advantage of a situation the Creator has created. They know that He believes we benefit from being tested, and that He wants our response to be a sincere and free one, not something that has no options and is forced. So He gives human beings free choice, and then does everything He can to help us make the right ones. As we see in the history of the Hopi, people do not always choose well, and the price we pay can become an impressive one. On the other hand, holding on, as the Traditionalists show us, has superb benefits. Not the least of these is the special opportunity we are given to walk with and to serve the Creator, and the rare satisfaction that comes from measuring up to a worthy challenge.

As the days of history flow by, we see that more and more of the Hopi were not able to measure up either. The Hotevilla kikmongwi, Pongyayouma, had to be removed from office for disciplinary reasons, and another "high spiritual religious leader" took over the leadership of the Village. This chief was Dan Katchongva of the Sun Clan. He was a son of Yukiuma, very wise, charismatic, and while in office, distinguished himself in many ways. More is said about him in Chapter 5. After he died in 1972, Tewangyouma of the Corn Clan, a close relation of Yukiuma's, became chief, and remained in office until he died. Both of these men proved to be strong leaders, who in their administrations followed the footsteps of Yukiuma. As a result, they received similar kinds of punishment from the Government and opposing Progressive forces. And during their administrations, the Government was able to make enough inroads into the village to cause concern among the Traditionalists. It was enough to make them wonder how long the village could stand as a stronghold of the Covenant and the Traditional life-way.

When Tewangyouma passed on, a brilliant religious leader named David Monongye was recognized by the leaders as acting regent, and then functioned as traditional chief of the Hotevilla community until his death. He became the editor of the newsletters and remained a stalwart Traditionalist, keeping the yearly cycle of life intact and fiercely resisting Government inroads. Once the Hopi Tribal Council was installed in 1936, he became its implacable foe.

When the Shongopavi Day School was built in 1910, Hotevilla parents continued to balk at permitting their children to attend school, and in 1911 military force was once again employed to gather in the children, an action that only intensified the anti-Government feelings of the Hostiles. Opposing positions slowly solidified on the three Mesas, and to widen the breech, the Government built day schools in other areas. The Bacabi Day School was opened in 1912. Since it served both communities, in 1916 its title was changed to the Hotevilla-Bacabi School. In 1913 the Government opened a hospital at Keams Canyon to care for the Hopi and surrounding Indian peoples, who were mainly Navajos.

Once the Government had achieved some of its primary goals, and a sufficient number of Hopi had become dependent upon them, some of the hardcore policies were toned down and the compulsory schooling rule was relaxed somewhat. Children were accustomed to going to school by now, and a number of them had been successfully weaned away from traditional life. The Government was pleased, but the work was not finished. So new policies were instigated that, while they were said to be mandatory for all of the villages, were in truth intended to cause more suffering for the "obstinate" people of Hotevilla. Other villages would not really be a problem since their way of life already included compliance with Government demands.

At this early point in time, then, Hotevilla was being separated from the other villages and treated as an isolated thorn in the Government's side. While so far the Traditionalists had no reason to worry about defections, everything the Government did from then on was shaped to wear down resistance. In the Government's mind, breaking the back of Hotevilla was an absolute must, for so long as it held out, it would be an embarrassment to both the Government and the Friendly Hopi. They could not say all Hopi wanted to live the Bahanna way. We can see how personally the Government was taking the situation by observing how malicious and far reaching just a few of the new rules were:

1) Using Hopi marriage ceremonies was prohibited: Prospective Traditionalist brides and grooms frequently were arrested and put in jail, and kept there until they yielded to the Bahanna and agreed to have a Christian wedding ceremony. In other words, the Hopi couple was not permitted to begin their new life together on a Traditionalist basis, and it was a factor that tainted everything they did thereafter, even making it impossible for them to participate in some of the most important religious rites.

2) Chemical sheep-dipping was enforced, and herdsmen had a choice between complying or being arrested and jailed. Led by Navajo police and Hopi rangers who were hired from other villages, including Tewas from First Mesa, Hotevilla families were forced to herd their sheep several miles away to dip sites, where it became the accepted custom to slaughter some of the sheep to provide meals for the police and rangers. Hotevilla people—both men and women—who resisted these thefts were themselves stripped naked and dumped into the chemical troughs. The shame of this rude treatment mattered not at all to the police,

who openly joked about it and derided the Traditionalist Hopi. The fact that the Hopi had no serious problems with their sheep prior to this time was of no consequence. Government control was what counted, and any opportunity for abuse was welcomed and enjoyed.

3) Stock reduction was instigated. Having made land allotments, the Government Agency people determined how much livestock they thought each parcel of land could "sensibly" support. As we might expect, this number was always smaller than what each Hopi family already owned, so there was always a surplus that had to be sold. Those who refused to comply with this fraudulent rule were jailed and had all of their stock taken away from them. Whatever was appropriated was either divided up among Friendlies, and the schools sold to Whites for some ridiculously low price, or destroyed. It was a clever rule that made self-sufficiency impossible and insured that Hostiles would become more dependent upon the Government. Thus there was a cruel method behind this madness. Since the Hostiles had little in the way of monetary income, they could not pay for what they had to obtain from the Government. The moment they defaulted, the Government simply took over their property, and immediately parceled it out to Bahanna commercial interests.

In 1917, the United States entered the First World War, and Hopi men were required to serve in the armed forces. Even though they were not recognized as citizens and could not vote in national elections, they were subject to the draft. When the Traditionalists explained that they abhorred war and asked for exemptions from military service on religious grounds, they were imprisoned until they changed their minds. Some never did, so they remained in jail for the duration. Whites could be exempted from service, but Hopi couldn't. In all, approximately one-tenth of the men in the Hopi tribe served in the United States Army.

During this time, the Traditionalists were reminded that at Oraibi Maasaw had predicted that there would be three major wars involving most of the people on the earth. The Hopi leaders went to look again at the Road Plan pecked into the cliff side, and saw that the three circles indicating the wars were still plainly there. The patina on the stone was a richer and deeper brown. But time and weather had not removed the drawing. In a Kiva at Hotevilla, they unwrapped their Pathway Stone tablet and pondered the four-pronged symbol that was on it. Not until World War II would they be able to compare it to the Nazi flag and make the German connection. Then they shook their heads in amazement. More than coincidence was involved in this. Another prophecy was being fulfilled. By the time the war ended, its devastation and the heavy loss of life had given the Elders a grim picture of what a world war amounted to. The prospect of another one to come, and of a third and cataclysmic battle to top off both of these, left them shaking their heads in concern.

The outside world kept moving in. In 1926, the Lee's Ferry Bridge was constructed over the Colorado River, bringing increased tourist and commercial travel into northeastern Arizona. Hundreds of curious outsiders visited the villages, and when the Cameron-to-Gallup road was completed, it brought even greater contact and pressure. The main tribal income for all of the villages except Hotevilla in 1930 was still farming, but it was progressively supplemented with a modest amount of agency and off-reservation work, and by increased arts and crafts activities.

Dan and the other Traditionalists watched with intense interest as more prophecies were fulfilled. The first Hopi of Oraibi could not have known what these predictions had meant, but out there for everyone to see at this stage were the "roads in the sky," for airplanes were flying overhead. There were "moving houses of iron" travelling on the railroads. "Horseless carriages" were everywhere present; even on the Reservation. "Men had the ability to speak through cobwebs" as telephone lines criss-crossed the nation. Soon too, "Men would even have the ability to speak through space," as relay stations took their places in the infinite blue sky overhead. "Men's clothing was taken over by women," who found it fashionable for dress, and best for workplaces. It was duly noted that as prophesied, "Women's skirts were being raised above the knee, devaluing the sacred body of the female, indicating many things would be devalued from the original." I will not be so foolish as to pursue this latter prediction and have myself burned at a stake as a prude. But some of you might want to think about raised skirts and ask yourselves whether they may have led the world to a general pattern of behavior we would be better off without. Maasaw seemed to think this was a reasonable assumption.

As these miracles came to pass, the Traditionalists became certain that every prophecy, save in instances where there would be choices between endings, that would be fulfilled. This kept them watchful for signs of other happenings, and it fortified their assurance that they were following the right road. It also made them more determined than ever to keep their vows.

They tried to tell the Government representatives about these predictions and fulfillments, but no one listened. Instead these representatives rolled blithely along, continuing their efforts to change the Hopi from an independent to a dependent people by tempting them with Bahanna's lifestyle. Now that the traditional way of farming provided no income to pay for amenities, dry farming was regularly criticized by Progressives as passé and inadequate. The Elder Traditionalists protested this and warned others about the prophesied consequences of shifting away from self-sufficiency. Progressive Hopi waved them off. They were derided as obstructionists who did not understand what was going on in the real world, and who did not want the people to get ahead. They were portrayed as "Conservatives" as opposed to "Progressives," who were depicted as dynamic, enterprising, reformative, broad-minded, and liberal. Morning, noon and night the children in boarding schools had this difference pointed out to them, and were told that if they followed the old ways they would never be able to get ahead or function in the wonderful White world.

Traditionalism was, the Bahanna teachers said, simply an outmoded hinderance. Contrasting examples from the modern White world were shown to them in posters, books, and photographic slides. Escorted trips to the cities featured visits to the finest of the White man's amenities. The approach was a persuasive one, and it reached the youth. Families started to fall apart as young people began to trade Traditionalist religion for baseball, football, Bahanna-type dances, and the other sports and common pleasures so cherished by the youth of the outside world. They gladly spoke English instead of Hopi, and as prophesied, could no longer discuss matters with their parents or grandparents in the original language. Nor could they understand the chants and commands used in the ceremonial performances, which guaranteed that there would be fewer keepers of the Covenant with every passing year. Dan Evehema and the other Elders ached when they were derided by young Hopi, and mourned as they watched this circumstance gel, for Maasaw had told them that people must be given the freedom to choose. No true relationships with the things of the Creator could come from coercion, and true relationships between individuals could not be forced either.

Another prophecy was fulfilled as wage work increased in economic importance, and as automotive transportation became available. Winslow, which was the closest town of reasonable size to the Reservation, replaced Flagstaff as the key municipality in the Hopi world. Although even today Winslow is not a very large town, Hopi moved there, or commuted there, and it became harder than ever for them to carry on the Pattern of Life Maasaw had given them. By the same token, the town dwellers and those who remained in the villages began to lose their religious strength and energy. To outsiders, everything at the Reservation looked the same, but it was not. The ancient stone buildings were misleading. Even the majestic public dances were misleading. And the Traditionalists knew it. Deep down the Progressives knew it too, but deluded themselves into thinking that eventually everything would be made right. They convinced themselves that a Hopi whose intentions were good could walk simultaneously in two worlds without difficulty. Meanwhile, prophecies pointing to the developments of this period were being fulfilled at a rapid pace, and the Elders began to sense that the time had come when they would need to do as Maasaw said and reveal their secret message to the world. They talked and prayed about this in the Kivas, and shaped their ceremonies to reflect their feelings.

The Great Depression of the 1930s affected Hopi economic life drastically, especially that of the Friendlies who had grown so dependent upon wage work. It left them despondent, unable to cope, and searching for relief—even of a temporary kind. Lacking immersion in the INSTRUCTIONS given by Maasaw for just such a time as this, they turned to one of Bahanna's solutions. Previously, the Hopi were known as a tribe that was remarkably free from alcoholic beverages. But all this changed as liquor became readily available in the nearby towns and cities and was easily brought home to the Reservation. For the first time, drunkenness and its associated abuses became problems in Hopi Land.

Passage in 1934 of the Wheeler-Howard bill, commonly known as the Indian Reorganization Act, led directly to one of the greatest changes in the Hopi life-way. Unlike others that proceeded it, the act was at first thought to be well-intended and one that signaled a dramatic modification of federal attitude. But it also reflected prophetic warnings in that it did not prove to be a blessing where the Covenant was concerned.

In 1935, writer Oliver La Farge, a longtime friend of Indian causes, drafted a constitution for the Hopi, and in a contrived election in 1936, a tiny minority of Hopi voted to accept the terms of the Reorganization Act. This first constitution was printed in English, and only a few of the Elderly Traditionalists could read it. Most of the Hopi adults did not know how to vote, were suspicious, and registered their disapproval of the whole idea by staying away from the polling stations that were set up in each village. The printed ballots consisted of two simple boxes—one marked yes, and one marked no—only one of which was to be checked. The voters were not told what the vote entailed, and especially that it included a Tribal Council whose constitutional powers were loosely defined and wide open to Council interpretation. Less than 200 out of several thousand who were eligible to vote did so. But this did not bother the Government Agency people. They declared the vote to be a valid and binding one, and immediately thereafter seated a Tribal Council that consisted entirely of Progressives. Whenever the Tribal Council is considered, we should bear in mind how deceitfully it came into being. Adding these facts to its subsequent behavior, we are able to see why the Elders refer to it as a bogus puppet organization. As of today, the Council's longevity is the only thing that gives validity to its existence, and it has no right whatsoever to claim that it is the rightful head of the "Hopi Tribe." Nor does it have the right to formulate laws that it claims must be obeyed by the sovereign and independent villages of Hopi Land.

The Council has had one basic purpose. It was funded by and directly answerable to the Bureau of Indian Affairs, and as such provided the United States Government with a channel through which the use of Hopi land could be gained for industrial purposes. Tribal Councils at other reservations often have done the same thing.

Maasaw predicted that this exact thing would happen. And being forewarned, from the beginning Traditionalist Hopi recognized that the Council was not formed for the good of the Hopi nation. In confirmation of this, the Council did not once disagree with anything the Government wanted to do. This was why the Elders continued to speak of it in the newsletters as a "Puppet Government." Stung by this accusation, the Council dragged its canons to the walls of the stockade it was building and quickly fired back in kind. Since then it has never let up. Knowing itself for what it truly was but wanting to divert attention, the Council accused the Traditionalists of using their religious stance to cloak their politics. I taped a telephone call from the Director of the Hopi Council's Cultural Preservation Office that made this exact allegation.

So the perpetuation of factionalism was assured by the Council's existence, and the Government's advantage was that it could operate behind the scenes, reducing the heat from the Traditionalists, yet accomplishing even more than before. After all, if it was Hopi who were perceived as doing these dastardly things, who could complain? Differences of opinion would be a tribal problem, something they needed to work out for themselves—but always after the damage had already been done.

On top of this, there were certain new things that Washington, D.C. wanted to set in motion, things that had "touchy" written all over them. Government and corporate surveyors had been busy, and had learned by now that under the surface of Hopi land lay vast amounts of coal, water and other valuable resources they needed and could profit from. Consequently, our Government played, through the Council, the lead role in establishing prices for the use of tribal lands and what was taken from them, and priced this so cheaply that it defrauded the Indians. So it was less expensive by far for corporations to obtain whatever they could on Indian land than it was to contract for land elsewhere in the United States. Added to this reprehensible tactic was another wedge the Government knew they could count on. Even though the Hopi were being routinely cheated and knew it, they were so poor and desperately in need of funds and jobs that they neither wanted to, nor could, do anything but play along.

Hotevilla, Maasaw said, would be a microcosm of the world. The Elders knew that something like what was happening there, but of greater magnitude, would happen somewhere else in the world. In 1936, the Tribal Council took office. In 1936, Adolf Hitler took his first overt steps toward World War II. Factionalism and the appropriation of land and resources swept across Europe, Northern Africa, and Scandinavia, just as they were sweeping across Hopi Land. The second circle on the Road Plan petroglyph became another prophecy fulfilled, and the swastika symbol on the stone tablet was fully understood.

A few years later, when World War II was full blown, Japan entered as an ally of the Germans. The Elders looked at the Pathway Stone tablet again, and saw that a sun symbol, the symbol of the flag of Japan, was there to join the swastika symbol in denoting those who would be the perpetrators of this second global war. In the throes of combat, the Elders saw human beings in their most reprehensible state. They saw now how modern weapons behaved and what they could do. They learned about shattered communities, fractured bodies, and massacred Jews, and they could project this gruesome picture into the future. The horrible loss in lives and property by the time this savage war ended caused the Elders to be more alarmed than ever at the prospect of a third war to come—one that will, with the extended development of nuclear, chemical, and biological devices, be more devastating than the first two wars put together.

Dan Evehema was in his prime by this time, and a strong person in every way. His influence was felt throughout the village. He was married and part of a caring extended family. Hotevilla was still a mainly Traditionalist village, although inroads were being made by Progressives and in the Bahanna schools. Hotevilla was no longer a monolithic shrine. The leaders discussed this in the Kivas and debated what they should do about the situation. When they looked at the stone tablet, the Road Plan, and reviewed the prophecies, they were not encouraging. But the leaders continued to believe it was a battle they would eventually win, and so they kept at it.

The word "purification" was in the prophecies, and from their elevated position alongside the Creator, the Elders were starting to see what would be involved in bringing purification to pass. It was a chilling situation. To retain their own stability through all of this, the Elders and the other Traditionalists immersed themselves even deeper in following the INSTRUCTIONS. This enhanced their closeness with the Creator and Mother Earth, and developed within them the serenity and wisdom they needed to survive.

Interestingly, after functioning sporadically and ineffectively for four years and receiving little support from the Hopi villages, the Tribal Council was disbanded in 1940. The Traditionalist

Elders celebrated the collapse and rejoiced over the absence of Council attacks. But as they reflected on the matter, they knew that the departure of the Council would not be permanent. The Government needed this Hopi channel, and was not about to let go of it. The only question was how the Government would get its channel back. Further assurance that this would happen rested in the prophecies, which told the Traditionalists that their own people would become their enemies, and would serve as the tools of the foreigners who would invade their land.

Hiroshima and Nagasaki are names that became etched in minds the world over. They caught the attention of the Traditionalists too. In the prophecies, reference was made to a "House of Mica," or in our terms a "House of Glass," that would be built on the eastern shore of North America. At this place, distinguished representatives of the nations of the earth would gather to watch over, help balance, and harmonize the affairs of mankind. The prophecies regarding this auspicious spot told the Hopi that when a mysterious "gourd of ashes" was dropped upon the earth with horrible consequences, a Traditionalist delegation was to go to the House of Mica—four times if necessary—to warn the delegates of what would ultimately come of "the bomb," which is what the Hopi now knew the gourd represented. If the delegates did not stop its use immediately, far more tragic things would come of it in the future. But the delegates were burdened with world problems of great consequence, and in the end the reception was a token one. In fact, all four of their attempts seemed fruitless—or at least so the Elders thought. But *Hotevilla*'s translation into French by UNESCO seems to challenge that conclusion. At the time, however, it appeared that a third world war was assured. The prophecies described such a war in searing detail. Although the Elderly Elders feel this battle could be very close, they attach no date to it.

Nostradamus pinned it down for us. He said that, unless mankind changes its course drastically, Armageddon will begin in July of 1999. Simple arithmetic tells us that is only a few years from now. Seems impossible, doesn't it? Some parts of the world are presently in turmoil, but here in America things are still looking pretty good, and life is going on almost as usual. Before we discount the idea as preposterous, we need to make a careful survey of what is going on in the world today. Then on the basis of what we find, and recognizing that the full truths are often hidden from us, we need to ask ourselves whether or not there aren't a number of things whose combination can easily be the catalysts that will inexorably lead to World War III. I consider some of these "things" in the warnings given in Chapter 10.

Oraibi High School was established in 1939. Dan was forty-six years old then. It opened with about 200 pupils, and, in the sense of equipping students to understand and deal with the outside world, it has proven itself to be beneficial. But like every other school, it has done nothing for the Traditional Culture or the Covenant. In fact, the educated youth have for the most part separated themselves from the Traditional life-way, and in so doing, have become another prophetic fulfillment. In this same year, 1939, Hopi representatives, concerned over Navajo encroachments, met with the Commissioner of Indian Affairs, John Collier, to enlist his support in confirming the boundaries of Hopi Land and enforcing the exclusivity of at least the 1882 reservation. But the meeting, like most others, produced no tangible results.

Hopi fears that the United States would not protect the Hopi' special relationship to their land were heightened when the Hopi and Navajo reservations were divided into grazing districts, and the Bureau of Indian Affairs assumed administration of the Hopi districts. In 1943 the BIA's Hopi Indian Agency took charge of

District Six as its area, even though District Six included only 631,306 acres that immediately surrounded the eleven Hopi reservation villages that existed at the time. The anxious Hopi were assured that District Six would not become the new Hopi reservation, but it in fact did. The Elders lamented this further loss of sacred land, and reflected once again upon the fulfillment of prophecy that it represented. Given their choices, this was one time they wished Maasaw might be wrong, for access to the original shrines was harder to obtain day by day. They could hear the rumbling and see the end of the Fourth Cycle coming now, and they found it frightening.

When another unilateral federal stock reduction plan was introduced in Hopi Land, it was strongly opposed, but the Hopi could do nothing of significance about this either. For the Government, stock reduction continued to be a means of establishing control and dependency. The Government used stock reduction to establish an allotted amount of grazing land for each farmer. It then forced the farmers to reduce the size of their livestock herds to what the Government told them the new property could sensibly support. The opinions of the Hopi were neither solicited nor valued. Dependency would be incurred when the limited number of livestock sufficiently diminished the Hopi economic base.

When the Hopi complained, the Government Agency claimed that it had implemented stock reduction to improve the grazing potential in District Six. But the interesting fact is that it placed the rest of the reservation stock reduction plans in the hands of Navajo agencies. These stock reduction procedures, together with a soil conservation program, shrank the Hopi land base to a fraction of the enshrined area that had been venerated in Hopi ceremonies for thousands of years. There was another byproduct that benefitted the Government further. Despite the professed astonishment of Government employees, in some "strange and unexpected" way it turned out that the total of the allotments did not use up all of the Reservation space. A lot of the land was left over. Naturally, the Government couldn't let this orphaned property go to waste. So they leased part of it to outsiders and the Tribal Council took over the rest—free of charge.

Land allotment and appropriation was a devastating regulation for all Hopi, and even some of the Progressives began to grumble and admit that the Elders might be right in their opposition to the Government and the Tribal Council. But what to do about it—that was the conundrum.

By 1940, the Hopi had seen tremendous changes in their social organization. Outside pressures had increased radically, and the world view held by the Progressives had undergone irreversible changes. Once magnificent Oraibi had declined in population to 112 residents. Most of the buildings were empty, and many were crumbling. It was a sight that brought tears to the eyes of passers-by. The village was spiritually lifeless, while Hotevilla remained strong. Several new and modern villages had been founded and were developing. During World War II, a lot of Hopi Progressives left the Reservation to work in neighboring cities. Others were drafted. Some Hopi men registered as conscientious objectors, and rendered alternative service. Two of the few laudable consequences of the war were that missionary activities were reduced to a minimum, and the influence of traders waned.

Since the Hopi population was increasing and land was becoming an increasingly precious commodity, the subtle movement of Navajos who were settling closer and closer to the Hopi villages brought reservation landholding problems to, at least in the mind of the Hopi Tribal Council, a boiling point. Harsh words were exchanged, but, with their numerical superiority and political dominance, the Navajos were able to hold their positions. To this day the land issue has remained a key point of contention between the two tribal councils, and has even made the national news. The Elders, on the other hand, have taken an unexpected and surprising position in the dispute, suggesting that the Navajos be left alone, since the problems that will come with the closing of the Fourth Cycle might make the spiritual Hopi glad to have the support of spiritual Navajos.

Two issues that became central in the 1950s and 1960s were land and resource use, and cultural sovereignty, for the Hopi ceremonial cycle centers in the land and its generative powers. Throughout the 1960s and 1970s, the Hopi elders continued to speak reverently and emotionally of what in their migrations Hopi ancestors had established as Hopi country, referring to the whole of it as a huge "shrine" that encompasses the Grand Canyon, the San Francisco Peaks, the northern reaches of Black Mesa, Zuni Salt Lake, and even territory south of Route 66. They use the Bear Clan's stone tablet to reinforce this claim. Naturally, the United State's government has not acknowledged it. For them, the 1882 executive order that established the original Reservation included only two and one-half million acres, and it completely excluded the Hopi settlement of Moenkopi. Mind you now, there was no treaty made to establish the reservation, and no battle was fought. This was a unilateral decision on the part of the Government.

The postwar years brought increased Government attempts to establish its presence in Hopi land and also led to, for the first time, conscious action by Hopi to deal with the consequences of non-Hopi jurisdiction over their lands.

The Indian Claims Commission was authorized to rule on claims for monetary compensation that were brought against the

United States by any tribal entity recognized as representing a tribe or identifiable Indian group. By far the most common proceedings were those concerning lands taken by the United States without rendering just compensation or without due process of law. According to Indian Claims Commission statutes, however, once an award was made and the money was in the hands of the Indians, such payment disposed of all rights, claims or demands that the claimants could make. The Commission knew the awards received would not be sufficient or fair, and that once accepted, the money would soon be gone. Therefore, the Government's problem in this area would be ended. Does it, then, surprise you to learn that the Agency superintendent prodded the Hopi to submit a claim for monetary compensation?

Government agents knew full well that seemingly large sums of money are an irresistible temptation to poor people. While looking in awe at the total figure, no one thinks to divide the amount to be received by the number of people who are to receive it. Consequently, the small amount for each is never acknowledged.

In 1950, Progressive Hopi from Second Mesa were joined by Progressives from First Mesa and Moenkopi in an attempt to press their land claim. They lacked a cohesive position, and had no representatives from First and Third Mesas. This turned, however, a light on for the Government, for it saw here an opportunity to lobby for the reinstatement of the Tribal Council. At a meeting held in the national capital the Hopi were told that they needed a unified body to speak for them, "that the only salvation for the Hopi people was to revive the Hopi Tribal Council." Seven of the thirteen villages were persuaded to select representatives, and the Tribal Council was resurrected in 1951—just in time to retain a Bahanna lawyer and submit a claim before the deadline expired. By some happy coincidence, all of this happened at the same time Government attention was being focused in another way on the Hopi and Navajo reservations. A Navajo-Hopi Act had authorized the expenditure of $88,570,000 for the general improvement of both reservations. On the Hopi reservation, the expenditures included such enrichments as schools, houses, roads, fences, wells, stock troughs and flood-control dikes. The revival of the Tribal Council coupled with the credit they received for many of these improvements, solidified council presence among the Hopi. It was broadly intimated that it was they who were really providing the jobs and services, when in fact they were not responsible for any of these. No one mentioned that the improvements also promoted indebtedness, and that the Hopi were being encouraged to think of the United States and its agencies as part of the normal state of Hopi affairs.

To everyone except the Traditionalists, all of this looked promising. The Traditionalists knew better. Mother Earth had told them in the Kivas that what the Government really wanted was not on the surface of the land. It was underground—coal, oil, gas, uranium, water, and whatever else of value might be there. Moreover, they were told that the rejuvenated Tribal Council would become the paid channel the Government needed to reach these things. Thus while the Progressives who lobbied for the Council's revival supported the Government's presence, there was a renewed resistance by the Traditionalists. This difference of opinion was publicly expressed to the Indian world in 1949 when two Hopi spoke against the Navajo-Hopi Act at the annual meeting of the National Congress of American Indians. Their viewpoint reflected a growing concern that Hopi cultural sovereignty could be easily compromised and lost. Understandably, what was happening now became an "inside" intrusion the Tribal Council could not ignore, and it began to use its tribal newspaper to assault the Traditionalists, particularly the elder and most formidable members.

The Traditionalists responded with a message sent to President Harry Truman. Later, they posted similar letters to other presidents, senators, congressmen, and to the heads of special Government committees. Each of these documents dispelled any thoughts that Hopi religious elders were detached from everyday life. They rejected outright the notion of Hopi asking the Government for compensation for land that had been taken from them when it was already rightfully theirs, and for which no agreement had been made. They refused to allow oil companies drilling access on Hopi lands. They denounced the Navajo-Hopi Act appropriations as an effort "to reduce the Hopi people under this plan," and they refused participation in any military action resulting from the North Atlantic Treaty Organization alliance. In part they stated, "This land is a sacred home of the Hopi people. . . . It was given to the Hopi people the task to guard this land . . . by obedience to our traditional and religious instructions and by being faithful to our Great Spirit Massaw. . . . We have never abandoned our sovereignty to any foreign power or nation."

The documents the Hopi presented were signed by twenty-four ceremonial leaders from four villages, and once again reflected the firm belief that Hopi prophecy was unfolding in a manner that necessitated action on their part. The two opposing strategies with separate leaderships that had existed from a time before the 1906 split, once more burst into the open among the Hopi, with each side communicating a different ideology to the agencies of non-Indian jurisdiction. Since the Hopi had never signed a treaty with the United States, the Traditionalists asserted that each of the Hopi villages was an independent nation that had not even extended diplomatic recognition to the United States. In other words, the Government could not assert a claim that never existed.

Reflecting the influence of sixty years of Government persuasion and Christian missionizing efforts, Progressives asserted that, as the younger generation of the Hopi who were not baptized into Hopi ceremonial customs, they had in truth chosen the civilized method of democratic government in dealing with others for the welfare of the people. It was a backwards way of justifying the Council's existence, and of saying that the Elders, who had maintained their vows and the ancient ways, were not using civilized methods. Everything the Progressives did was what the prophecies had said they would. And the results were just as predicted. Dan and the other leaders made note of this, and met in their Kivas to discuss what was happening, and sought to relate it to the time lines on the Road Plan and the Pathway Stone. It was clear by then that Hotevilla Village, the illustrious shrine of the Covenant, was in danger of being won over, and heroic efforts would be required to save it.

Throughout the 1960s, land remained the central focus of attention for both the Traditionalists and the Progressives. While the Traditionalists asserted their role in the Covenant and caretakership of Mother Earth, the Tribal Council claimed also to be traditional in its actions, and employed its economic interest in Hopi land resources as a basis for political strength and influence. Since the Council talked a great deal about tradition but few of them participated in it, the Elders knew that everything the Council members said had an ulterior motive attached to it.

After filing a claim with the Claims Commission, the Hopi Council started negotiations with the Navajo Council over areas outside District Six, which by 1953 had become occupied almost exclusively by Navajos. After several years of fruitless negotiations between the councils, Congress passed a bill authorizing the Hopi to sue the Navajos to settle the land question in court. The suit was resolved by a three-judge panel in 1962, which ruled that Hopi had an exclusive right and interest in District Six, but with the Navajos had only "joint, undivided and equal rights and interests . . . to all of the executive order reservation . . . lying outside . . . district six." The Progressives blamed the Traditionalist Elders for this convoluted settlement. It gave the Progressives no choice but to pursue an aggressive strategy to enforce their rights, and it officially diminished the land base they were counting on to enhance Council coffers.

Recovering quickly and undaunted, the Tribal Council intensified its efforts to promote economic exploitation of Hopi land and resources. The Elders said that an examination of what the Council had wrought called into question any Council claims of success. In 1956 the Bureau of Indian Affairs published a report by assessing the economic feasibility of mineral exploitation. Between 1961 and 1964, and ignoring the wishes and warnings of the Traditionalists, the Tribal Council secured leases for prospecting, exploring, and drilling for oil, gas, and minerals. These brought the Council $3,139,104.43 in royalties. It was an unheard of income that bolstered the Council's image of itself, and in their view made it more like a real government. From this largesse, the Council became openly magnanimous, and authorized an incredible payment of $1,000,000 for legal fees and services to their Bahanna Mormon attorney. They reserved about $500,000 to be used for operating expenses, built a large new and modern meeting hall and headquarters at Kykotsmovi, and arranged for regular monthly compensation for Council members. In other words, being a Council member became a full-time job. There was a discrepancy of sorts in populations, but in their view this made them equal to those of New York, Chicago, and Los Angeles. These latter moves further cemented the relationship of the Council and the Government, and if it had not been completely there before, in the Elder's view put the Council fully in the Government's pocket.

Rejecting the advice of the Elders of Hotevilla to be cautious in what it did, the Council used the remaining $1,600,000 to join with Navajos in constructing an undergarment factory for the B.V.D. Company. It was not built on Hopi Land where residents could easily get to it. It was built on lands donated as a "Hopi industrial park" by private individuals and the representatives of the off-reservation city of Winslow. After only two years of faulty operation, the factory was close to closing down in 1971. Worker dissatisfaction, Hopi complaints of B.V.D.'s failure to pay rent, and lack of enthusiasm for either making the long drive over poorly maintained roads or relocating to Winslow suggested that the B.V.D. factory was destined to fail. Nevertheless, the Hopi and Navajo tribal councils, the Bureau of Indian Affairs, B.V.D., and the city of Winslow did everything they could to pump new life into this foundering venture. The attempt was not successful, and in 1975 the factory closed for good. By this time, nearly two million Hopi dollars had, like the flooding from intense summer storms, gone rushing down a colossal desert wash and disappeared.

When the Council began its B.V.D. venture, it also started to provide additional services and employment for Hopi under the BIA's "buy Indian" policy, and under various programs of the federal War on Poverty. A grant-loan from the Economic Development Administration coupled with $144,700 of Hopi money enabled the Council to construct a modern motel, museum, and shop complex on Second Mesa. Known as the Hopi Cultural Center, the building opened in 1970, featuring excellent displays of contemporary Hopi weaving, carving, and paintings, and providing craft sales and a restaurant. It had continued to be a great place for tourists to stop, and has proved to be one of the most rewarding Council investments.

A Council move of special significance was the employment of policemen to enforce its regulations. Before long, these police were threatening and harassing Traditionalists and seeking to subdue them to the point where they would submit to the Council. Needless to say, the Traditionalists were not cowed, and, if anything, pressed their arguments against the Council more forcibly than ever.

The undergarment factory was a failure of considerable proportions. But it is by no means the largest and worst economic development scheme the Hopi Tribal Council has gotten the Hopi people involved in. With the blessings of the Government, and in conjunction with the Navajo Tribe, in 1966 they leased a portion of the joint use area of Black Mesa to the Peabody Coal Company. Once again, the Traditionalist Elders warned them not to do this, saying that the consequences would be catastrophic. And once again, the warning was disregarded.

Maasaw prophesied several unique things. One of these was that "One day a man will go to the moon, and he will bring a piece of it back to the earth. When he does this, something big where the future is concerned will begin in Hopi country."

In July of 1969, Apollo Eleven carried our astronauts to the moon. They walked on it, and they returned to the earth with samples from the lunar surface. So we have another theological statement with a scientific fulfillment, but more was to come.

In late 1969, Peabody began strip mining the northern area of Black Mesa, agreeing to pay the Hopi Tribe an annual royalty of at least $500,000. Later, after renegotiation, this figure would rise substantially. In addition to coal rights, Peabody also obtained the right to pump *thirty-eight billion gallons of water* from underneath Black Mesa to use in transporting the ground-up coal through a pipe 275 miles long to a power plant in Nevada. Although the mining operations guaranteed a steady income to the Tribal Council, and a worthwhile number of jobs to Hopi and Navajos, the Traditionalists feared that runoff from the mining area could adversely affect Hopi crops, and that Peabody's plans for reseeding and recontouring the mined area would not reverse the environmental damage to the fragile ecosystem. They also knew that no amount of money could undo the possible harmful effects of pollution from the area power plants, and that pumping operations would seriously deplete accessible water supplies.

The Elders told the Hopi this, but Peabody officials put their arms around Hopi shoulders and assured them that none of these misfortunes could possibly happen. What, they asked, did uneducated Hopi Elders know about industrial operations? On the other hand, Government and Peabody technicians had considered every eventuality, and declared that the operation was as benign as ever one could be. The Hopi should rejoice, they exclaimed. A near-perpetual blessing had come to them. It was like manna from Heaven. For the next forty years or more they would not need to worry about a thing.

But the operation was so huge that the fall-out came quickly. By mid-1970, every accusation was already threatening to become such a stunning truth that Hopi Traditionalists were able to muster impressive opposition to the strip mining. In 1971, following months of village meetings at which Hopi, environmental experts and advocates, lawyers, and anthropologists aired their opinions. The kikmongwis and ceremonial leaders of ten of the thirteen villages joined in filing a lawsuit against the Secretary of the Interior and Peabody Coal Company. In the discussions, there was a great deal of talk about Hopi prophecy, the significance of Black Mesa as a portion of the Hopi holy land, and the advisability of subjecting Hopi sovereignty to arbitration under United States law. The suit also alleged that the Hopi Tribal Council did not constitute a proper quorum when it signed the lease, and charged the Secretary of the Interior with exceeding his authority when he approved it.

A further basis for the suit was that the strip mining violated "the most sacred elements of traditional Hopi religion, culture and way of life." Six Hopi elders explained that Black Mesa was "part of the heart of our Mother Earth," granted to the Hopi to "hold in trust in a spiritual way for the Great Spirit, Massaw." "Title," they added, "is vested in the whole makeup of Hopi life. . . . If the land is abused, the sacredness of Hopi life will disappear."

Correlations with the moon landing did not end with the mining. In 1970, the Navajo Tribal Council stirred up a hornet's nest by offering to purchase the Hopi's half-interest in the joint use area. For once the two rival Hopi forces were united in their opposition. The Hopi Tribal Council denounced and rejected the offer, and the Hopi Traditionalists issued their own statement to the same effect, stating that no part of Hopi land was for sale. Reasons for the rejection differed considerably however. The Traditionalists maintained the position the Keepers of the Covenant had held for almost a thousand years at Oraibi and Hotevilla. While the Tribal Council said it wanted the land for Hopi families, it really wanted the land so that the Government could obtain its use through them.

It was evident that at this point in time a clear split had developed between the Traditionalists and the Progressives, who were epitomized by the Tribal Council. The Elders looked again at their Pathway Stone tablet. Along its time line they saw the three v-shaped symbols that now began to make sense to them. The first one was slightly larger than the second. It indicated, they knew, the division that had taken place at Oraibi in 1906, with each of its two legs displaying the different ways the people would go. The Elders remembered also the prophecy which promised that at the time of the first split, a second split would be foreseen. They looked for it, watched it begin, and saw its development. The division had so clearly happened that it could not be denied. All of the Hopi people were divided into Traditionalists, on-the-fence Hopi, and Progressives.

Even Hotevilla itself was separating into factions, and the number of Traditionalists dwindled day by day. The stomachs of the Elders were churning. Even though it was predicted, the fulfillment of this truth sickened them and it hurt. Until now, the Elders had clung to the hope that the worst would not come to pass in their generation. They had hoped they could push it off into the future so that at least some Hopi children and their children's children could experience the joys of the ancient Pattern of Life. But this had become a dimming hope, a wish that might never be fulfilled. Unless . . . unless . . . they could get through to the people and turn them around. And so the thoughts that led David Monongye to the *Techqua Ikachi* newsletters began to germinate.

Meanwhile, the Government and the Tribal Council followed their chosen path and the division grew wider. The gorge at Hotevilla became a canyon. It was a microcosm. Countries all over the world started to have internal divisions that increased until the people were fragmented and torn apart. But divisions like this had happened before. They were not new to the history of humankind. And so no one related them to the end of the world.

Natural disasters were also happening in record numbers and at the very time in history that Hopi prophecies had said they would. Having stated this, it is vital to recognize the magnitude of what is involved here. You see, Hopi prophecies are not proven by the fact that natural disasters of record proportions are manifesting themselves today. What is significant is that Maasaw said that as the closing prophecies are being fulfilled, natural disasters of record proportions will occur. Those who would like to debunk the prophecies would be in "hog heaven" if they could ask how we can claim that the end prophecies are on the verge of being fulfilled when there aren't any natural disasters? But they aren't able to ask this, are they? The entire globe is experiencing record floods, earthquakes, volcanic activity, rising heat, and wide-spread fires right now, right at the very time when the prophecies said they would.

On top of this, the environmental problems that Maasaw predicted were already mounting in 1970. Cloistered as they were on the Reservation, where these abuses would lead was not clear to the Elders yet, but they knew where to look for answers. At the shrines, Mother Earth would talk with them about the situation. The Peabody operation was giving them personal experience every passing day. Newspapers and magazines would tell them what scientists were saying and predicting. The signs Maasaw had given them would reveal vital information. They also knew what the possible endings were for the Great Play of Life. But they did not know which of these the Creator would send.

This much they learned quickly: From what was going on, it was obvious that poor choices had the Fourth wheel wobbling. Even the peculiar aching in their stomachs confirmed what Mother Earth told them—that she was in poor health. The Great Play of Life seemed to be moving into its final act. An enormous effort would be required to stabilize the world. Keeping the earth in balance would no longer be a pleasure. Maintaining it would entail a fight. Should the wheel of the Fourth Cycle come entirely loose, it would be awfully bad for everyone.

The world needed something to hold on to while it steadied itself. There was one hope. If it could reach as far as Hotevilla, it would find this security in a few gnarled "old roots." The

Elders were in a quandary too. They, of course, knew what was going on. They wanted to tell the world the secret. But the way to do it had not yet come to them.

CHAPTER 4

The Amazing Story
Part Three

By the spring of 1975 the Tribal Council was overflowing with confidence and hounding the Hotevilla Elders unmercifully. In the Council's mind, the Elders represented the final hurdle it needed to get over if it wanted to win the full support of the Hopi villages. Having managed that, Council members could speak with immunity about a Hopi "Tribe" that was united under the Council's leadership, and it would have what it cherished above everything else—absolute control.

But the Elders were far too committed to their Covenant vow to give in. They did not think the Council merited control. Had they been asked how they felt about the battering they were getting, their answer to the Council members would have been, "Why don't you try something we aren't used to?" The Elders themselves would never use weapons to accomplish their purposes, but they knew that quiet persuasion would not prevail either. The severity of their losses through natural deaths and to the Tribal Council and schools had in fact brought them to where they knew the battle was close to over. If anything was to be preserved for future generations, and the message had to be, they would need to put their thoughts in print and pass them on to the outside world. They knew that the Progressive Hopi would not receive these efforts well, but they hoped there would be some of the Hopi and outside friends who would listen. That would keep a spark alive for the future. It was imperative to buy time. And, the Creator gave it to them in a way they never expected.

Five of the leaders felt themselves being pushed together by an unseen Spirit, and being urged to discuss what they should do. They knew that anything public would be risky, for it would bring the Council down upon their necks more harshly than ever. When David Monongye proposed that they publish their own newsletter, the others were surprised. But their eyes glinted, and they didn't say no. The odds of success were not good. None of them were writers. And while they could express themselves well in Hopi, this would need to be done in English. That compounded the problem. But David waved them off. He had already discussed it with Bahanna friends at the Agency, and remarkably, four of them, two men and two women, said they would ignore the risks and help out. The men would translate and the women would type it up. Then they would have it printed and the Elders could distribute it.

It was too wonderful a possibility to be ignored. The steadfast little gladiators wearing the armor of Maasaw shook hands and agreed to do it. For how long, no one had any idea. It depended upon how well they got along with the first issue, and somewhat upon the reception.

No one was likely to buy it, so it had to be free. That meant they would need to pay any expenses themselves, and as farmers they had very little cash. One further consideration remained.

If they tried to do it in Hotevilla, someone might discover them and report it to the Tribal Council, who would assuredly send the Tribal Police to arrest them and make an example of them.

So Dan proposed that they write it at his ranch, which was remote enough to afford them privacy. Besides, his family ancestors had for centuries lived on the mesa top from which point they could see anyone coming for miles. That would be the ideal place to do it. So, near the stone ruins of the ancient dwellings of the Evehema family, they built a shade shelter, commonly referred to as a "ramada," and in early June of 1975 secretly gathered there with their White friends to work out the first issue. They had no idea that they would continue to do this for nearly eleven years, and would produce forty-four issues and a bulletin before David's eyesight failed to where he could no longer serve as editor. All of them, actually, were well along in years by this time. Dan was eighty-two when they started, and ninety-three when they stopped. Their ages were remarkable to undertake such a task, let alone face the danger. They were not wrong about that. As soon as the first issue was distributed, the Tribal Council was furious, and, for the entire period of their publication, had the Tribal Police searching constantly for them. But the writers deceived them by meeting at random times, and were never discovered. We can certainly be glad for that!

They called their newspaper *Techqua Ikachi,* a phrase whose meaning we know by now. It expressed, they said, "The Traditional Viewpoint." The first issue was printed and distributed in August of 1975, and it explained that articles and messages "would deal with issues concerning the continuation of the traditional way of life, and world peace."

Its editorial staff was listed as: D. Monongye, J. Pongayesva, P. Sewemanewa, D. Evehema, and A. Howesa.

It featured a shield symbol that meant: "Together with all

TECHQUA IKACHI

LAND AND LIFE—THE TRADITIONAL VIEWPOINT FROM THE HOPI NATION

Issue Number 20

Hopi maiden with squash blossom hairdress, 1901

The time will come to pass when the minds of men will become deluded and the words of the wise will be ignored. When the influence from foreign sources has taken hold the spirit within the Native People of this land will wane, perhaps even be destroyed. We were warned of this by the prophets of old.

nations we protect both land and life, and hold the world in balance."

The first issue was longer than most of the others, and special in that it covered the problems the Elders felt they needed to confront at that time. The following summary of its material enables us to see what these issues were.

Introducing Techqua Ikachi...

"*This newsletter is the first of its kind.* It is a periodical which speaks from the viewpoint of the Traditional Hopi. It is printed for thinking people, especially those concerned about the future and fate of the Hopi in today's world, and as an educational help for the young people of the Hopi and all other native nations.

"We shall attempt to set straight the things that have been said and printed about the Traditional Hopi by people who oppose the Hopi way of life, and who are working hard to modify the ageless Hopi teachings. We hope this will bring more insight into Hopi life and help the children of today to understand their elders and not to hate them. We shall not attempt to indoctrinate, but merely to bring out the teachings that have enabled the Hopi to survive for centuries, and organize their minds for full efficiency."

Why Are There Factions in Hopi?

They begin by asking why the Hopi are continually breaking up into factions, and define the three current sets as the *Traditionalist Hopi*, the *Progressive Hopi,* and the *On-the-Fence Hopi.*

They emphasize that "the *Traditionalist Hopi* are those who strongly adhere to their aboriginal law, which they believe the Creator, or Great Spirit, laid out for them." As they see it, "this is the most important thing. To stray from this pattern would be to stray from life itself. The Hopi believe that life and nature are of the same body, and that we must keep harmony with each other and keep the earth in balance . . . through religious ceremonial duties which require profoundest concentration, and can only be done rightfully without interruption and by remaining free from evil elements."

They then explain in greater detail why this stand is vital to the Hopi and the world. The scurrilous activities of the U.S. Government that led to the breakup of Oraibi are discussed, and also the conditions that led to the formation of the Tribal Council.

After this, the land dispute problem with the Navajo is treated. The Elders ask why there even is a land problem when it could easily be solved by the traditional leaders of both sides rather than the tribal councils or the United States Congress. Neither of these, the writers point out, understands what is going on from a prophetic point of view—especially the Tribal Council, which is frantically seeking to establish an image of being traditional Hopi so they can be involved in the arbitration. They are doing this by encouraging Hopi awareness programs throughout the schools while at the same time the Council has nothing to do with the original Hopi: "In fact they diminish them and force them into extinction. They replace them with a law to protect dead ruins, and restore ceremonial kivas. . . . Are they really interested in saving the ceremonies? We wonder, for they are Bahanna Christians. To them the ceremonies, kivas, and shrines are taboo, the work of devils practiced only by heathens."

"The Traditional Hopi leader," they add, "does not accept money for his office. He is more strongly and deeply devoted, for the original Hopi came into this world together, and their *instructions* and *teachings* have remained the same to this day. He is, therefore, willing to follow the path set out for him and fulfill the prophecies no matter what the consequences. He knows what help will come as planned by the Creator. If no help materializes from other people, it will come in the form of destruction by nature. If none of this materializes, then Hopi is wrong. This much we know."

Next, the writers address the issue of the fence the Council is attempting to put up on Titus Lamson's land, and how the Agency is supporting the Council in this illegal action. The writers are not buying the Council promise that this will be a temporary act. They know it is "a wrongful claim of jurisdiction over their land, which the 'Hopi Tribe' will not regard as temporary."

"But," they declare, "we will stand to the last, whichever way they drag us out, feet or head first. The Traditionals put in their last word, we will tear the fence down, we are ready."

Great Spirit's Peace, or Government Police?

"For thousands of years," the writers declare, "we Hopi have lived in villages by a pattern established by the Great Spirit, whose teachings go all the way back to the dawn of time. *All the prophecies are being fulfilled*, including the period of great trial in which the world will be engulfed by efforts to force one's will upon others. As predicted, these efforts have grown so great that mankind has reached the brink of self-destruction."

Respect Requires Good Example

As their final statement, the writers take a look at an editorial in *Qua'toquti,* April 24, 1975, regarding respect, in which they point out that it is something that is earned and cannot be forced. "Who is following the example set by countless generations of Hopi ancestors to whom we owe our life? . . . We agree with the statement that the Hopi philosophy is beautiful and always in the same pattern. It is so beautiful that the Hopi have lived by that pattern since the dawn of time. The survival of all people, their land and life, depends upon that pattern. . . . Yes, we agree with the 'glorious' Hopi doctrine and philosophy laid out by the Creator Himself. Each Hopi has been born into it, grown up with it, believes it is sacred, and a part of himself with which it would be wrong to part. Respect for elders would exist today if the world leaders would conform to their teachings, constitutions, and laws by which they intend to lead people. . . .

"Meanwhile the Traditional Hopi wants simply to live his way of life without expense to anyone. . . .

"It has been argued, 'Let these young ones experiment with gentle things that would be good for their future, that will not hurt anyone, and can be easily canceled.' But unfortunately the immature actions of the Tribal Council prove difficult, if not impossible to reverse. . . .

"We agree that the Hopi world is changing rapidly. So is the Earth and all its people. Each person has a right to change, and no one can control that. This is up to each individual. It is also right not to change when one has found the right way. But this editorial seems to imply that the Hopi way is extinct. On the contrary, it is very much alive. It's not the resistance of the Traditional Hopi that puts the pressure on the young people, but rather the Tribal Council has led them into a circle where they are vulnerable to unemployment and economic conditions. . . .

"But the Tribal Council and their followers try to turn the young against their elders by building an image of doubt. They create division, whereas the elders would have unity. They misrepresent themselves to the outside world as the leaders or 'Chiefs' of the Hopi nation, while twisting what the Traditional leaders say. . . ."

So here we have the "sons of the Anasazi" twenty years ago, and after a thousand years they still have in them the steel and wisdom it took to build majestic Mesa Verde Cliff Palace and the spiritual center at Chaco Canyon. As is seen, the Elders hid while they did their writing, but they did not hide entirely. They published a business address where they could be reached, and they appended their names. Everyone on Third Mesa knew exactly where their houses and farming lands were. The Council had fits over not being able to criticize them for secrecy. When the police failed to catch them in the act, the Council members lashed out at them in issues of *Qua'toquti,* the Tribal newspaper. As the Elders replied, the encounter took on the nature of a running battle. To emphasize their points, someone drew for the Elders several barbed cartoons that were included in the newsletters. Most of these have been reproduced in the *Hotevilla* book.

The spacing out of the forty-four *Techqua Ikachi* newsletters is easily explained. All of these old men were still physically active. They worked in their fields and around their houses just like the younger people did. Maasaw's INSTRUCTIONS were followed to the letter. And when they weren't in the fields or otherwise occupied, they were involved as leaders in village affairs or in the ceremonies in the Kivas. The cycles of rituals alone occupied 216 days out of every year. So an average of four issues a year was all they could manage, and it is surprising that they were able to do that many.

Remember that if it had not been for the efforts of these men and the extent of their newsletters, the Traditionalist viewpoint would not be available to us today. There would be no secret to divulge. There are younger Traditionalists who are still living the Traditional life, but none of these is as able to tell us what the true Elders can, which is why the Council would still like to prevent the newsletter and Dan's information from getting out to you, and to the world.

As a rule, each of the newspaper issues received a mixed reaction. Traditionalists in Hotevilla and other villages applauded them. The Progressives dismissed them out-of-hand. The on-the-fence Hopi read them, but had already put themselves in the position of not being able to do anything about what the papers recommended. The Tribal Council underlined passages, fumed, and increased their attacks. The Government Agent sloughed them off. He thought he knew where the power was. Sooner or later, nearly everyone trashed their copies. Hopi Land had entered a new world, and the excitement of that overshadowed everything else.

Except for some high points that are mentioned further on, the general routine at Hopi Land from then until now has duplicated what we have already covered. Every problem that has been referred to has continued to increase, and we know that the combined result has brought the Traditionalist Elderly Elders to the brink of extinction. In the prophetical sense, we are poised at the end of something past and the beginning of something big.

Several times in their newsletters, the writers mention how amazed they are to see that all of the prophecies are being fulfilled. The Hopi Elders are just like we are when we consider the prophecies. We read them, we wonder about them, and we are fascinated by them. We note that all of the prophecies that should be fulfilled by now have been, but we just can't bring ourselves to believe they are continuing to happen before our very eyes. The Elders tell us in the newsletters that they are not only awe-stricken, they are trembling. For as they see the Creator acting to fulfill His promises, they also face the fact that they are caught up in the destiny of the world. And, it is a huge world in dire trouble. The responsibility is enormous. In the backs of their minds lurk the really awesome prophecies destined for the years immediately ahead. The Elders know that humanity has stepped into the closing phase of the Fourth Cycle of the world, and they know that the time has come for intense watchfulness and public action. They cannot act quietly anymore. They must stand in the open where everyone can see with their own eyes how fully the Traditionalists hold to their Covenant vow.

The Tribal Council confirms the need for Traditionalist action by becoming more open in its activities too. It has either put its own cattle and sheep onto land that was not allotted, or has opened parcels to outside companies that can lease them for mineral development. Since in these circumstances borders need to be established, the Council decides to identify and isolate the allotted Hopi properties by fencing them—beginning with those owned by the Traditionalists who are giving the Council the most trouble.

Notice now the newly established disparity there is between privileges. When it suits the Council's purposes, outsiders can come onto and exploit Hopi Land, even lands that do not rightfully belong to the Council. This fact acquires even greater significance when we discover in future chapters how the Council treats the guests of Traditionalist Hopi who are on their own private lands.

As we learned in the first issue of the newsletters, the Council chose the land of Elderly Elder Titus Lamson, a close friend of Dan Evehema, and a fellow member of the Men's Society, and without notifying Titus, sent a crew in to dig holes for the fence posts. Titus, however, was a stubborn man who knew what the rights of the individual villages were, and particularly those of Hotevilla. He confronted first the fence builders and then Council members, threatening to tear down the fence as fast as it was being built. Hopi Land, Titus reminded the Council, was owned by the Creator, and it was not to be partitioned off. An old man by then, he nevertheless stood his ground, and was supported by fellow Traditionalists and a group of young White followers who made a public issue of the affair. Eventually, the Council backed down, and the fence was not built. But it promised that workers would be back on another day to build it. What they eventually did to relatives and friends of Titus was even more despicable. You will learn about this in Chapter 11, and it has already made headline news.

At the same time the fence issue was smoldering, the Council joined forces with the BIA and the U.S. Department of Health and Human Services to build, without consulting the Hotevilla Hopi, a large, modern, metal-sheathed water tower on Hotevilla land. From it, they laid a water pipe to the nearby Hotevilla-Bacabi public school. A well was dug to supply the tower, and the protests of the Hotevilla Elders that it might contaminate the village springs were ignored. While they were at it, the BIA laid telephone lines to the school, to a small market on the edge of Hotevilla land, and to a few of the fringe residences owned by Progressive Hopi. My chronology for all of these things might not be exact, but it is close enough to serve our purposes. At the Council's urging, an attempt was made to extend sewer, water and telephone utilities into the village proper. They had no mandate from the majority of Hotevilla people for this, but claimed that certain families had requested it. When the Elders protested, even to the point of jumping into trenches in front of bulldozers and tearing up pipes, tribal police were called in to arrest the protesters. The invading workers, who were on sovereign land and had no permission from the majority of the residents to be there, were neither abused nor arrested.

But for the moment at least the intrusion stopped. During the next ten years, three more attempts were made to install utilities. None of these succeeded. The fact that the people did not want the utilities was of no consequence. And, why they were not wanted was of no consequence either. Although boasting that they were the leaders of efforts to maintain the traditional culture, the Council knew little of the actual tradition as it was practiced by Hotevilla. Nor did they really care about it. Their actions betrayed their words. What they continued to want was absolute control over the villages of Hopi Land, including Hotevilla, Shrine of the Covenant. It stood in their way, and something would have to be done to bring the village down. Between their failed attempts at intrusion, the Council met and conspired as to how it could accomplish its goal.

Before long it occurred to someone in the Council that there was a good-sized tract of open land between Hotevilla and Bacabi. The Government had already promoted HUD housing projects in several of the other villages. Since Bacabi had been a "friendly" village from the day of its founding, its natural orientation had been toward modernization. Its residents were Progressives, and its attachments to tradition were marginal. Of course! the Council members exclaimed. Bacabi should be expanded! The Council had no difficulty whatsoever persuading the Bacabi people to endorse a HUD housing project to be built on the open land. The fact that by historic grant Hotevilla had charge of the land was simply ignored. The announcement of the project was made, and plans to execute it begun.

The land theft was bad enough, but a thinly-veiled scheme underlying the project was even meaner. The modern water tower that sits alongside of the main road leading from the highway into Hotevilla Village was a disconcerting contrast to the antiquity of the village. It was as if invisible graffiti, "Tribal Council," had been written all over it. But a tract of modern HUD houses would be worse by far. The idea was so delicious the Council members salivated whenever it crossed their minds. Each time people drove through this new tract on their way from the highway to the old-style village, it would make a glaring statement about the progressive successes of the Tribal Council. The impact upon everyone who favors Traditionalism would be severe. It was compellingly clear that the Tribal Council has no conception of what it meant to be compassionate, fair, or loyal to the Covenant and to the message that must be preserved and at the proper time proclaimed. We might expect this kind of deception from the missionaries and the Government. On the basis of ignorance, they can perhaps be excused. But can fellow Hopi? The Elders mulled this question over, and thought not.

Once again, the Traditionalists stood firm, and like the fence, the HUD project was put on hold until another day. Nevertheless, it was a fact of life that postponement was the common reaction for the Council. It did not cancel anything. It retained its agenda, put its failed attempts on a back-burner, and looked for an alternate way to accomplish its intentions. The history of its actions and statements proved this conclusively. Between its forays, it carried on an active propaganda campaign in conversations, meetings and the schools as it laid the groundwork for the next foray. In the Tribal newspaper, called *Hopi Tutu-veh-ni* now, the Traditionalists were portrayed as doddering obstructionalists who hadn't the sense to see that the Hopi "Tribe" must move ahead.

No thought was given to the Covenant mandate, the prophecies, or to keeping the world in balance. Day by day the Council grew more determined that those responsible for the newsletters must be eradicated. But not being able to catch them in the act, they weren't able to jail the "old roots" and make an example of them. So the Council fumed, and it ridiculed them by proclaiming they should give up every vestige of Bahanna life and return to the old ways. The Elders were mildly amused, and answered that it might not be a bad idea—if the Council would act in kind and leave the Reservation to live with the Bahannas they have embraced. Of course, no Hopi can ever again live entirely in the old way. The Government has seen to that. It has eliminated many clothing and food sources, and curtailed the economic ways so that most of the people can no longer be independent and self-sustaining. At the end of this chapter you will see that changes about to take place in the Government budget are going to bring this problem resoundingly home to every Hopi in Hopi Land.

As more of the ancient prophecies were fulfilled, the Hopi people grew restless, and began to wonder where they should look for solid leadership.

The Council knew that it must convince the Hopi people that it was truly traditional, and that it had replaced the Elders of Hotevilla as the reliable authority in this regard. Then out of the blue a windfall of major proportions floated unexpectedly into the Council's hands. In July of 1978 two young White pothunters who were scouring the Reservation in search of Sikyatki pottery they could steal and sell came across a small cave of the type used to store Hopi sacred items. Its mouth had been partly closed by a wall of rocks, and inside it were four wooden figures that lay on a bed of prayer sticks and feathers with their heads resting on a log pillow. The thieves had no idea what the figures were, but they knew they might be valuable to collectors. So they removed them from the cave and hid them under a bush by the highway. The next night they came back to get them, and, when a Hopi game warden stopped to see why they were there, they were forced to leave the smallest figure under the bush while they explained that they were out of brake fluid. He gave them some, and, in relief, they drove off with the three figures they had already placed in the car.

For a while, nothing happened. It was only when a priest came from Shungopavi to make his prayers to the deities that the theft was discovered. The predicament was especially serious, for the figures were so sacred that most Hopi don't even know they exist. This being the case, should anything even be said, or should the theft be hidden? After debating for several days, the religious leaders made the unheard of decision to call in the FBI. The choice was actually unavoidable. These were central deities used in the initiation ceremonies, and without them it was possible that the ceremonies could no longer be held. The men who had stolen the *Taalawtumsi must be* tracked down. As word got out about the enormity of the disaster, the villagers were in shock. When a White trader who had obtained these irreplaceable deities learned that the FBI was looking for them, he panicked and did a foolish thing. He burned them—or at least claimed that he did.

Eventually, the entire story about the great theft of the *Taalawtumsi* came out, and only the single figure remains for ceremonial use today. Since the matter of initiations remains secret, what the Shongopavi people have done to compensate for this inexcusable loss is not known. But they have made recent adjustments, for the initiation rites have resumed at Shungopavi.

Before the resumption, Leigh Jenkins, Director of the Hopi Office of Cultural Preservation, claimed that the initiation figure theft was the worst thing that had ever happened to the Hopi people. He did not mention that during the division at Old Oraibi, initiations were suspended for a much longer period of time, or that when a disagreement occurred in another village, initiations were suspended there too.

We need to note here that the differences between villages extends even to major religious areas. When Shungopavi lost their figures, one would normally assume they could borrow replacements from another village. This is not done, for ritual variations between villages require different kinds of figures.

The theft of the *Taalawtumsi* was held up to the media as evidence of the kinds of terrible things that were being done to the Hopi. Shortly thereafter, Jenkins and some of his group made a television appearance to lament the theft of the initiation figures, and pointed out in graphic detail the unfortunate things that, as a result of "curses associated with such things as the theft," had happened to the perpetrators. I found this particularly interesting, for I am in fact banking on the Director's personal belief in curses. It could prove to be the best thing there is to deflate his attack on Hotevilla.

As stated, this unfortunate situation became, however, a boon for the Tribal Council. By publicizing it, even the Christian members could project an image of their being concerned about traditional life. I do not know when exactly The Hopi Cultural Preservation Office came into being. But the *Taalawtumsi* theft probably justified its formation. The new office seized upon it as the perfect issue to promote the Council's position as the "protector of traditionalism." They proclaimed to one and all that the theft of the initiation deities was the continuing example of endless thefts of Hopi artifacts that began with Rev. Voth and the anthropologists at the turn of the century. Omitting the fact that a number of Hopi had themselves sold religious items, with righteous indignation, the office set about the formulation of a plan to gain control of everything having to do with cultural and historic resource protection and preservation. What the office really wanted was absolute control over anyone having to do with any of these things, be they Hopi or outsider. Lacking formally enacted laws to accomplish this, Mr. Jenkins became the single acceptable authority in these matters. He let everyone, including the Elderly Elders of Hotevilla, know that information was not to be dispensed without his express approval, and he made it clear that outsiders were not to do anything on the Reservation other than through him. He even had the audacity to chastise Dan Evehema and two other Elders for making a video that had snippets of actual dancing in it. Jenkins warned that active dancing should never be shown in films.

Not long after that, rumors got around to families of Elderly Elders that it was becoming apparent that some of the older people on the Reservation would be better off in Government retirement homes. To the Traditionalists, the Council's implication was clear: if they couldn't shut them up one way, they would do it another.

Remember now, the basic motive of the Two-Hearteds and the forces of evil has been to keep you and me from obtaining and implementing the great message needed to save ourselves and the planet. What was threatened to the Hopi Elders was only one clear example of what was being done on a broader scale around the world. "Don't let the good news get out," was the message the two-hearteds dispensed.

On one occasion cited in the newsletters, the Council issued an edict refusing outsiders entrance to Hotevilla—particularly to those who were part of the "flower-child" movement that was going on in San Francisco at the time. Katchongva countermanded the order, and told the Tribal Chairman to mind his own business. Hotevilla was, the chief said, a sovereign village that would make its own decisions. One decision was that the village dances were open to all who came with respect, whether they were Hopi or Bahanna.

When a British film crew came to Hopi Land to film simple things like Hopi farming methods, the Tribal Police hauled them in and told them to explain their intentions to the Tribal Council. The Council said that nothing was to be filmed without the proper permits and written permission. The Council even said they would censor the film. The crew was flabbergasted, and said they had never before encountered such dictatorial laws. Wherever they went at Hopi Land after this, they were hassled and threatened. Were it not for someone guiding them to the Traditionalists at Hotevilla, they would have returned to England empty-handed and disgusted. One of the British crew told an Elder that, before they found the Traditionalists, they had concluded there was not a Hopi left of the gentle kind written about in books.

Last year I received documentation that Mr. Jenkins had become the consultant and procurement agent for a Bahanna firm making a promotional film to sell clients on a full-length film to be done on the Hopi Tribe. When they solicited Dan's participation, he refused, but not until he gained copies of their ambitious proposal and the promo film, which he passed to me. This was interesting stuff, for it even included active dancing segments of the Snake Dance. The message was clear. When any Hopi other than Mr. Jenkins did anything with the media, archaeologists, or writers, it was not acceptable. Whereas whatever he did in whatever areas he chose, was just fine. Leigh Jenkins had proclaimed himself the impeccable Hopi authority.

A few other questionable Council activities are mentioned in the final chapters. One of the most blatant is currently in progress. Jenkins wants his personal views incorporated into Hopi Tribal Law. Almost everyone who has learned about this, and knows what else he is doing, speaks of him as attempting to turn Hopi Land into a police state.

In the summer of 1995, with the Elderly Elders nearing their physical end, and most other Traditionalist opposition badly outweighed, Mr. Jenkins began to formulate an extensive "Historic and Cultural Resources Protection and Preservation Ordinance of the Hopi Tribe." It is a document that would do justice to any police state on the planet. Parts of the proposal have been published in the Tribal newspaper, and, I assure you, there is nothing even remotely like it in force in any state in the United States. The typewritten document is a long one—already in its fifth chapter—and he is still working on it. It is called a proposed document, but he intends to have it enacted into Hopi Law. I doubt, however, that any court in the land would support it. But in the meantime, he will use it as though it is already law, and no one will be able to move in Hopi Land without first securing "a permit issued from the Hopi Tribe." His brass astounds the Elderly Elders—and me.

Among the typical provisions of the ordinance is the following: "No person shall conduct ethnological, archaeological, historical, medical, cultural research or other studies, whether oral or written, scientific or nonscientific, make recordings, whether visual, motion, sound, multimedia or other, regardless of mechanical device(s) or technology discovered or not yet discovered, or attempt to do any of the foregoing, on the Hopi Reservation or on lands within the jurisdiction of the Hopi Tribe, without first obtaining a permit issued by the Hopi Tribe or by the express consent of a Hopi village and/or Hopi individual(s)."

Reading it makes me glad that Dan Evehema gave me his signed permission to do the books.

The consent rules do not apply to: "Hopi practitioners, Hopi traditional clan and religious leaders or Hopi groups engaging in bona fide customary and traditional activities relating to the practice of the Hopi culture, religion or traditions; or to employees or agents of the Hopi Tribe engaged in official business relating to cultural resource management activities approved in accordance with established rules and regulations."

Who do you suppose will decide what is "bona fide," and what is not?

The last exclusion is an interesting one; the rule makers

exclude themselves. You will see how this exception works out as "The Amazing Story" reaches its awesome conclusion in Chapter 11.

Since the collapse of the ancient Hopi life way has come so far as it has today, I think it would be fair to ask where the Hopi people would actually be without the stubborn defense by the Hopi Traditionalists? Would there be anything worthwhile of the ancient way left, and what hope, through the Covenant, would there be for the Hopi (and our) futures? If the Tribal Council had been its keeper, the secret would have been lost long ago.

Perhaps some readers would like to hear the Tribal Council's side of this portentous issue. They certainly have one, and have consistently expressed it in the Tribal newspaper. You can be certain that my *Hotevilla* and *Survival Kit* books will get ample treatment, and I'm glad you will have the books to compare with what they say. In the meantime, anyone can subscribe to the paper or contact the Council and Office by writing to:

Hopi Tribal Council
P.O. Box 123
Kykotsmovi, AZ 86039
Tel: (520) 734-2441, fax: (520) 734-6648

Because of recent developments, the Council does have its hands full and might be a little slow in responding. The September 1, 1995 issue of their newspaper carried a lead article the first paragraph of which read as follows: "The Hopi Tribe is facing a potential fiscal nightmare, as tribal officials travel to Washington and attempt to reverse a tide of budget cuts which could reduce the BIA budget by 23%, and cut tribally operated program funding by one third."

The Senate Appropriations Committee had proposed slashing the BIA's 1996 budget by $434 million, and was cutting 3,000 of the BIA's then 12,000 employees: "The greatest impact on tribes would be the reduction of approximately $160 million in Tribal Priority Allocations, contracts issued to tribes to operate their own programs."

The rest of this lengthy article spelled out the specific areas potentially affected in Hopi Land—the elderly, youth, poor families, education, health, law enforcement, tribal courts, and social services. I saw nothing in the article about possible cuts in Council salaries, or cuts in the Hopi Cultural Preservation Office. Perhaps more of the Peabody money could be used to make up the deficit, and surely a reserve from earlier income had been put aside. This was just natural good government, wasn't it?

Once again, the Tribal Council ignored the Hopi prophecies. Prophecy said "the Bahanna government will gradually cease their responsibility in caring for Native people. The government will release us from their protective arms, wanting us to be on our own feet."

So another prophecy was being fulfilled, and from the Government's general financial circumstance, it appeared that these cuts were only the first of many.

Our Amazing Story does not end here. It's astonishing climax does not come until the last chapter of the book. Even then, the story will not be over, for it is a living account filled with astounding developments that will continue to change until the cycle has closed. Since every change affects us, we who follow the INSTRUCTIONS will want to keep in touch with what is going on at Hopi Land and Hotevilla.

Perhaps though, the time has come for a moment of honesty. No matter how you resist it, you will be troubled by the fact that, in spite of all we do to praise and recommend the Traditionalist way of life, it is a way that appears to have succumbed to Bahanna's power. No one can be blamed for asking does this not indicate a weakness in Hopi Traditionalism. Is the Bahanna way actually best for us and for the Hopi? Does might, after all, actually make right?

If I did not know how the Bahannas accomplished what they did with the Traditionalists, I might be tempted to answer yes to the question. But you have seen that the Hopi have not made a free decision. It was not persuasion or good example that brought any of the Hopi to where they are. It was force, unrelenting pressure, orchestrated deceit, and what the Elders call "brainwashing." For a long time now the children born in Hopi Land have been raised in a non-Traditional environment that includes White-oriented schools. They have no personal experience to tell them how it really was before the changes took place. And even if they really wanted to, how would they go back? The last of the capable teachers have been brought to the edge of extinction. Who could teach the young people what they need to know?

Dan talked about Hopi stepping off of the narrow beam and not being able to get back on it. That was the past. Today there is an entire generation of Hopi who never got on the beam in the first place. Therefore, where the INSTRUCTIONS are concerned, when you make your decision as to what you will do with your own life, contrast Hopi life before White intrusion with what it is like today at Hopi Land. Do you think that 100 years of Government encroachment has brought the Hopi happiness and a better life? Do you think Hopi life has improved with Tribal Council control? Who speaks of life there as "good" or "beautiful" today? There is no freedom, and the people go from one frustration to another. The isolation they appear to choose on dance days by closing their dances to outsiders is actually a defense mechanism. They want to hide the truth of what they have become—Bahanna Hopi. Except for the Traditionalists, they make themselves prisoners in their own land, and, with its proposed Protection and Preservation Ordinance, the Office of Cultural Preservation is taking steps to set that misfortune in concrete.

The last little gladiator, Dan Evehema, has followed the ancient Pattern of Life through every temptation and tactic the two-hearteds have thrown at him. Yet not once has he wavered or looked back. He has followed the straight road shown in the Road Plan, and he has survived beautifully. At the same time he has been off the Reservation and, from New York to San Francisco, seen most of what the Bahanna world has to offer. In the light of Hopi prophecy, and in personal experiences, he has carefully evaluated where the Bahanna world is heading and what it is doing to itself. I doubt that Dan would agree with Nostradamus's prophecy regarding the timing of Armageddon. But he would say that unless something effective—more expressly the following of the INSTRUCTIONS and WARNINGS—is done to change the scenario, a major part of the Bahanna world does not have many years until it is going to be in grievous trouble.

Having made a comparison of the two ways, Dan has chosen to stay where he is. The course of his play is set. Not many of us are going to join Dan in the solitude of his arid mesa land, and he does not suggest that we attempt to become Hopi. He did, however, tell me when I was last there that anyone who follows the Traditionalist Pattern of Life is welcome to come and live free on his land. But that would require those who do to live the simple life he does, and I doubt that many of us would be up to that. It is just not the life we were raised to lead. Still, there are jewels in his Pattern of Life that are universal, and, wherever we are, they can change the pattern of our lives and the nature of the planet for the better. No matter how bad things look today, there is a way we can survive.

On the other side, we have been given a good look at the Bahanna Hopi Progressives. There is little in what they have said or done that recommends our following them instead. They talk the Traditionalist life, but they do not live it. Anything they have gained by giving in to the Government, we already have out here, and more. Where survival is concerned, they have absolutely nothing to offer, and it is easy to understand why this is so. Materialism, rather than the True Maasaw, has become their god. Having tasted power and what they mistakenly believe is the good life, they will not give themselves over to the simple life of a digging stick, seeds, a gourd of water and a plain cloak unless their existence depends on it. Even though they don't realize it, it does. Actually, the continuing cuts in BIA appropriations may send a lot of Hopi back to their fields. As for the Hopi conversions to White ways, any Hopi needs to realize that their opportunity to be something special to themselves and the world is to be what they are by birthright. To be Traditionalist is to be the possessor of a wondrous gift. To become Bahanna Hopi in one's life-way is to become absorbed by the Bahanna world, and essentially, lost to view.

As we consider all of this, we need to pause for a moment to get to know the true Maasaw, for he plays a vital role in everyone's present and future. Maasaw has been a misunderstood deity. Yet in terms of the Covenant and the great secret where blending with the land and celebrating life is concerned, we find in him the best friend we are ever going to have.

Chapter 5

Beauty Behind the Mask

While it is spelled Maasaw, Masaw, Massau, Maasau'u, and other ways, each of these names for this awesome Hopi deity is pronounced the same: *Maa,* like the sound a bleating sheep makes, and *sow,* like the noun for female pig. We have already seen that where Hopi history is concerned, Maasaw plays an extremely important role. As a Helper Spirit serving the Creator, his assigned task is to be the Guardian of the Earth. He lives on the earth, and he watches over it. When I described him in "The Amazing Story," you learned that his appearance was so gory the Hopi who met him at Oraibi thought it must be a mask, one like the typical Maasaw mask worn by Hopi men who impersonate him during ceremonial performance. The difference is that the real Maasaw was not wearing a mask. His real face was so beaten and blood-spattered that everyone simply assumed it had to be a mask.

How does it happen that the Creator uses someone so ghoulish to be the guardian of the earth and all of its inhabitants? Why not a more attractive person? And how did Maasaw get that face? Was it like that when he was begotten by the Creator, or did something happen after he came to earth to take up his assigned responsibility?

I think his face was battered when he fought a gargantuan battle with the forces of evil for control of the earth. In a sense, it ended in a draw, since neither was banished. Yet, in the end, it is Maasaw who will triumph, for he told the Hopi at Oraibi that he is "the first and he will be the last," taking full control as the Fifth Cycle of the world begins.

In the meantime, Maasaw is the Savior of the Hopi, just as Jesus Christ is the Savior of the Christian world. You will recall that Jesus also said he was the first and the last, and in his titanic struggle against the Devil and evil, he too was bloodied and battered on his way to the cross. Even the instructions and warnings the two of them gave to their disciples are similar in nature, and the prophecies of the end times are remarkably alike—all of this, even though they appeared on opposite sides of the globe and had no known contact with one another.

What am I saying here? Is it that there are two Saviors?

Or, is it that Maasaw is really Jesus Christ who has come to the earth in a different guise? The Hopi do not say so, but some Native Americans tell us that legends handed down by their people teach that Jesus once walked the Americas and ministered to the natives.

I am not so foolish as to attempt an answer to either one of these questions. Having raised them, I feel like newspaper columnist Louis Grizzard who, when asked, "Why don't newspapers tell the truth?" answered, "Hey, what the heck? Only costs a quarter. If you want the truth, gotta pay $3.75."

The Survival Kit will cost more than $3.75, but not enough more to get me to stick my neck out where the above questions are concerned. My aim is to provoke thought, not to end it.

As a Christian, I cannot accept that there is any other Savior than Jesus Christ. Yet at the same time, Maasaw fills this role for the Hopi Traditionalists, who are not Christians. Moreover, in learning about all that Maasaw does, you may have decided that he fills the role for a lot of other people too. Since no word of Jesus Christ would come to the Hopi during the first thousands of years of their existence, it appears that the Creator provided Maasaw for some very special servants who needed him. Even when word of Christ did come to the Hopi, it was carried by Spanish individuals who were miserable representatives of the Savior they proclaimed. It would be pretty hard for any of us to accept the God of a people who had disdainfully overturned our lives and culture, and after knocking us down because we wouldn't agree with them, were standing with a booted foot on our throats and swords poised over our hearts while they demanded our conversion.

Of course, the Hopi wouldn't give up Maasaw. Of course, the Hopi shouldn't give up Maasaw. If and when it is necessary, the true Creator will do whatever He must to reconcile Christianity and Maasaw on the basis of right choices and right behavior.

Remember, also, that it is the Hopi Traditionalists who are telling you their story. I am only the bearer who is passing it on to you. I believe in the reality of Jesus Christ, and I also believe in the reality of Maasaw. Both of them are too well attested to be dismissed from history's stage. We Lutherans believe that the just live by faith. But where the validity of Christianity as a whole is concerned, people who are telling a lie do not, as hundreds of first-century Christians did, let themselves and their children be burned at stakes for the enjoyment of drunken Roman audiences. And as for the validity of Maasaw, no one would have held on to his message as the Hopi Traditionalists have if it were in any way false.

Cult mentalities excepted, people do get caught up in lies they have trouble getting out of. But when the game is up, and they are faced with exposure, they will say, "All right, I give up," and weasel out as best they can. When given the choice between renouncing their faith or being burned alive, the Christians in Rome told the Romans to go ahead and burn them. They were not about to deny what they had seen and heard. I find that especially convincing.

Well-educated Christians and Traditionalist Hopi are not cult members. They do not brainwash others in an attempt to convert them. They don't bomb buildings. They don't place chemical or bacterial bombs on subways, and they don't send soldiers in the name of God to conquer others. The fact that some—like the leaders who sponsored the Crusades, or the priests who headed the Spanish Inquisition—claimed to be Christians, did not make them such. True Christians and true Hopi do become involved in conflicts, but where it is at all possible, they solve these through peaceful efforts.

How should we think of Maasaw? One of the best ways is to compare him with the Ogre Kachina who was, until recently, common and popular in the Hopi ceremonial cycle. Dan told me that the Ogre has become another casualty of White education. Young Hopi are much too sophisticated now to believe in Ogres, so they appear less and less in the villages, including Hotevilla. In a way, the situation is like that of our children who become "old enough and mature enough" to no longer believe in Santa Claus. Parents see this milestone as the end of a time when Christmas is a field of dreams come true. Something changes then. After that, the national holiday gets to be pedestrian. Shopping for toys can be a pain in the neck, but watching the children when they open the packages and recording it on film is something else entirely. Those who complain about the secularization of Christmas ought to think about this, and should realize that we can do this and keep Christ in Christmas very nicely too.

What is lost for the Hopi is that the Ogres filled an important position in the educational scheme, and where children are concerned, there is nothing in Hopi lore to replace it. Today, this loss is attended by a general loss in respect for parents and elders at Hopi Land, and a loss in respect for almost everything else of value. As is the case with so many families in the outside world, the Hopi families who have chosen to imitate the Whites have also fallen apart. One of the prophecies says that "the raising of women's skirts above the knees will lead to the devaluation of the woman's body, and of many other things." There isn't much of anything that is on a pedestal anymore. And, the heroes and goals that we do put there are often as inconsequential and meaningless as could possibly be.

What matters is what the Ogre accomplished for the family and the community. Like Maasaw, the Ogre Kachinas were fearsome looking creatures. They wore huge and frightening masks that had bulging eyes, gigantic snouts, mouths filled with sharp teeth, and whose crowns were topped with wild bunches of long hair. They carried weapons such as yucca whips, bows and arrows, lances, clubs, and, in modern times, even meat cleavers and hand saws. Their bodies were painted with garish colors, and they wore any kind of clothing that helped them seem bigger and more vicious. Animal blood was often poured on the weapons and the masks. You can see why Ogre Kachina dolls were fun to carve, and became popular with collectors. I have three of them.

Ogres hunched up their shoulders and uttered fierce sounds as they walked through the village, making themselves as menacing as they could. One of their most important duties was that of

Ogre Kachina

disciplining small children. In past times this was a different situation than it is today, for by and large, children behaved quite well, thanks to training and to the ever-present threat of the Ogres. Sometimes though, a few of the kids kicked over the traces, and word of this got around. Villages were so small that not much of anything could be hidden for long. The father would also say something about this when he was in his Kiva with men who filled the Ogre role. When the time neared for the Ogres to appear, parents told such children that, since their behavior left something to be desired, the Ogres might just come and take them away. They would probably be disposed of in a fearful place like the bottom of a lonely canyon, where they would never be heard from again.

The threat was laid on as heavily as grout on adobe brick by both parents, who would shake their heads in sorrow and tell their child they wished something could be done to prevent the abduction. Quite likely though, they would say, nothing would help. Following this announcement, the tone of life around the house became noticeably subdued.

When the child was sufficiently impressed, the mother would tell him in an inspired way, as though she just thought of it, that the Ogres loved sweet things like piki and cookies. If some of these were available, she would tell him with a frown on her face, they might take them instead.

"Can we make some?" the child would ask expectantly, his jet-black eyes pleading as he did so.

"Yes," his mother would reply, "We can!"

So the child would enthusiastically join his mother in preparing a basket full of sugary gifts. He might never again in his life work as hard as he did now. His sisters would be amazed. At the same time he would, of course, be on his best behavior, and a smidgen of hope would edge its way into the picture.

Then one dark and gloomy night, while the family was gathered together and "by chance" discussing what might happen, they would hear loud banging, followed by moaning sounds that came from outside their house. "They are here," the parents would whisper frantically to the child, "Go and hide someplace." In less than an instant and as if by magic, the child disappeared.

At once there would come a horrendous pounding on the door, followed by harsh voices announcing they were Ogres who demanded to be let in. Ignoring the child's pleas that they not do so, the parents would slowly open the door, whereupon the Ogres would push them roughly aside and come storming into the living room. Knowing who the child was, they would call out his name, and insist in bellowing tones that he come immediately to them. All the while they did this, their bulging eyes searched the room, their great mouths clapped open and closed, and they made menacing gestures with their weapons.

"Where is he?" they would roar.

It was all the boy could do to keep from dying on the spot, and it was all the parents could do not to laugh and give everything away.

When at last the wide-eyed and trembling child crept slowly from his hiding place, the Ogres grandly announced to one and all that they had heard he was not behaving as he should, and that they had come to take him away. Then they lunged at him and attempted to grab him. In tears by now, the child would run to his parents, who pretended they were filled with anguish over the idea of losing their precious child.

When they felt the child had suffered enough, the parents would tell the Ogres that their son had been bad, but not so bad he didn't deserve another chance. In fact, they would say, he had done a number of good things at home and in the fields, and while the boy vigorously nodded his head in agreement, they would tell the Ogres what some of these things were. Why, they would triumphantly add, he had even made some delicious desserts for the Ogres, and hoped that, if they came to his house, they would take those instead of him. By now the boy was nodding like a cork on a fishing line and, in hearty agreement, getting ready to defend himself.

For a few minutes, then, the Ogres would grunt like hogs and act as though any substitution was out of the question. Then they debated among themselves as to whether they could even do such a thing. Did the ancient laws permit it?

"I heard of something like this over at Mishongnovi," one would say. Before he could finish his statement and, while the boy was hanging on every word, his voice would trail off.

At this point, some of the Ogres would raise their enormous snouts and, for the first time, smell the fragrant odors coming from the delicacies. Then they would sniff their way over to where they were and look at them. By now, they would show signs of weakening, mumbling at the same time that to take them might set a bad precedent for the rest of the villagers. Meanwhile, the boy cowered behind his mother with his arms clutched tightly around her waist.

After what seemed like an eternity, the Ogres would repeat their routine, and finally agree to take the gifts. With these in hand, they offered a reluctant thanks to the boy and the parents, and left the house, promising to return if they heard any rumors about the child's bad behavior. As we would expect, the moment they were gone and the door closed behind them, the grateful child hugged his parents and thanked them profusely for rescuing him. Then, while the parents acted as though they were amazed that their son had so narrowly escaped his abduction, the son ardently declared he would show his appreciation by being a better child. The entire enactment of this centuries-old drama cemented the parent-child relationship, and was always a beneficial educational experience. The next morning he would seek out his best friend to tell him about the tortures of the dammed he had been through the night before, and warned the friend that he had better make certain the Ogres didn't come to see him.

As we might expect, by the time their rounds were completed, the Kiva of the Ogres was filled with delicious foods, and they had a grand and rollicking feast while they laughed about what each of them had experienced.

Sadly though, the Ogres, like the Snake Dance and a number of other performances, are vanishing in some villages and already gone in others. We can chalk up another victory for White-run schools and the United States Government. Hopi kids are too smart to fall for this sort of thing today, and too smart to behave as they once did also.

In a broader and more encompassing sense, Maasaw fills this same role as the Ogres for the adult Traditionalist Hopi. His fearful presence keeps them ever mindful of punishment and death, but what he is truly seeking is their rescue. He delivers prophecies that are harbingers of death and destruction, but at the same time points to the instructions and warnings that will accomplish survival.

Behind the true face that people think is a mask, there is beauty that is wondrous to behold. Maasaw is a deity who sacrifices himself, and who cares tremendously about those who are placed in his charge. His entire way of life affirms this truth. Maasaw's character also tells us something important about the Creator Himself: He often masks what He does in strange ways to test our willingness to hang in there until we learn the important lessons that are involved. He does not want us to make shallow commitments, or to take for granted that our life with Him is assured simply because we announce to one and all at a revival that we "are saved."

We have seen that when the Hopi asked Maasaw if they could live with him at Oraibi, his answer was to look askance. In an unspoken way he was asking, "Why in the world would you want to do a thing like that? Can't you see that I have nothing here? My life is simple. All I have is my planting stick, my seeds, some water, and my cloak. If you are willing to live as I do, **and follow my instructions** for the life plan I shall give you, you may live here with me and take care of the land. Then you shall have a long, happy and peaceful life."

The implication was that they ought to consider their decision carefully. Once it was made, it would not be an easy one to change. And, as sure as anything, they were going to be tempted. What if it turned out that they were like so many folks whose lives were already centered in fun and games, and who were bored with such tiresome things as consequences and responsibilities?

Some of those who have made this latter choice might respond by saying that Maasaw's concluding promise was a hollow one. That over the past century, and during the Spanish occupation, Hopi life was anything but peaceful. But the Hopi can remember 650 other years that were, to them, near bliss. Whenever the Traditionalists have been questioned about their problems, they have been quick to point this out.

While Chapter 10 deals more comprehensively with warnings, let me give you here an example of the kinds we get from Maasaw. I hope it baffles you as much as it did me before I figured out how it works.

"The teaching," we read in the newsletters, "is that **there are two Great Spirit Massaus,** a poor and a wealthy."

Confounding, isn't this, and seemingly at cross purposes? Yet it fits the picture of temptation as it is applied by evil forces. If they want to get to us in a sly manner, what better way than to follow the old adage of "the wolf in sheep's clothing." Do you think this means that someone dresses up their own Maasaw to look and act like the real Maasaw? A costumed figure might work. Unsuspecting people who don't look too closely anyway might think they are dealing with the good, or poor, Maasaw, and then be lured into a situation they could not easily get themselves out of.

"The poor Massau," the newsletter continues, "lives in simple and humble ways. He travels the good path, and teaches good ways of life. He only has a planting stick and the seeds in making his living. He is the caretaker of the land. When we destroyed our last world by our own corruption, he permitted us to live on this land with him and use the land for all our needs and protected the land from harm. We made a commitment to obey his laws. We asked him to be our leader. He refused and said we have great ambitions in our hearts, that not until we fulfilled the journey ahead to good or bad, would he be our leader. For he is the first and shall be the last.

"**The wealthy Massau** lives in carelessly evil ways. He is crafty and wicked. He is boastful that he knows how to use his influence to sway people to his ways. He can destroy and teaches no love, only hate. We must always be aware of his intentions.

"We believe that the meaning of this knowledge and wisdom in Bahanna terms is that one signifies moral law and the other signifies material law. Perhaps few will accept what we say. The sad fact in this period of time is that not only Hopi, but people throughout the world are forsaking the teaching of poor Massau and his laws for better things. Or they could be choosing doomsday in following the wealthy Massau. We are hopeful there may be one or two who still believe and are standing firm behind the poor Massau and the Great Spirit."

Have you figured out who the two Maasaws are yet? We know there is only one legitimate Maasaw. So what are the Elders really saying? They are showing us that the two Maasaws in this parable are the Traditionalists on the one side and the Tribal Council and the Office of Cultural Preservation on the other. Both sides look like Hopi, and both sides talk like Hopi, and both sides claim to be the group that truly represents Maasaw. Each of them wants to lure Hopi into its fold.

Looking at the descriptions given above however, which would you say is the poor and true Maasaw, and which is the rich and false Maasaw? Which lives the humble and sacrificial life? Has anyone seen Council or Office people out in the fields with a digging stick and some seeds lately? Which of them is living in houses where all of the amenities of Bahanna life are present? Which is it that handles all of the money that comes to the tribe? Which of them is in the Kivas? Which is doing the ceremonies, and which is keeping the Covenant?

Sometimes those who play the wealthy Maasaw try to convince themselves that what they are doing is best for everyone, even though deep down inside they know it is not the truth. We see, however, that if their Maasaw wins, they at least have more company to keep them warm during their constant winters of discontent.

The Elders tell us that the two Maasaws are both between us and within us, which poses still another mystery to be solved. What they mean is that we are in the middle, or *between,* them, while the two of them seek to lure us into themselves. Once we have made our choice we move into that one, and are *within* him. After that, we are that one's follower, and we are, with an exception, controlled by him.

Related to the choice of Maasaws is another parable that speaks of one seed in which there are two seeds. This refers to the individual who has chosen which Maasaw he will follow, and yet retains the freedom of choice. In other words, he is never locked in. He can opt out whenever he wishes, although when he does this, in the case of the true Maasaw, getting back in is not easy. Every time a person steps off of the balance beam, it costs him something, if nothing more than his carrying with him thereafter the awareness of his own vulnerability. It happened once, and he can never be certain it won't happen again. Like those who join AA, they need to keep to the mark with particular zeal for the rest of their lives.

Before Bahanna came, and even for awhile afterward, the impersonators of Maasaw would appear as line dancers during the Kachina season. Twenty or more of them dressed as Maasaw would form a long line and dance in the central plaza in remembrance of the great meeting at Oraibi. Everyone who watched felt the impact when the dancers made the long moaning howl that was peculiar to them, and shook their Pattern of Life rattles as they moved back and forth here at this place the villagers called "the center of the earth." We can be sure that the rain clouds above them were thick as grapes on a vine while this was going on.

But, over the years, the Government made its inroads. Maasaw dancers were a prime target. It wasn't long before they appeared less frequently, and finally they did not appear at all. Interestingly enough, at the 1995 Bean Dance at Hotevilla, the masked Kachina dancers who danced at the public performance were led by a single, imposing Maasaw figure. There is no question but that the Traditionalists arranged this to make a powerful statement against what the Tribal Council, Office of Cultural Preservation, and Progressives were trying to do to the village. No spectator who watched this could have failed to see and understand the message. Some of them must have trembled and held their breath. Council members must have clenched their fists and grumbled recriminations. They were coming to Hotevilla by then, because they were gaining control and wanted everyone to know it. I wish I had been there to share the face off. It was like a day in the old west, except, for the moment, there were no guns. Those would appear on the Council side at the renowned Home Going Dance a few months later.

Outnumbered as the Traditionalists were, everyone in the village knew that, when a move like the promised utility installation was made against Maasaw's followers, the consequences could be grave. This was why, months after they were first placed there, the pipes still lay around the perimeter of the village. They were there at Bean Dance time in February, and they were there at Home Going in July. The two-hearteds had found it difficult to summon up the courage to make their move. There was also the matter of guilty consciences to be considered. The decent members of the Tribal Council knew that putting in the utilities at Hotevilla Village was a rotten thing to do. And they were concerned about having to live with that truth.

If, through reading the *Hotevilla* book, the presence of the "sacred object" becomes known before or during the installation, it is going to become even harder to make their move. But sooner or later the Tribal Council has to complete the job. They know they are being confronted by Traditionalist power, and at this point in time they can not afford to lose face again. If they don't move soon, their authority and control will be finished, and the other Hopi will begin to stand up to them too. Now that they have a copy of the *Hotevilla* book in their hands, if the Council and Office have already gone ahead with the installation, there will be absolute consternation over their not having known about the buried village marker. Dan has tried to warn them, but as usual, they are not listening.

I know that authors are supposed to exercise self-control and place a damper on their feelings. But isn't what is going on up there at that tiny village in the midst of nowhere something impressive? What makes it even more dramatic is that, while it sounds like a fairy tale, it is actually happening. I never imagined on that day in May, when I entered Covenant Land, that the Creator would be drawing me into something as important as this.

Meanwhile, Maasaw carried on with his duties as Guardian of the Earth and shepherd of the Traditionalists. In one of the newsletters, the Elders described a moment when they prepared for an important meeting with Agency officials, and the words they used give us a marvelous feeling of what it has been like to be a Traditionalist involved in momentous events. The statement is beautiful and stirring. Would that all of our days began with the same kinds of thoughts and emotions:

"As dawn appeared over the horizon in Hopi Land, one would dimly notice movements of dark figures against the Eastern sky. There was an air of extra awareness and feelings for those who were up at that hour. *One could almost feel the movements of the Mother Earth getting ready to care for her children and even the jogging feet of Guardian Massau returning home after an all-night vigil over Man.* Dogs were barking, cocks and mocking-birds were sounding the arrival of dawn. Before long, Father Sun would take over the task he does everyday.

"One by one, bowed darkened figures would whisper and breathe their prayers upon the cornmeal that their hands held: 'Our Father Sun, all the Unseen Living, help us this day with your Supreme Power. Echo your voices into the ears of men so that they may hear and understand our purpose here this day.

Protect and guide us in the right way. May our body, mind, and spirit be wholesome this day, I humbly ask Thee.'"

This is the kind of prayer Dan makes to the Creator and Sun in the morning, and to Maasaw each evening. I have italicized the lines regarding Mother Earth and Maasaw so that you would not fail to notice them. For clarification, you need to know that every morning Mother Earth gets ready to care for us, and that every night Maasaw also flies four times around the earth to see for himself what is going on there. He assumes the form of a fireball, and what we often mistake for a falling star or comet is really Maasaw going by. Maasaw also spends part of his time jogging around Hopi Land to see that, despite the problems there, all is as well as can be expected. As he jogs, he carries a lighted torch, both to illuminate his way, and so that Hopi who might accidentally come upon him will know to give him a clear berth. He has work to do, and does not want to be slowed down. He tours all of the villages of Hopi Land, and reports from Hopi who have sighted him are common. I asked Susie if she had ever seen him while he was making his rounds, and she said that she had seen him trotting across their property several times.

There is something else we need to know about Maasaw and his relationship to the entire globe. Reference is made in the prophecies to a "gourd of ashes" that will fall upon the earth and cause great devastation. Hopi leaders have interpreted this gourd as the atomic bomb, and relate it to nuclear bombs that will be used during a Third World War, the description of which is similar to those of Armageddon predicted by other prophets. Most Hopi do not know about this other little gourd that Maasaw carries, but Dan Evehema told me about it. It too is filled with ashes, but they are miracle ashes that do not cause devastation—they end it. The prophecy is that when, during the great Purification, the Hopi are about to be ravaged to the point of extinction, Maasaw will pour his ashes upon them and the rest of Hopi Land, and all of the fighting in the world will stop. Then a new harmony will come upon mankind, the Fourth Cycle will close, and the Fifth Cycle will begin.

How does anyone make a deity of death out of Maasaw?

Let's consider some other examples of his true nature.

The Elders say, **"In our language, the name, Hopi, has held the same meaning from the beginning. It names those who live by the plan laid out by the spirit, Maasauu,** and today hold the land in trust for him. Although our bloodline is very important, the word refers to our whole way of life, as well as to the foundation of the authority of our traditional leaders, and our claim over the land."

They make reference to the way it used to be at Hopi Land during the Harvest season: "Let us step back to our past, before our way of life was disturbed. Our life was of happiness, our activities, entertainments, and ceremonial patters were complete. Let's take a glimpse of one of the ancient ones.

"Long ago, when the first Hopi met Massauu, they asked for his permission to live with him in Old Oraibi. So Massauu would watch activities from his house top.

"Perhaps, for some reason, he thought of the idea of getting the people together to make them happy during the Harvest Season. He gathered the leaders and explained what he had in mind. He made a request that was announced from the house top, that during four days the people would harvest for him: women would prepare the meal, while girls, boys, and men, together would harvest his cornfields.

"On the fourth day, they gathered and went below the mesa. There, they formed two groups at one fourth of a mile from each side of the field. At a signal they ran towards the field while shouting and whooping. Boys and girls worked side by side, shy at first until they began to laugh and talk. They had great fun and took advantage of this occasion, for, at that time, girls were respected so that one could not talk to a girl just anywhere or at anytime.

"Suddenly, Massauu would pop out of the cornpile and start chasing the men around. Everybody would be laughing, hollering, and, at the same time, fearful of him, for his face looked ugly, horrible and bloody with the look of death. This ended the harvesting, and they returned home.

"After the meal, Massauu entered the plaza, where men were dressed in different costumes to tease and challenge him. Finally, he would knock out one of his victims with his weapon, a drumstick. He acted like a clown and would strip his victim, who pretended to be dead. He would then dress up himself with that costume in the opposite manner of him who he stripped. Dressed like that, Massauu would chase the men around, and everyone would laugh and have a good time. It would end with them killing him with a hot torch to the mouth. Then he was carried to the outskirts of the village, where he was dumped. But he came alive when they hollered and shouted.

"Those were days when men communicated openly and verbally with spirit beings, animals, birds, and men could talk and understand each other. At that time there were no 'animals of burden.'

"Then, Massauu was part of the ceremonial cycle until he hid himself from men. Later, he was impersonated. Finally, not long ago, this was discontinued. Is it possible that this has meaning the Great Spirit himself has drawn up?"

You see by this intriguing story that, in the beginning, the real Maasaw participated in the harvest, which always has been the most joyous of the four seasons for those who have continued to farm at Hopi Land. In this account we are introduced to a

Maasaw who is fun-loving and who has a fondness for performing. He wants to share this side of his nature with the people, and he does not mind being made fun of. This brings him closer to his people. As was made clear at that first meeting at Oraibi, he is, therefore, a very warm and personal deity, not imperious, remote, and reeking of death. Being able to humble him for even a moment was something the Hopi relished, and it gave them a healthy perspective regarding their Guardian. Maasaw is awesome in appearance, but has the proverbial heart of gold.

So too did the menacing Ogres, who carried out their duties in an effort to bring understanding to children that would assure them the very best kind of life. This is consistent with the nature of the instructions. One of their first lessons is that children must be taught to have respect for others, and especially their elders. At the same time, the adults, by what they are taught to do, must show their respect for one another, and for the Creator and his Helper Spirits—the "Unseen Living." Can you imagine what a chore it was for the Ogre impersonators to wear their heavy masks and costumes, and to behave as they had to? But they did it because it was a task that brought lasting and important results.

We often see the nature of the deities themselves as they are reflected by the people they choose to represent them. By looking at the servants, we can see what their Creator and His Helpers are really like. Several of the Traditionalists I mention often in my books have made prominent contributions in this regard during the last century.

Yukiuma stands at the head of the line. This gritty little man, who is given special attention in the *Hotevilla* book, assumed the leadership of the Hopi at Oraibi who refused to give in to the United States Government. He did whatever was necessary to hold to his vow during the division of Oraibi, and in 1906 led his followers away from the village and to Hotevilla Springs, where the new village was founded. So firm was he in his convictions that he endured eight imprisonments and endless harassing during his term as kickmongwi of Hotevilla. He set a precedent for all of the Traditionalist leaders to follow, and is remembered by Traditionalists as one of the greatest Hopi ever. He is the closest thing to a hero that the Traditionalists have.

Dan Katchongva was one of the most charismatic leaders to serve as kickmongwi of Hotevilla Village. A son of Yukiuma, he inherited his father's determination and wisdom. An eloquent orator and teacher, he remained, until his death in 1972, one of the most sought after guides to the Traditionalist life-way. One of his final acts was to dictate an abbreviated memoir that included some details of his life, and also some of the most important of the Hopi prophecies. That memoir is included in its entirety in the *Hotevilla* book, and stands as one of the most valuable documents to come out of the Traditionalist era at The Shrine of the Covenant.

David Monongye served as the last Traditionalist kickmongwi of Hotevilla Village. He was an extremely intelligent man, who was as familiar with the outside world as he was with Hopi Land itself. He was a kind man, but also firm. He was able to communicate effectively with Bahannas who were open to Traditionalist needs, and gave them express guidance as to how they could help in the most effective ways. He also foresaw the dire consequences that would come from the operation of the Peabody Mine, and did his best to alert everyone regarding the dangers. Once the Tribal Council and the Office of Cultural Preservation were installed, he fought them at every turn.

Titus Lamson and Dan Evehema were lifelong friends who shared their loyalty to the Creator and Maasaw. He went to join the Kachinas in December of 1995, at the age of ninety-four. Titus was an outstanding Keeper of the Covenant, and a strong defender of individual Hopi rights. At the same time he was a warm friend to several young Bahannas who joined him and the Traditionalists of Hotevilla in their attempts to defuse the destructive efforts of the Tribal Council. His most noteworthy act in recent years was to confront the Tribal Council publicly when it attempted to fence in his land. That defense was successful, but now that Titus is gone the Tribal Council is extracting a price from those Bahannas whom Titus permitted to live on his land and to farm it. Details regarding this situation are included in Chapter 11.

Caroline Tawangyama is Dan Evehema's sister. A happy and wise lady, she was the first child born at Hotevilla after the split at Oraibi. Therefore, she is probably 90 years of age. She has been a staunch and spunky Traditionalist for the whole of her life. Caroline has often led those who have resisted what the Tribal Council has attempted to do. In particular, she was in the forefront of those who, during at least three earlier attempts, kept the utility pipes from being laid in Hotevilla Village. On one occasion, she even jumped into a trench in front of a bulldozer, and challenged the driver to run over her. Tribal police dragged her out of the trench and threatened to arrest her. But the Council changed their minds about the utilities, and decided not to put Caroline in jail. In recent years, she has been slowed by diabetes, and requires dialysis, so has been less active than usual. Caroline was at the village at the end of August to meet the workers when they made their current attempt to begin to put in the utilities.

Dan Evehema. Dan's story has been told in the *Hotevilla* book and in this book. My opinion of him as a remarkable individual is not a secret, and my gratitude to him is unbounded.

Susie Lomatska. You learn a little about Susie in this book, but a lot more in the *Hotevilla* book. Generous to a fault, she was an indispensable helper in bringing that book into existence, and is a cherished friend. She makes piki bread in the old way, and is an excellent Kachina doll maker. When the Department of Health and Human Services acceded to the Council's request and published information heralding the proposed establishment of utilities in Hotevilla last year, she did what none of the men volunteered to do. She went alone to the Tribal Council Headquarters and confronted them, demanding to know where their authority to do this came from. She wanted to see the names of those who had signed authorizations for the intrusion. All they did in reply was to stall her, and eventually gave her no answer whatsoever. She was with the other Traditionalists to meet the workers when they came to Hotevilla Village to install the utilities at the end of August. Susie has spent a good part of her life caring for Dan and assisting him in every possible way. His general happiness is mostly due to her making sure that he is secure and watched over.

Our own wealthy Massaw comes in the guise of materialism to tempt us, and uses the same approaches that he does with the Hopi. Therefore, all of the warnings given to the Hopi at Oraibi in A.D. 1100 are lessons we need to listen carefully to. When we add them to the warnings the world itself is giving us, we can see that our situation is not a good one. We need to know what the secret is, and we need to follow its INSTRUCTIONS and WARNINGS.

THE SECRET!

Chapter 6

Prophecies Past and Present

Everything having to do with the secret begins with the prophecies. Up to this point in time no more than a half-dozen of the prophecies have been revealed. All of them, totaling about a hundred, are given in this chapter and in Chapter 7.

The Hopi Traditionalists do not need to convince us that their prophecies are valuable and extraordinary. They differ from other prophecies in that the Creator has designed them to perform several unique functions. So please read what I tell you about their unique qualities before you read the prophecies themselves. I describe how the prophecies work and I tell you how to interpret them properly. Once you understand these things, there will be no limit to what the Hopi prophecies can do for you.

The Source of the Hopi Prophecies

I assume you noted my assertion that "the Creator has designed them," and wondered why I said it. It is because any consideration of Hopi prophecies begins with the recognition that their author is the Creator Himself. This is what the Hopi have resolutely claimed for nearly a thousand years. And when we consider Hopi prophecies, we too must think of them as coming from the Creator. The information the Hopi were given at Oraibi was routed through His assistant, Maasaw, but it did not originate with him. Where the prophecies are concerned, he is a bearer, and nothing more. In the same way, the Hopi are not producers of the information. They are channels through whom the Creator and Maasaw speak to us.

Since we receive the prophecies from the Hopi, we call them "The Hopi Prophecies." This is really a misnomer, just as it is misleading to call what you are reading "*The Hopi Survival Kit.*" I use the word "Hopi" on the book jacket for simplification, and for familiaritiy's sake. We know who the Hopi are and we can identify with them. We must, however, be clear in our understandings. It is imperative to recognize that the Creator Himself is their Author and Source. They are what He sees, what He plans, and, as such, are infinitely superior to any predictions that have a human origin. Knowing where the Hopi prophecies originate, we can expect every one of them to be lucidly presented and accurately fulfilled. They will not be phrased in some strange language that needs decoding, and most will not need to be explained.

These insights regarding the Source should give everyone special confidence in the Hopi prophecies. Recognizing their Source is an admission that we acknowledge His concern for us, and accept that He cares enough to warn us and provide us with the means of defending ourselves.

Despite the fact that our amazing story opens with an adventure into the unknown Underworld, Hopi prophecy has a clearly established historic origin. Its realities cannot be contested. It was etched in stone at Oraibi and has been reviewed and proclaimed by the Hopi loyalists every year for nearly a thousand years. If all of this is not true, the Traditionalists of each succeeding generation will have gained nothing by basing their lives on it and expounding it.

Where Hopi understandings are concerned, the exceptions to the Principal Source just mentioned are where Maasaw and other Spirit beings continue to commune with the Hopi when they pray individually or as a group in a Kiva ceremony. When the Hopi do their rituals, these Spirit beings send power and strength and wisdom into the celebrants. The performers receive it first, and then pass it on to villagers and friends who in heart and soul and mind are identifying with them. This is power for understanding, power for the growth of crops, and power for the deepening of the love relationship that bonds creature with Creator. The process is part of a melding that has been established through the Covenant and maintained through tribal initiations, the making of shrines, and the living out of the entire Pattern of Life. There is also power for uplifting one's spirit, and for the positive transformation of an individual or a group.

In countless places throughout the southwest the Hopi have built their sacred shrines and sunk their roots into Mother Earth. The shrines are not elaborate, but through them She sends up to the Hopi Her personal power. At these places the fibers of the Hopi heart and soul interweave with Hers to establish a bountiful union. It is a fusion that is kept alive by rituals performed at them by Hopi. Every past and present-day village has numerous shrines in and around it. These are sacred places that are not to be disturbed by outsiders. When a Hopi is at one of them and performing a ritual or saying a prayer, he or she is able to commune with Mother Earth in ways that others cannot. Knowledge is acquired about creation that the rest of us can only envy. Since they have obtained this valuable information, it is especially wonderful that the Traditionalists are willing to part with it, particularly in this critical moment of environmental need and stupendous natural disasters. Of course, not every Hopi can claim this blessing. Not all of them are linked with Mother Earth. On-the-fence Hopi still use the shrines. Progressives do not. But many of those who seek to walk simultaneously in both the Red and White worlds are as deaf to Her as those of us in the outside world who have no shrines, and who have established no useful connection with Her.

Beyond the things already mentioned, the Traditionalist Hopi have a conditioned sensitivity that comes from following the annual cycle of rituals and duties. These keep them attuned to the Creator and the highest Spirits, and hold them in a state of readiness to meet any problems that arise. How wonderful it is then that the Traditionalist Hopi believe the time has come to share this gift with us so that we can enjoy the same advantages. We should be eternally grateful, and listen carefully to them as they reveal the marvelous secrets they have learned about the Creator and survival. Moreover, this gift is freely given. It does not and will not cost us a cent to take full advantage of it. The Traditionalists want nothing in return, except perhaps our support.

We should remember too that what we are experiencing here is a rare treat. **It is the first complete rendering of the Hopi prophecies ever made to the outside world,** and it is all the more valuable because the Hopi Elders know the time has come to reveal it. Until the newsletters were first published, and actually because of their mysterious disappearance, until today only a few of the prophecies have been disclosed. The major portions were kept secret and discussed only in the privacy of the Kivas. Even then, it appears that they have been discussed by only a select, highly trained, and dedicated few. The prophecies were not a subject for loose talk or inattentive ears. Where the prophecies are concerned, the little that has been told by anyone indicates there is limited knowledge among the Hopi in general.

It may even be that only Dan Evehema knows the broad amount we include here. And, when he does put on his cloud mask and goes to be with the other Kachina spirits on the San Francisco Peaks, there will probably not be another person who knows and can relate all of the Hopi prophecies, instructions, and warnings without having to refer to *Hotevilla,* or this book. Fortunately, the Elders put it in the newsletters and their other accounts so that it could be preserved for this propitious time.

Since the Hopi prophecies sound modern for information received so long ago, we need to know why they do. During specified Kiva ceremonies, it has been the Hopi custom to repeat annually in the Hopi language all of the information pertaining to the Life Pattern. I say "has been," because it is doubtful that anyone will be equipped to do this after the Elderly Elders are gone. Until now, the prophecies and instructions were memorized so that they could be passed on word for word in the exact form they were first received. But needs have changed, and the language has been adapted to our time and requirements. This is why the revealed information seems modern today. What we read in the newsletters has been brought up to date for present day Hopi and ourselves.

Contemporizing was a difficult task for the writers of the newsletters. But they knew that if the legacy was to be passed on, it could not be avoided. Thanks to their education in White-controlled schools, far too many Hopi are no longer able to read, write or speak the Hopi language. They can only understand Hopi when it has been translated into modern English. The Elders commonly claim that young people can no longer comprehend the commands of the Fathers who lead the ceremonial dances, and that they do not understand the words of the ancient songs. Accordingly, many dancers follow the routine, but lack the profound understanding the Traditionalist Elders have. So spiritual power flickers like a failing candle. Precious energy is lost, and it can not be recovered.

HOPI PROPHECIES POINT BEYOND THEMSELVES

An incident at Dan's home will introduce you to Hopi attitudes regarding the prophecies and how they work. While we were sitting on the couch in his living room I opened my notebook and showed him how I was removing the prophecies from the newsletters and putting them in order. When I explained that I was doing this so that they could be studied as a separate unit, he smiled and shook his head in amazement. "Bahanna's ways," he said, pitying us for having to go to such lengths. But he turned a few of the pages, grunted, and then nodded his head in approval. I knew what was running through his mind. He had expected me to do this, because it would be the only way we could reach Bahannas.

When we were out in the yard later on and sitting in the shade of the ramada at the picnic table, he picked up an ear of corn that was lying there. It was golden-yellow sweet corn, the kind Hopi eat when they celebrate the harvest at the great Home Going Dance. A brief rain that morning had brightened its color and made it shine. Rain is always a good sign. He turned it back and forth and admired it as we do a precious gift. Then he bent over and cradled it in his arm as a mother does a child. He stroked its kernels and sang a song to it. It was a short melody whose words were those of gratitude to Mother Earth and the Creator. As he straightened up he looked toward his corn fields across the road. His eyes softened and for a moment he was lost in memories. Decades of farming had blended him in an amazing way with those fields. Compared to the sweeping corn fields of Minnesota they didn't look like much to me, but for centuries they had been life itself for his family, and his feelings toward them were powerful. I understood then why he did not like being away from the fields for very long.

He turned to me and made a dispensing motion with his hand, saying as he did so, "Prophecies come, prophecies go, but we live on. That is what happens to those who follow the Road Plan and the Pattern of Life."

What he meant was that the prophecies passed on by Maasaw do not dominate life, and they are not an end in themselves. They are a direction arrow and a catalyst. They point to and push us toward something that is beyond them, yet which works in tandem with them. This something is a superb way to fortify ourselves against the prophecies when fulfillment is threatened, and when they are actually fulfilled. Therefore, even the most terrible of the prophecies have a good side to them. It is one that is amazing in that Hopi prophecies can be self-defeating. They tell us what will take place, and immediately thereafter lead us to the instructions and warnings that enable us to either lessen their impact or keep them from happening—at least from happening as soon as they otherwise would.

PROPHECIES THAT ARE DIRECTLY RELATED TO THE HOPI HELP US AS WELL.

As I have said, there are about 100 Hopi prophecies. Since some prophecies contain several within their descriptions, the exact number is difficult to determine. As we study them, it is intriguing to discover that while most have to do with the Hopi themselves, they are also useful to us. This is not difficult to understand. The Hopi and we share the same Creator, and as human beings we have a lot in common. The Traditionalist Hopi know that, and it is unfortunate that so many outsiders, Christians in particular, fail to realize it.

Maasaw implants a special kind of assurance within those

who respond to his call to serve. As prophecies are fulfilled in Hopi Land, and as the Traditionalists carry out their assigned responsibilities, the Guardian of the Earth helps them grow in strength, self-esteem, and conviction. Then the Hopi are able to speak from personal experience and with confidence. They know they are dispensing first-hand knowledge, and they know what they are talking about. Since many of the prophecies deal with the personal aspects of individual lives, they enable the Hopi to see the Creator's concern for them, as individuals, as a group, and in terms of their relationship to the entire world. Above all, the prophecies lift the Hopi up and let them sit at the right hand of the Creator. From this extraordinary vantage point, the Hopi are able to see what is going on around them, what is coming, and what they must prepare for.

As we view the prophecies that are personally related to the Hopi, we learn to identify with the Hopi, and we discover that what happens to them happens to us. We learn what the Creator's true nature is, and are no longer able to think of it in terms of what we would like it to be. Most of us prefer the "good" Creator who is always understanding and permissive, and who treats us as innocent victims of circumstances that are always beyond our control. We want a Creator who protects us from evil, and who thinks we merit a long and untroubled life. When life doesn't work out that way, we are mystified. We simply don't understand it. But at the same time we insist upon freedom and free choice. In short, we want to be indulged. Whenever something untoward happens, we ask "Why me?" or, "Why them?" Our personal contributions to the situation are conveniently overlooked. As long as we are pretty good on a relative scale, we think the right kind of a Creator ought to appreciate that and take good care of us.

Fortunately, and in certain circumstances, He does take better care of us than we can rightfully expect. In this regard, it is helpful to observe how prophetic fulfillments affect the Hopi, why they do, and what their answer to them is. Then when our own pattern of thinking finally gets straightened out, our chances of survival will be greatly enhanced. We will have obtained a clearer picture of human nature; and of what kinds of creatures the Creator has to deal with. Then, as we watch the fulfillment of a succession of prophecies in the lives of the Hopi, we will no longer doubt that future prophecies will also come to pass. Centering upon prophetic fulfillment in the lives of the Hopi is much less complex than having to view it in terms of fulfillments throughout the entire world.

PROPHETIC HOPE

We usually think of prophecy as something that has to do with disasters that will happen in the future, either to a person, a group or a place. In this view, there are no nice prophecies. Most are so foreboding they only incite fear, and so are derisively called "doomsday prophecies." A book that is filled with them can leave us gasping for breath. Since we have enough bad news and don't need more, we usually turn our backs to prophecies, and hope they will go away.

In terms of how they work, the Hopi prophecies are not, however, doomsday prophecies, and only a fraction of them have to do with world-shaking events. Some point to useful commodities that will be invented, and others have to do with changes that will take place in society.

When it comes to deciphering them, the prophecies of outside-world prophets can, by comparison, be extremely frustrating. We are seldom told why a certain prophecy is going to be fulfilled. Figuring this out is something we must do for ourselves. We must deal with the fact that, while some prophecies come to pass, others do not. We are left with the dilemma of not knowing what, if anything, we should do about any of them.

At the same time, we cannot deny that the prophecies of the Bible have proven their accuracy, and we know that a few prophets, like the well-known Nostradamus, have compiled impressive track records. His interpreters admit that of his more than 1,000 prophecies 800 continue to defy translations that are acceptable to everyone. He appears also to have made a few inaccurate predictions. Yet he made incredibly accurate predictions concerning some of the most important individuals and events in history. Where a few of his predictions about the future are close to duplicating those of the Hopi, I make note of them in the material ahead. Even the details he gives of how things will happen inspire awe. Now and then, Nostradamus does reveal how history will shape itself to guarantee the fulfillment of certain prophecies.

John Hogue, one of Nostradamus's foremost interpreters, claims that the reason the prophet made his predictions known was to give people the opportunity to do something to prevent them from happening. But the fact that he used encoded quatrains belies this assertion. It often takes his interpreters years to figure out what he really said, and even then they can't be sure they have it right. If Nostradamus wanted people to be forewarned, why would he make it nearly impossible for them to understand what he was saying? Why wouldn't he just state his revelations plainly and in terms anyone could understand?

We have considered some of the ways in which the Hopi prophecies differ from those of Nostradamus and other prophets, but there are more. Hopi prophecies substantiate themselves in that every one of them that should have been fulfilled by now has been, indicating that the rest of them will be. Some are in the process of being fulfilled at this very moment. The track record to date is perfect. These important prophecies tell us in advance what we should anticipate and prepare for, teaching us caution and awareness. They tell us why things will happen, thus helping us understand ourselves, the nature of the world, and the nature of our Creator. And, since they point beyond themselves to the instructions and warnings, we are given active ways to get ready for them and to counteract the damage. Note the word "active." We are not left to sit, to wonder, or to live in fear. We can get to work immediately on specific solutions. More importantly, we are trained to be constantly doing, as an automatic process of life, everything that is necessary to keep us alert and ready. Therefore, we are able to live in abiding hope. Above all, there is a splendid gentleness in what we are called upon to do, a gentleness that clothes us in an attitude that affects everything we think, say, and achieve. Our life takes on a rhythm that is synchronized with the universe. We learn to touch, to care, to relate, and to find the ultimate joy in life, which is a state of one-ness with the Creator and everything he has created.

PROPHETIC IFS

We are seeing that the Hopi prophecies separate and distinguish themselves from others. Taken together, the ways tell us that, because of our sinful natures, the Creator has no option but to deal harshly with us. Yet at the same time, He has provided us with a way to redeem ourselves and find an escape from any dilemma. Even now we have not exhausted the ways in which the Hopi prophecies work. There are more. When Maasaw gave his prophecies, instructions, and warnings to the Hopi at Oraibi, they were often conditioned by "ifs" and "maybes." This is why the Elders often preface or punctuate their statements with conditioners such as, "If we are fortunate, this will happen," or, "If we are not fortunate, this will happen."

This is neither indecision nor an admission of not knowing the answers. It is a recognition of how Hopi prophecy works, and it says that the final outcome does not rest in human hands; it rests in the hands of the Creator Himself.

HOPI PROPHECY FUNCTIONS AS A STAGE PLAY.

In Hopi prophecy, life functions as a global play in which all of us are the actors. There are possible things that can happen in each act, but we ourselves determine which of these it will be by what we choose to do. The course that the act follows is determined by an initial choice, and by subsequent choices. The Traditionalists believe we are in the midst of the final act today, as the Fourth Cycle of the world closes down, and we can shape and reshape its form if we make the right choices. In Hopi prophecy, there are no fated endings that are set in concrete.

But the actual end of each act, and the beginning of the next, are left to the Creator to decide. He also determines the conclusion of the final act of the play, although He makes this decision in consultation with His Principal Assistant Spirits, including Mother Earth. Therefore, the ultimate blessing or punishment to be rendered is one that, in their combined minds, will be appropriate in light of human behavior.

Since all of us who are alive are in the play at once, we face yet another question. Human choices are bound to be different. Does this mean the Creator will face the difficulty of having to choose which of us He will respond to? This is not really a problem. Our choice is a basic one. Whenever we are faced with an option, we must decide whom we will follow. Will it be the Creator or will it be the two-hearted forces of evil? Will it be the good Maasaw or the bad Maasaw? For instance, the Hopi have been told by the Elderly Elders that the time has come when they must end their vacillating. They must choose now whether they will follow the Creator's way, or the Bahanna way of materialism. Once this basic choice is made by any of us, however, what follows may be involved and complex. Free choice remains, and the two seeds are still within us. Walking the narrow beam will never be easy, for temptations are constantly placed before us by the two-hearteds, and if those don't work, pressure follows. In each instance, however, the "punishment will always fit the crime." In a sense, we ourselves establish what it will be, and pretending ignorance about this will not change the situation. We make our own bed, dig our own grave, puncture our own balloon.

PROPHETIC TIMING

In response to the question as to when any of the prophesied things will occur, Dan usually says, "It may be in your lifetime, or in your children's, or in your children's children's lifetime." We could take this as an indication that it might be a thousand years from now before the worst of them happens, and that we really have nothing to worry about. Haven't we, we say, time and time again proven ourselves to be creative people who rise to the occasion and conquer critical situations? You bet we are, we answer. Our human resourcefulness and ingenuity has been impressive. So shouldn't we conclude that we have plenty of time and that we should just go on doing the same things we are doing now? But time and events are accelerating, and problems are growing exponentially. They magnify themselves at an amazing rate of speed day by day. And, what we have accomplished in correcting them so far has hardly dented our entanglements. As for the actual magnitude of the problems we face, what do we know the truth about? Who can we rely on to tell us how it really is with any dangerous situation? Will industry? Will governments?

In any event, time and indecision are not the points Dan is

making when he speaks of alternate possibilities. He is simply admitting that he has no way of knowing which it will be. How the play goes all depends upon the choices made by succeeding generations and individuals. So, the Creator did not attach fulfillment dates to his prophecies. Nevertheless, He didn't leave it entirely loose. He gave the Hopi a list of signs that they could associate with certain prophecies and, so, would know when they were in the midst of a fulfillment, or that a certain one was about to take place.

Here is a newsletter quote that will serve as an example: "When a Hopi sees these things happening, his response is simple, it appears that we are now at the beginning of something." All you need to know now is what these things are.

The Hopi also know that, as choices change, a given prophetic fulfillment might be redirected, pushed back, or watered down. "The situation itself, or the destinies of humans varies," they say, "with time and space." In the next chapter we learn what these signs are, and how the Hopi make use of them. Their sophistication may surprise outsiders who think of the Traditionalist Hopi as uneducated and only able to do things by rote. But they do surprisingly well, and, in fact, are impressively sophisticated.

THE NEED FOR SELF-EXAMINATION

Another important point for us to recognize is that, when the Traditionalist Hopi know that things are not going well or that danger exists, they look within themselves for answers. They examine themselves, and then do something about what they learn. Likewise, our problems today are more often than not the result of our own acts, thoughts, and desires, and the consequences have been exacerbated by our inexcusable laxness in admitting our personal responsibilities and doing something about them. In a global sense, we have even jeopardized our own existence by waiting too long before we have faced facts and acted upon them. We also do a great deal of compromising. If we are participating in something we know to be a sin, we are delighted when some adroit social authority finds a way to excuse it. We must change this pattern and begin to develop the kind of honesty that Maasaw expected from the Traditionalists.

It is not fair to indict everyone when accusations such as these are made. Some individuals and groups are making careful choices and performing herculean efforts to rectify environmental and other problems. It is just that there aren't nearly enough of them to accomplish what must be done in the seemingly short period of time we have before the Fourth Cycle closes down. I use the term "seemingly" because the closing time can be pushed back. But to accomplish this, those who are already in the battle need massive help. Every one of us who puts *The Hopi Survival Kit* to work will become part of the effort.

We can understand now why the Hopi prophecies, unlike so many others, have no dates attached to them, and why they are always couched in general terms. Everything is laid out by the Creator, but options are there and nothing is settled. Specifics regarding prophetic fulfillments are carefully avoided, and it is only when a prophetic possibility begins to kick in that the Elders can say, "It might happen now, but we will wait and see," or, "It appears that we are in the midst of something." They say this, however, with confidence. From the long list of prophetic fulfillments that have already taken place, they know that one day the rest will follow.

What is predicted will not evaporate. Sooner or later certain of the prophecies assigned by the Creator will come to pass, and, in the end, the Fourth Cycle of the world will close. In a way, the options would seem to be an unsettling factor. In order to prepare in advance, we need targets and target dates. In Chapter 11 we learn there is a way to narrow down time periods by viewing Hotevilla as a microcosm that helps us establish intensities, trends, and sequences. When we consider this, however, we must never forget that following the INSTRUCTIONS will keep us in a perpetual state of readiness, so that, whenever a fulfillment comes, we will be prepared for it. There will be special and last-minute things to do, but that is all.

Is all of this hollow boasting? You will need to follow the essence of the Hopi Pattern of Life to find out. It is evident that, compared to the nature of other prophecies, the Hopi form is unique. It is broader in scope, more comprehensive in its details, and carries with it constantly the greatest possible hope. We always have a reason to choose rightly and to continue working, which is what the Elders and their ancestors have done so consistently. They have never, and will never, set a date for the end of the world and then go into seclusion on a mountain top to pray and wait for its fulfillment.

I continue to be impressed by the fact that the Hopi prophecies predate most, if not all, others by hundreds of years. I am also influenced by the fact that the prophecies and other information were given to a small, remote, and relatively unimportant group who, for the most part, could not in their time period have had any idea of what Maasaw was talking about when he made references to other races, modern accomplishments, global wars, and global situations such as those existing today. In fact, the Hopi had no frame of reference for most of the things he referred to. So they could only have sat there with open mouths and wrinkled brows, again and again scratching their heads in bewilderment. They heard what was being said, but they had no idea what it referred to or what to do with it, and the challenge from Maasaw to remember it word for word must have been all the more daunting because of this. I assume, though, that Maasaw told them not to worry, for the time would come when some generation of their descendants would open their eyes wide when they realized that a prophesied event was actually taking place. Then they would be able to make the necessary associations and to act accordingly.

It is worth noting that this priceless information was placed in the keeping of the very Native American people who would outlast all of the other tribes in North America in preserving their Traditional ways and vows. If this responsibility had been given to any other tribe, its keepers would be long gone by now, and there would be no one left to pick up the torch. Hotevilla Village and its few surviving Elderly Elder Traditionalists are the very last of all the Native American cultures to go down. When they do, as prophecy says they will, the auspicious end of something glorious and worthwhile will have been reached. In more ways that we know, we are all going to be poorer for that!

As you read what the Elders have to say about all of this, you will learn to recognize what things they have looked for in order to make their judgments, and you will begin to look for the same things. The *Hotevilla* book will be helpful to you here. It places each of the prophecies in the context of the situation being addressed and covers all of this information in much greater detail. Lacking that book though, there is enough here to tell you what you need to know.

Are the Hopi prophecies more reliable than those given by other prophets? I have my reasons for believing they are, and my guess is that as you have read between the lines you have suspected this. For one thing, I prefer their Source as compared to human origins. Also, their track record to date is perfect. I like the fact that they fit the nature of the God we meet in the Bible. The Gospel predictions of the end times are much like those of the Hopi, except that by comparison the Bible's are brief and summary, taking up little more than a few pages of text in both the Old and New Testaments. They don't give us as much to go on as the Hopi prophecies do. Jesus did include instructions for living and warnings, once again making the comparison of the two a favorable one, and I have already expressed some thoughts regarding a connection between Jesus and Maasaw. But I am afraid that is the best they can be—just thoughts.

It is time for you to be introduced to the Hopi prophecies, and then to the instructions and warnings that were also given at Oraibi. I trust you will find these revelations to be a stimulating journey. When it is finished, you will know which prophecies are related to you, the perils involved, and you will have been pointed to your own set of instructions and warnings to guide, protect, and sustain you. With all of these in hand, you can climb aboard the Hopi Ark and let the rain come down in buckets.

The prophecies that follow are organized in a time sequence, and divided into three categories: Those that have been fulfilled and part of those that are being fulfilled are addressed in this chapter. The rest of those that are being fulfilled and those that are yet to be fulfilled are cited in Chapter 7, together with the signs the Hopi watch for that tell them when something important is about to happen. My comments regarding some of the prophecies that need clarification are given in italics. For comparison with the Hopi prophecies, some of Nostradamus's prophecies regarding the future are also given in italics. The prophecies are given as they are in the newsletters. I think you will enjoy the quoted material more than you would edited versions.

Yukiuma knew all of this on that day in 1921 when he sat there in his jail cell and wished that the Agent and the Colonel would listen to him. As you read the prophecies, you may find yourself wishing that all of us had learned about them years ago.

PROPHECIES ALREADY FULFILLED:

- What Hotevilla Village did was in accordance with space and time and the guidelines set by our prophets long ago. They said, should we, along the way, find ourselves keeping out of step with the Great Creator, we must stop and think that we have become careless. Then we must act in some way not to follow those who become tangled in what we are told not to do.

- The Cherry Tree story clearly confirms the prophecy of the Hopi about the newcomers arriving in our land. Hopi called them "Bahanna"—the white race. It was prophesied that they will come in large numbers. They will be cunning and sly with forked tongue and sweet tongue. By deceit and fraud they will take over the land of the Native people. They will be ambitious in many ways and disturb the lives of the first inhabitants, disturb even the land and Nature. If we protest, they can seize the land through superior force of weapons and will attempt to annihilate all Native people. But a remnant of these people will survive to carry on for the future.

Bahanna will not end their conquests until the last Native disappears; this will be their goal.

Just as predicted, the Bahanna Government came to Hopi land with good intentions. Armed with a proposal of education for the children, with promises of many good things for the Hopi and for their children's future. After meeting over it, leaders from all the villages rejected the education, saying: Bahanna school is not good. It will not fit into their needs or blend with their religious ceremonials. That they will teach their children their own ways, as in the past.

The religious leaders foresaw it as trickery devised to destroy the minds of children. They foresaw the danger that the children would lose their traditional culture and identity.

Lose even their language and become the tool of the Government. They foresaw that they would destroy themselves and lose the Hopi way of life.

The Bahanna persisted but failed for a time. Then finally all the village leaders bowed to the inevitable only when threats of prison were used.

Among the Hopi this created great division and friction. Discord erupted between those who yielded to the powers of the Bahanna Government and those who chose to keep their position as Hopi. Knowing they could not live side by side, the devoted Hopi decided to escape to a better world of life so the traditional culture and their religion would not die. Thus the village of Hotevilla was founded and was firmly established to symbolize the protection of all life and land. It is important to understand the **sacred wall of defense** is erected to ward off the wicked in their attempts to annihilate the last remnants of the first native people. That **those who dare venture to disturb the sacred barricade will cause a great misfortune to befall us all.**

- So it was predicted by the prophets that one day we would encounter the presence of people of other races with ways different from our own. That they will erect their own kingdom upon our land; they will pose as good-hearted. Their words will be charming and they will multiply like ants. We must not be deceived by them, for the vines of their kingdom will spread throughout the land, diluting and dissolving everything that gets in its way. We must be cautious and not covet or adopt any of their ways, for it will forever be a curse upon our nation.

- The beginning of the new age of the prophecies of tomorrow has begun to unfold before our eyes. It was said, among Bahanna the people with the Cross will appear on our land.

They will be kind and helpful with good hearts. Beware, for they will be the instruments of Bahanna's kingdom and will seduce you into forsaking the laws of our Great Creator. The wicked of our people will join their flock to clear their sins, but this will be in vain.

- The new government order will be established on our land, our own people with short hair will take positions in this government disguised as the ear and tongue for our Nation. They will also be the tools influenced by the Bahanna's kingdom. They will, together with the Cross, help fulfill the desire of Bahanna to take over our land by diluting and dissolving our beliefs and traditional culture. The Hopi land will be their last target, the test of survival for the Natives of this land. If we weaken and fall, the extermination will be completed by Bahanna's kingdom.

To this day we are shadowed with deep sadness. Our attempts to communicate with the Bahanna government have failed completely. Our words of honesty and truthfulness did not move the Bahanna, it seems he looks at us as creatures of the past. . . . The Bahanna do possess high knowledge, they construct mighty tools, they drill into our Mother Earth and move mountains. They make mighty weapons and fly into the air like birds creating fear and terror in all around them. . . . As a whole, they do not have religion. We do not need any of that. We are satisfied with the order of our Great Creator, whose light does not blind us and does not lead us into confusion. Instead His light brightens the road, so that we can absorb its great wisdom and live like humans. While the Bahanna are destroying our world by their inventions, they are blinded to such an extent that they do not even know their own origin. . . .

Perhaps there is still time for this land to live on under the laws of our Great Spirit and our Great Creator. These are the things we desire. We are very sad for our life of today, it is heading down the direction you have created for us, the tide is gathering and the high tide which sweeps us away may not be far off.

- We, the Hopi, have a prophecy which foretold that one day a house built of mica (the United Nations) would appear on the eastern shore of our land. There the Hopi would visit the great world leaders within. The Hopi delegation would bring forth a message of their dangerous situation, that their way of life is threatened and may be demolished by lingering foreign encroachment. In case for some reason they are not welcome they must not be discouraged, for this will be the test of the prophecy. Four attempts must be made. At the end of that time if the door fails to open they were to throw their case behind them, toward the setting sun. . . .

  Perhaps some people will accept this as the final act in fulfilling the prophecy. The fact is that according to our elders fulfillment can be final if it is done according to the guidelines of the prophecy. Leaders in the House of Mica are supposed to recognize the Hopi as a living people endowed with all the human rights and equality with all mankind. They are supposed to receive and greet the Hopi with an open door. . . . What the Hopi say will hinge on divine laws and instructions for the future. . . .

  Just what are the Hopi prophetic instructions regarding the United Nations and what constituted fulfillment? Two misconceptions must be immediately dismissed. The Hopi are not charged with just another appeal for peace, nor do they request membership in the UN. One more voice added to the chorus of those calling for peace would add little compared to the true significance of what Hopi tradition has to offer the modern world through this forum. . . . The communication effort of the Hopi and the developments that led to the existence of the United

Nations are parallel responses to the invention of **the atomic bomb**. From the Hopi perspective these two efforts ought to enhance each other for the benefit of the entire world. . . .

Two monumental cultural factors have prevented the European immigrants from recognizing this process of widespread unification: **The presumption of racial superiority and the need to conquer and convert. And a recent tendency to discredit all knowledge which does not stand the test of scientific thought.** The Hopi insist that the coming of the light-skinned race, the invention of the atomic bomb and the development of the UN were anticipated by their ancestral prophetic instructions to be fulfilled by the Hopi, they must make four attempts to gain a genuine hearing. . . . If unsuccessful, a rare opportunity will be missed which would ultimately result in the elimination of all human life on earth.

The basic premise is that humans cannot simply make their own laws and enforce them with weapons without regard to natural order . . . the Hopi simply call out to a return to our common heritage before it is too late. "Perfect Consideration" could eliminate all war. . . . These difficulties can be overcome. To many, there is saving grace in the **pieces of the broken vessel of Hopi culture, in the person of a few elders** who still refuse to abandon their traditions, their understandings and their hopes for a truly peaceful world for now and generations to come. In them lies a great hope for peace. . . .

Hopi also have been given a duty to warn the leaders and people of coming danger. Also Hopi were to express their suffering, their sorrows of experience, at the hands of stronger powers. When the A-bomb was dropped on Japan the Hopi were prompted to warn the world leaders in the UN about the advanced destructive technology, about the danger to land and life. . . .

We received no positive response from world leaders. Our experience in the Geneva hearings is that activities there are political and are not based on the principles of spiritual laws. . . .We find that aggressive, violent activities are given top attention. . . . .

As we looked on the UN entered the Persian Gulf war. . . .

Therefore, we have come to the conclusion that world peace is becoming hopeless. . . .

During this time, we received no response from any official member of the UN. Since this situation lies within the guidelines Hopi received from Massau, we gave this our careful attention. We completed four trips there to speak to the General Assembly, all failures. On reaching this point we became aware there is little hope we will ever fulfill the prophecy concerning the UN. . . . So the religious leaders decided that what they have to do to fulfill the prophecy, actually the final instruction, is to throw their case behind them. Hopefully it will help us in reaching our goal. From here on Hopi will rely on three people behind them, the Great Creator and natural forces. One of these could complete the purification according to His plan.

A recent development changes this situation entirely, and shows that the Creator always fulfills his promises. You have already learned how UNESCO is underwriting the translation of the Hotevilla book into French.

- Before their migrations began, Maasaw let it be known, though perhaps not by direct instructions, that whoever would find him first would be the leader there at Oraibi, which became the mother village for the other villages established later on Third Mesa.

The expression, "not by direct instructions," is a sugges-

tion that as the Hopi worshiped in their Kivas, they were able to learn things that the Creator and Maasaw might not have told them at the beginning of the migration period.

- One day Hopi will encounter people of other races with ways that are different than the Hopi's own. They will erect their own kingdom on Hopi land. They will pose as good-hearted. Their words will be charming. They will multiply like ants.

- A prophecy told of a bear sleeping somewhere in the northern part of what is now called Europe, who would awaken at a certain time and walk to the northern part of this country, where he would wait.

  Later, the Bear Clan [who found the bear] took over from the Bow Clan of the Hopi at Oraibi, because the Bow Clan chief of the past had contaminated his standing by taking part in the changing of the life pattern.

- Human beings have many evil ambitions in their hearts that they will pursue throughout their lives.

- There will be roads in the sky.

- There will be moving houses of iron.

- There will be horseless carriages.

- Men will have the ability to speak through cobwebs.

- Men will have the ability to speak through space.

- Men's clothing will be taken over by women.

- Women's skirts will be raised above the knee, devaluing the sacred body of the female, indicating that many things will be devalued from the original.

- One day a strange people will appear in our midst, people who create man in their own image. Once given his language and knowledge, our own people will become the instrument by which he will try to rule over us and carve the rest of us into his image. Our own people will become his tools, and he will make certain they do a good job.

  But if we remain strong and firmly rooted, we will not be reshaped, whereas others will slump because they are rootless. So when the tests come we must possess the strength to preserve ourselves.

- As time goes by, for self-gain, people will struggle for power to rule.

- Each race will create a different system to go by, once their leadership becomes distorted by mistakes or destructive ways.

- Through the inspiration and the forewarning of the Great Spirit, man could foretell events centuries in advance, and therefore know that one day strange people would come ashore to take over the land.

- **Long before Bahanna (White man) came upon our land, when Maasaw still walked among us, He gave the Hopi special knowledge. He gave us instructions and prophecies indicating that along the way many things would come to pass. Then He pointed out a path, a way to travel, that was like the narrow edge of a knife.**

  Along the way, He said, we would face many evil obstacles, obstacles which would lessen our spiritual energies and the will to go on, causing us to stray off the path. But, if we reached the end of the path without weakening, we would be rewarded with a good, peaceful and everlasting life. Then Maasaw would be our leader, for He is the First and will be the

Last. This is the path our village, Hotevilla, the last remnant of traditional Hopi, has chosen to follow to this day.

- It was foretold that Bahanna would have all the tools necessary to protect our right to the exclusive use of Hopi land for those who wish to live by the Great Laws without interference. But it was also prophesied that this person of White skin who would come among us might gather us under his wings, feed us and take care of us like a mother hen, only because he sees something underneath us which he wants to get. Then when we grow big enough to suit his purpose, he would adopt us into his fold, and thereafter we would support him as his servants.

- It was foretold that one day, if we are fortunate, we will meet up with another race of people of peace who will respectfully request the use of the land, and who will accept our rules concerning the land without question. But if we are unfortunate, we will meet up with the wrong people. We will encounter many pitfalls, and once we are caught in this we will be cursed forever.

  This is a perfect example of how the "if" aspect of Hopi prophecy works. The result depends upon the choices that are made. Good choices lead to good fortune. Bad choices lead to bad fortune. The course of the Great Play wanders accordingly. In this instance, the bad prevailed, and the subsequent relationship with the Whites proved to be an unfortunate one. The same "if" applies to all prophecies in terms of which of them will be fulfilled, and which of them will not.

- But the high officials did not have to scratch their heads for very long for a new idea: Simply form a government within the tribe, one more easily manipulated. The time was ripe, for by now there were enough educated Hopi, and **the prophecies**

foretold that one day Hopi children with short hair or bald heads would be the ears and mouth for the elders, and in time become the leaders. So the Hopi Tribal Council was formed.

PROPHECIES BEING FULFILLED TODAY

- The beginnings of the new age of the prophecies of tomorrow have begun to unfold before Hopi eyes. It was said, among Bahanna [White people] the people with the Cross will appear in our land. They will be kind and helpful with good hearts.

- As foretold, the vines emerged and expanded West, North, and South, causing sudden changes throughout the country.

  Tragic events developed causing unrest throughout the land. . . . They have a forked tongue, two faces, two hearts both black and white at the same time. . . . As their way unfolds the Hopi see that their ancient fathers were right in their words.

- Human beings have many evil ambitions in their hearts that they will pursue throughout their lives.

- For thousands of years we Hopi have lived in villages by a pattern established by the Great Spirit, whose teachings go all the way back to the dawn of time. **All the prophecies are being fulfilled**, including the period of great trial in which the world will be engulfed by efforts to force one's will upon others. As predicted, these efforts have grown so great that mankind has reached the brink of self-destruction.

- The changing of our ceremonial pattern could be a proof of our prophecy about being forgetful of nature's presence.

- White men will continue to come. Great caution must be taken by Hopi to screen out the bad from the good.

- At the time of Oraibi's split, the people will remember that **the remnant will again be split in two** due to extreme pressure from the outside.

- One day our own children may become our enemies. Schools will destroy the sacred balance of Hopi life. They will interrupt the traditions and people will forget the instructions of Maasaw. This destruction will reach much farther than our village. The whole earth could go off balance.

- As foretold, all of this information must come out into the open at the period when we are about to be overcome by harmful elements and can step no further.

- **Mother villages are endowed with powers of self-protection, a weapon of mysterious power. Those who defy and disturb their roots without respect will suffer great misfortune which can extend to the whole of mankind.**

- We are now awaiting our White brother who traveled eastward across the great waters long ago, who was to return when he hears of our difficulties He will deliver the sacred Hopi stone tablets into proper hands.

  Since the reference here is to more than one stone tablet, the obvious meaning is that the White brother will make certain the various tablets are given to their proper keepers. In other words, he will take them away from the unworthy and give them to the worthy. As for the corner of the Fire Clan's stone tablet that is missing, and he apparently took with him when he went away, he will put it back in place. At that tense and exciting moment, the manner of the closing of the Forth Cycle will at last be known.

- One day Hopi children with short hair or bald heads will be the ears and mouths for the elders, and in time become our leaders.

- One day our land will be taken over for development. So today the housing projects are beginning.

- The dimensions in time and space will vary in accordance with the conduct of man and nature.

- As we follow the pattern of life, our individual lifestyles might change, and some of us might become mixed up and even fall to the opposing forces who have their materialistic advantages. But there will always be resistance from those of us who stand together and adhere to the great laws.

- As the authoritative leaders die out, people of bad intentions will seek out leaders with whom they can deal for their own ends. People with good intentions will also seek for the right leaders to help them regain what was rightfully theirs from the beginning.

- Children, and even grown-ups, will forget their language. Intermarriage with other tribes and races will deplete the identity of what we are. All these things have been foretold repeatedly by our elders, who taught us to beware that Bahanna education would lead us into pitfalls which we will never escape.

- Hopi prophecy says that if in the name of progress we link ourselves with a culture not our own, it will be difficult to regain what we have discarded. What happens toward the end will be the consequence of our carelessness.

- As was predicted in recent years, many problems have begun to form. They said that this would come to pass when we get hooked into a lifestyle that is not ours.

- Along the way, the people and the world will change. Factions will develop in Hopi land. The Hopi must search for and choose the path which will best satisfy his ideal way of life.

- The time will come when many of us will put material laws above the Great Spirit's laws. Yet in time of need, the wealthy, the poor, and the disbelievers will abandon those things and cry out to the Great Spirit for help.
- These issues of keeping or abandoning the original Hopi Law may actually be the fulfillment of our prophecy that "one must pay, or one must not."
- The prophecy foretells that Bahanna would be very persistent, and eventually might force his ways upon us. But should he reconsider and correct his mistakes, he would then decide who will pay and who will not pay.
- Our prophecies foretell that times will come when we will periodically recover our senses and find that some vital element is amiss. Then we will retrace our steps with fear, not bearing to look back at where we have been. So we will go forward, backward, forward and backward, our decisions uncertain. This is happening today in Hopi land, as it is happening in the rest of the world.
- Just two or three righteous people will be able to fulfill [the Creator's] mission. Even one truly righteous would be able to do it.
- So time passes on, and the prophecies of our ancient people begin to unfold. Many great events lie before us, and we are witnessing with astonishment today the fact that our ancients' words were right. Live long, for there are great and exciting adventures awaiting us!

CHAPTER 7

Prophecies Present and Future

MORE PROPHECIES PPRESENTLY BEING FULFILLED

- The following contains a prophetic warning for us to be aware of during changing times. The warning is clear, but sadly most of us ignore it because of the temptation of new ideals. We think we are ready to compete with the outside world because of some know-how we learned through education by the Western Culture—know-how that we believe will bring us prosperity and comfort. How long will this last?

  According to prophecy, the Bahanna government will gradually cease their responsibility in caring for Native people. The government will release us from their protective arms, wanting us to be on our own feet. Wanting us to be just like any citizen in the country. Wanting us to become civilized quickly and join the main stream of the American way of life. In this way their responsibility over Indians will end. There would be no more "Indian Problem." Any mistakes we make will be our own doing, the Bahanna government would not be responsible. Their influence would linger on in making sure we run our government the Bahanna way, not by our own traditional ways.

Knowing this would happen the Traditional Hopi refused to acknowledge the proposal of Western concept education and all the favors which were offered.

- **Hopi prophecy says that if we link ourselves with a culture not of our own the situation will develop that it will become difficult to regain what we discard in the name of progress.** Of course we can continue to practice what we lose, but it will have lost its value. What happens toward the end will be the consequences for our carelessness.

- According to our ancient prophecies, some day along our path we will arrive at the point of confusion because of the fast life due to the change from good to bad in our moral principles. Just as in our previous worlds, the lives of people and the leaders will become corrupted by greed and power. Honesty and truthfulness will wane. This will affect our children who will hassle us with nagging and annoyance which will finally cause mental distress resulting in failure of our health, perhaps to our graves because we become worry-warts. Many other things will come about which will be cloaked with mystery, which cannot be fully understood, and it will be difficult to explain how it will affect the world and people.

- **Time seems to be moving faster** in Hopi land and elsewhere. Sometimes we feel that we are keeping up with it, then sometimes we are not. Often the thing may look positive which would benefit man towards freedom and hope. Then suddenly the same thing becomes negative, darkness without hope. We mean the future of people and the earth. We can only say this:

maybe this is part of the cultural revolution which will go away when the global society becomes stable.

Perhaps most people frown on Hopi because of their doomsday prophecies. Such as when the first gourd of ashes (Atomic Bomb) was dropped on Japan, killing many innocent people in a few seconds. The Hopi had knowledge that this would happen someday, so we were not much surprised that this came about. Rather Hopi took it as a sign that things were getting out of hand. As instructed, Hopi promptly gave warning to the world that this powerful weapon must not advance further. If it did mankind and all life would face disastrous consequences. Sadly, no one heeds the warning so we keep marching on.

- **Our prophets predicted that there will be another split as there was in 1906** when there was no solution for both factions to live side by side when one side forsakes the Divine Law and our religious leaders for cultural change away from Hopi ways. This will lead to what they term, "One will pay and one will not." Meaning one is Bahanna way and one is Hopi way. This choice will be up to each of us, to choose either of the paths freely. There will be no pulling or pushing to get one to join the others. If this prophecy is fulfilled we will all live in harmony once again. That is if no one intervenes.

- According to prophecy **the Hopi are to be the last target.** We are to be conquered, not by the Army and their weapons, we are to be **conquered by our own people.** By our own sons and daughters without us lifting our hands. Their weapon will be what they learned through the education so kindly taught by the Bahanna. If we are lucky, they will be able to tell the light from the darkness. If not they will continue marching until they topple us. The Bahannas will pat the back of the conquerors while cheering and applauding. They will be satisfied that they were not required to finish the task which they set out to accomplish. It is our own people who bring this about and the Bahanna, therefore, cannot be blamed. The conquest will be over and all Native People will be finished. This is a sad ending and it is a pity that we must end this way.

- **It was foretold that this portion of Hopi land must be protected and was to be a shelter for mankind.** That it must not be harmed by man.

We wonder, do they read or hear the newscasts each day about widespread natural disasters, conflicts and wars? Have they totally forsaken the spirit of our ancestors and our Creator?

We feel it is of the greatest importance to carefully calculate our actions and restore harmony and balance or we all will perish. Since no one can tell what the next day will bring, suppose a natural or man made disaster strikes today, what will happen? You know all the water and electric mains will be knocked out first. Many of the dependent multitude of people in big cities will perish. On the other hand, our village will still be standing with no broken water mains, no lost electric service. Our wells and springs will still be usable unless the super-powerful gourd of ashes falls from the sky and the earth and all life will be burned to amber.

At this time we are very desperate. At any time our children will push us beyond the brink. Then we will be done, our original way of life will close forever. Our worries and tensions mount daily. Our children have come so far and it seems almost impossible to back away. Hopi believe we are to be the last victims of the great white forces. It is said if purification does not come, our Great Creator will take the land back because we do not care for the land and we don't deserve to be on it. The above subject, to our children, is soundless and has no meaning.

- **The Hopi elders look on with awe as the predictions of our prophets begin unfolding before their eyes.** The fast life, the changes in attitudes and behavior of the world's people, contesting for power, boastfulness in know how, increased immorality and materialism. The world's people do not realize these actions gradually diminish the life resources through opposing the laws of nature with our own designs. Clever as Man is, he did not see his actions set nature in motion toward disastrous consequences.

Upon this basis our religious leaders always opposed modernization. But for some years conflicting and distorted versions of our traditional wisdom and knowledge have been passed on by "progressive" Hopi. These distortions are now confusing the minds of Hopi people into going forward toward modern ways. People who don't understand the old teachings correctly are easily misled. Those with shortcomings are easily hooked into the very way of life that true Hopi are avoiding. These people are encouraged to follow the new system of a salary based life and education. They are told that modern ways will not harm them. While those who lack education and technical skills are encouraged to become dependent on handouts, welfare, food stamps, etc. This harms the traditional principles of self-sufficiency through farming and hand crafts. We feel that this is a shameful, not a proud way of obtaining necessities. It seems they would know better, but they appear to ignore the problems of the present crisis as if it were unimportant. Devoted Hopi regard this crisis as extremely serious. It could be the harrowing last chapter of the true Hopi way of life.

To show you how persistently willed the Hopi "progressives" are in doing their dirty work, only a month ago they made an inroad into our village with telephone lines without the approval of the village leaders. From informed sources we hear that they are planning to install water and power lines into our village. Can we stop them?

Our readers can compare our present situation with the ancient ones, our chances for survival are not yet gone. There is always a group of people who survive to carry on. The difference lies in that the ancients did not know about nuclear warfare, and today's big powers have more powerful weapons and have exploited many secrets of nature and used them wrongly. The Gods do not allow the secrets to be known unless for the benefit of all living things.

- Very often we hear the tune, **"Do the Hopi really hold the key to survival in their mysticism?"** We do not want to undermine any religious groups. Hopi does not claim the key, for all people on Earth are responsible for holding the key to survival. Hopi merely teaches alternatives by basing his knowledge on the past histories of humankind from previous worlds. **Hopi were instructed to tell of the Great Purification just ahead of a time when Humankind would once again become highly civilized, tending to become careless and leading us to self-destruction.** Survival is up to each of us to consider. Furthermore, we believe the instructions were given to all people long ago, according to where we are placed and how we were commissioned to fulfill our duties. Hopi brings this message to the world, hoping that there are pillars, however seemingly feeble, still standing by the strength of His knowledge. Only His way will endure.

- This situation confirms a theory found in our prophecy telling us that the choice of what to do with the land is ours. Therefore, **whatever choice is made will bring its due**

reward. We will see what happens. When we look at our past history, we see the actual fulfillment of our prophecies, and that amazingly enough many events were foretold centuries in advance. And even still some of us refuse to accept the reality of this ancient knowledge.

- **The time will come to pass when the minds of men will become deluded and the words of the wise will be ignored.** When the influence from foreign sources has taken hold the spirit within the Native People of this land will wane, perhaps even be destroyed. We were warned of this by the prophets of old.

The Hopi will be the last target because the traditional ways embody a high level of knowledge and strong ability to resist. In the effort to accomplish his ends the Bahanna will use many tactics. As time passes there are increasing signs within the Hopi Nation that the oppressors are succeeding.

Yes, the Hopi have come a long way, through one obstacle after another. Many of the ancient prophecies have already come to pass. At this time the Hopi live in two worlds, our traditional one and that of the Bahannas. We are now at the point where each of us has to make his own decision as to which world to choose.

Our ancestors were right in predicting that soon dances and music not our own will drown out the traditional teaching and knowledge of the Hopi. Our long tradition and customs of dress appearance, hair styles, our traditional sports for children and adults, many things uniquely Hopi will disappear. Most of our ceremonials will end.

In order to keep our village stable we must keep our thoughts on a spiritual level. This becomes the most important base for our village to stand on. We must not forsake the laws and instructions of the Great Spirit, the Creator, from whom we received our teachings and to whom we vowed to live them.

It has been said that if even only one or two stand firm it will accomplish the good result for all land and life. If we weaken and fall under the mounting oppression of the Bahanna as we did when we allowed our land to be cut up and put in writing and sold, then any possibility of recovery of our Tradition and our land is nil. When all that is ours, all that is Hopi, is taken away and all our powers of reaching the spirits of heaven and earth are gone, we are dead. We may stomp our feet to the beat of the drum and sing ever louder when praying, but, sadly, we will not reach the spirits, the guardian spirits and the producers of food and rain. We will know then our identity, our spirit power and values have gone. Though we may walk the crowded streets of our village, in truth, we will be dead.

SIGNS

- The Hopi must plant his seeds and watch them grow, he must pay attention to the **signs of change in natural order**. He must watch with close attention to the behavior of all life on earth. Any change or odd behavior will be the sign that the natural order of the earth is getting out of balance. Hopi believe that Hopi land is the Spiritual Center where changes will be visible to the trained mind and sight.

A recurring theme of prophetic tradition is that of Mother Earth's revenge for abuse by mankind. Nostradamus sees this lashing back as reaching its apex between the years 1993 and 2000. In the spring or autumn of 2000, he says, the earth will either suddenly or slowly shift on its axis. By October, there will be such a great movement that people will think it has lost its gravitational pull and is plunging into perpetual darkness.

This is not a prediction we will like or accept. Everyone will prefer the Hopi prophecy that, depending upon changes in human behavior, pushes this kind of global change off into the distant future. Of course, we don't have long to wait to find out, do we?

- The earth is like **a spotted fawn,** and each spot has a duty to make the body function. Hopiland is the center of the earth's body. It is the spot of power with the duty to foretell the future by **comparing the actions of mankind with the prophecy told them**. Hopis teach caution and awareness.
- Now we enter the time of testing which only the Great Creator can confirm. The **alignment of the planets,** we were so kindly informed of by the star watchers. The Hopi have expected this to happen and have been waiting. According to ceremonial tradition following the stars one day certain stars will come together in a row as has happened thousands of years ago. It is a time of purifying the land. Changing climate and many catastrophes may occur as we pass through this stage. What may happen no one really knows.

Although the alignment of the planets does have an exact time, according to legend it may be in your lifetime, your children's or their children's. **But as the time nears the predicted behavior of the people accurately describes the people of today.** Perhaps it is the time to repent and pray that our earth will not be totally lost. It has been said that this event may bring about one of two things, destruction or the prosperity to renew the earth to its original wholesomeness. This much we do know.

Nostradamus's predictions include an alignment of the planets that will lead to sudden and violent phenomena occurring in the spring, a date his translators set as May 5,

2000. On this date, scientists say, the new moon will align with earth, the sun, Jupiter, and Saturn. This will bring to pass a gravitational tug-of-war between them and the earth. It could result in powerful earthquakes, tidal waves, and winds that will cause tremendous damage on earth. The earth could be toppled off of its polar axis. Solar activity is expected to increase 20 percent, further aggravating the next great drought.

Depending on the degree and suddenness of the shift, scientists theorize that any or all of the following phenomena may take place:

1. The sun or moon will appear to stand still and turn blood red in color.

2. The stars will swing out of position and the sky will turn black.

3. Arctic, temperate, and tropical climate zones will wander across the planet.

- **When the end is near, we will see a halo of mist around the heavenly bodies. Four times it will appear around the sun as a warning that we must reform,** telling us that people of all color must unite and arise for survival, and that we must uncover the causes of our dilemmas. Unless man made weapons are used to strike first, peace will then come.

- So the time will come when we will experience late springs and early frosts, this will be the sign of **the returning Ice Age**.

Knowing what the prophecies have said thus far, we can see that the majority of them deal with the Hopi themselves, and that it is these prophecies that have been fulfilled. Unfortunately, there are some that tell us things that are painful to hear. It is not encouraging to see that Whites have

done to the Hopi every terrible thing the prophecies said we would. It is also not encouraging to know that they have called out for help many times, and although Americans are the most responsive and caring people in the world, few of us have responded to them.

Now we switch to a new phase where the prophecies deal directly with us, for they deal with the future and fate of the entire world. These are comparatively few in number, yet so awesome they confront us in a reverberating fashion. As we analyze them, we will recognize that portions are already coming to pass. World conditions easily confirm that the downturn of the Fourth Cycle is underway, and that the prophecies are beginning to be fulfilled. Therefore, I suspect that in the near future one of the prophecies will be so clearly fulfilled there will be no mistaking it. Perhaps that will gain our full attention and get more of us to put the INSTRUCTIONS to use. The problem is that we usually delay such things as long as we can. Whenever solutions for improving and redirecting life are presented, critics often ask for proofs that the proposals will work, implying by their request, that without these guarantees, we will be wasting our time.

Fortunately, where the Hopi instructions are concerned, that kind of proof is ample. With these, we are not talking about a new and untried scheme. For nearly a thousand years now the Traditionalists have been living testimonies to the fact that their instructions work exceptionally well. Dan Evehema is the perfect illustration. Still in remarkable condition at the age of 102, he shows us a true fountain of youth in action. An example of this truth is that, when I took the first copy of the printed *Hotevilla* book to him, I drove onto his property and found him in front of the house, looking for

all the world like an elf, and wearing on his head a cone-shaped red bandanna. He was standing in the middle of a huge wood pile and using a hand axe to split wood for his winter fires. Have you wondered what your chances are of doing that kind of thing when you pass 100?

PROPHECIES YET TO BE FULFILLED

Please remember that the prophecies I include here are quoted from the newsletters, so that they are what the authors themselves wrote and are not edited:

- Today, once again, the world is facing a new crisis. This is **a war of retaliation against terrorism**. A war to save the innocent and to punish the guilty. But who is innocent and who is guilty? Well, this depends on how you look at it. Life would be good if all men were innocent. Let us focus on minorities and figure who is guilty. Minorities such as the Native people of both North and South America and elsewhere. We believe militarism is born out of injustice, poverty and ignorance where absolute government refuses to hear the grievances of minorities or to help in resolving problems. So the people resort to violence, demonstrations and even terrorism or other recourse when they see no other way to be heard. What can we do when our world leaders and the people are acting like fools in attempts to solve the problems confronting us? Once again we will quote the prophecy of our elders. We hope it will interest you so that you will be more aware of it as it has been happening for some time.

- It is in the prophecies of the Hopi that in a case like this the Navajo may help our cause. Also the Bahannas or the Paiute Tribe may help. We doubt that the U.S. Government will easily concede our sovereignty. If possible both Hopi and Navajo traditionals would like separation from those who want to be assimilated. Both tribes could thereby retain their identity and lay the foundation for a self-respecting community.

- There are **two water serpents,** one at each pole with a warrior sitting on his head and tail. These command nature to warn us by her activities that time is getting short and we must correct ourselves. If we refuse to heed these warnings, the warriors will let go of the serpents, they will rise up, and all will perish.

- We are much concerned about the **climate**. No one seems to be able to predict the weather accurately from day to day. However, we know according to our time markers that it is past due for certain seeds to be planted at their proper time. This spring we are reluctant to plant due to the late snow and cold weather. Once more maybe our ancient prophecy is right, that one day we will plant wearing finger sacks [gloves] clearing away snow with our feet before planting. The summers will become shorter for maturing the corn for harvesting. The result is anybody's guess.

  "Anybody's guess" is another reference to the "if" aspect of Hopi prophecy—the end result being determined by the choices the participating individuals make. The Hopi sensitivity to "signs," irrespective of whether or not their assessment is accurate, causes them to examine their own behavior and, if necessary, change it.

- It is said that if the **future generations** find out through records that we did nothing to preserve the good ways, they will pull and box our ears, and even throw us from our houses into the streets. This suffering will be of our own making. The lack of peace in our own spiritual being could trigger the revolution.

- Our **White brother** might come and find we have forsaken the sacred laws and instructions. Then he will whip us without mercy. Either this, or nature herself will take over.

- Let us take a look into the future through the eyes of our prophets. They say that **along the way the industrialized world will have certain problems.** Throughout the world people will be uncomfortable because of the changing times. The worldly woes people will be going through. People will have to make adjustments to fit themselves into new life styles and environments.

  The industrialized nations will become careless in getting more of the resources they need out of the earth, oil, coal, etc. Believing all these things will last forever. Soon natural resources will be depleted. Fuel shortages will occur, industrial machinery will come to a standstill. The machinery used for planting, harvesting and transport will become useless. Supermarket shelves will become empty of farm produce. The farmers and those who grow their own food will not sell their produce. Money will become worthless. The white man (Bahanna) with all his intelligence and technology will not be able to repair the damage.
- Now let us review our knowledge briefly, the centuries old prophecies which warned us what would happen when we forget the principles of right and wrong in our behavior. **We will see extraordinary events in Nature and Earth, including mankind;** because modern man ignores the wisdom of ancient culture and religion. Modern man looks upon old wisdom and knowledge as dead, useless and no longer respected.

  Modern man began to depend on the money system and no longer on Mother Earth for food. According to prophecy when this happens Mother Earth will hide the nourishment which she provides because of the view that ancient food is poor man's food.

When all food disappears modern man will try to correct his mistake, the conditions he caused upon the earth through his inventions. He will try to achieve some kind of method to heal the wound, but this will not be possible when we reach the point of no return.

Only through peace the survival of mankind and our planet Earth is possible. **Only if we, the human race, are willing to change.**

- The Hopi play a key role in the survival of the human race through their vital communion with the unseen forces that hold nature in balance, as an example of a practical alternative to the suicidal man-made system, and as a fulcrum of world events. The pattern is simple. **"The whole world will shake and turn red and turn against those who are hindering the Hopi."**

- This is a prophecy related to the Biblical version of "Armageddon" which may yet come to pass. This prophecy goes on to say that the time will come when common people will become concerned and frustrated because they no longer can live with their hectic world. They will be particularly against the bloodthirsty policies and the deceitfulness of world leaders. The unrest will be world wide as they foresee that the hope of living in peace has become hopeless. **The world over the common man will band together to fight for world peace.** They will realize that their leaders have failed in accomplishing peace. People in high places will be hunted down like animals, perhaps through terrorism. In turn leaders will retaliate and begin hunting each other. This condition will gather strength and spread far and wide. It will get out of control the world over. Revolution could erupt on our land.

The liberators will come in from the west with great force. They will drop down from the sky like rain. They will have no mercy. We must not get on the house tops to watch. They will shake us by our ears, like children who have been bad. This will be the final decisive battle between good and evil. This battle will cleanse the heart of people and restore our mother earth from illness and the wicked will be got rid of.

The prophets dare say a peaceful new world order will be drawn in Hopi land. The people will live under one God and leader. We will speak one language, the Hopi. The earth will bloom again.

If this fails to materialize, our Great Creator through nature will do the task according to their plans. It could be total destruction in any form. Only brother and sister will survive to begin a new way of life.

- Eventually **a "gourd full of ashes"** would be invented, which if dropped from the sky would boil the oceans and burn the land causing nothing to grow for many years. *This would be the sign for a certain Hopi to bring out his teachings in order to warn the world that the third and final event would happen soon.* That it could bring an end to all life unless people correct themselves and their leaders in time.

  Hopi leaders now believe **the first two events were the first and second world wars and the "gourd full of ashes" is the atomic bomb.** After the bombing of Hiroshima and Nagasaki teachings formerly kept secret were compared and released to the world. The details presented here are part of those teachings.

- The final stage, called **"The Great Day of Purification,"** has been described as **a "Mystery Egg" in which the forces of the swastika and the Sun plus a third force symbolized by the color "red" culminate either in total rebirth or total annihilation**—we don't know which. **But the choice is yours,** war and natural catastrophe may be involved. The degree of violence will be determined by the degree of inequity caused among the peoples of the world and in the balance of nature. In this crisis rich and poor will be forced to struggle as equals in order to survive.

That it will be very violent is now almost taken for granted among Traditional Hopi, **but man still may lessen the violence by correcting his treatment of nature and fellow man**. Ancient spiritually-based communities, such as the Hopi, must especially be preserved and not forced to abandon their wise way of life and the natural resources they have vowed to protect.

The man made system now destroying the Hopi is deeply involved in similar violations throughout the world. The devastating reversal predicted in the prophecies is part of the natural order. If those who thrive from that system, its money and its laws, can manage to stop destroying the Hopi then many may be able to survive the Day of Purification and enter a new age of peace. But if no one is left to continue the Hopi way, then the hope for such an age is in vain.

The forces we must face are formidable, but the only alternative is annihilation. Still the man-made system cannot be corrected by any means that requires one's will to be forced upon another, for that is the source of the problem. If people are to correct themselves and their leaders, the gulf between the two must disappear. To accomplish this one can only rely on the energy of truth itself.

This approach, which is the foundation of the Hopi way of life, is the greatest challenge a mortal can face. Few are likely to accept it. But once peace is established on this basis, and our original way of life is allowed to flourish, we will be able to use our inventive capacity wisely. To encourage rather than threaten life. To benefit everyone rather than giving advantage to a few at the expense of others. Concern for all living things will far surpass personal concerns bringing greater happiness than could formerly be realized. Then all things shall enjoy lasting harmony.

- How can there be peace? Nowhere is there peace, not even within Hopi peaceful society. Bahanna society, every nation on earth, from people in high places down to the lowest cast are not at peace. How can peace be accomplished when weapons are made to kill? How can there be peace if people hate, not love? Perhaps the only alternative now is **"Purification."**

- **Three people** were named who were to help the Hopi when we reached the crisis of no return. The Paiute Indian was to help according to his wisdom, but if he is unable the Navajo Indian will help also, according to his wisdom. If their efforts fail then Bahanna will come to aid. This is where we are now.

  The time has now arrived to do something for the Traditional Hopi of Hotevilla. Why only Hotevilla? Our answer now is that it is time. Now we stand alone according to our prophecy.

- Most of us don't know how important Winter is in Hopi land. We shiver and complain when our houses fail to warm up the way we want. Perhaps we begin to run short on coal and firewood. Soon we begin to complain to the snow clouds to stop dumping snow on us. In this we are acting silly, snow is a must. Without snow the Spring months will be dry and can cause problems in planting. So we were concerned and sad when snow failed to come. This Winter has been mild and Spring like. The fruit trees bloomed a month early, a beautiful sight they were. We had hoped the weather would not turn cold and ruin the fruit. Sadly, we lost out to a more powerful force than man, that is our Mother Nature. We take it as though she has boxed our ears for being deaf to her environmental laws. She has snatched the food from our mouths as punishment. For four days and nights now a freezing cold wind has been beating on our doors and windows.

Most people will not think much about this kind of incident, but to the Hopi this means much in the light of traditional prophecy. For one thing, this cold spell could continue late into Spring. This is unusual and would shorten the growing season. It is said we will clear away the snow with our moccasins before we plant and finger sacks (gloves) will be worn. This prophecy may sound impossible, so let us wait and see if Grandpa's prediction will come to pass. The question is: will this occur the world over? This would depend on the geographical areas, in the regions with different climate, things will happen in different ways. **For instance, tropical land could become a land of ice, the arctic region could become tropical. This may occur due to a pole shift according to Bahanna's concept. But this need not happen if we, the people, get our leaders to do something about the harmful things being done to the environment.**

- Most people will view this story as just another legend or myth. However, the Hopi were instructed not to forget this knowledge about the **power of the land of Ice**. It is a prophecy handed down to us from generations ago and the Hopi still believe it has a true historical basis. No doubt critics will frown on our statements and take it as just another Hopi doomsday prophecy. We will summarize our story so it will not be too lengthy.

When the first people emerged upon this land from the underworld they were met by the Great Spirit, and Massau, the Caretaker of the land and His helpers. He saw they were identical so He divided them into groups. Each group He gave a name and a separate language. Each group received a religion and instructions. Each group was given a special food for nourishment and shelters of different types then clan memberships within each group for mutual respect and different tasks which they must uphold for the benefit of all life and land.

From the Hopi group (the name they received), He selected four clans: Bear, Fire, Spider and Snake clan members, for special duty. He endowed them with magical powers of warmth and taming powers over a cold climate. They were to go on a special mission to the Land of Ice. They were instructed to melt the ice with the Magic Songs and Prayers He taught them. They were told the ice is growing and sometime in the future will mature and will travel southward or will explode bringing grave misfortune, for this had occurred before.

They began their preparations, storing food, weaving coverings, and making other things needed for travel to the Land of Ice. Finally they started traveling Northward for some years. This took some years, for they had to stop to rest, build their houses, and prepare fields for planting so as to have food with them always. After years of traveling they finally reached the Land of Ice. First they made shelter, for it was very cold. Then they commenced to sing their Magic Songs and smoked and prayed. The ceremonial began with the Bear clan, next day it was the Fire clan, followed by the Spider clan. The

Snake clan was last. Each day the ice defrosted to some degree until only about four inches were left when their songs ended. But they were instructed not to repeat the ceremonial. They had done their best and must return to continue their migration. We were warned the ice will grow again. Should the clans with the controlling powers vanish or stray away from the great laws of the Creator, there will be no way of stopping the ice build-up. **So the time will come when we will experience late springs and early frosts, this will be the sign of the returning Ice Age.**

Now, let us give our attention to scientists and researchers findings regarding **the Solar Ice Age.** The question is how much time is left before it is hopeless to make an attempt in preserving civilization by stopping the fast approaching new ice age?

They are now doing their best to inform people and the top leaders of the world. They claim it is absolutely essential to take action in preventing a new glacial period, otherwise we face serious consequences.

The theory is that approaching glaciers will be well on their way by 1995. The earth warming 'greenhouse effect' will play a big part because of the increasing rise in content of atmospheric carbon dioxide gas. The effect would be a changing climate worldwide, droughts, high winds and storms resulting in increased erosion and an increase in volcanic activity which would result in an increase in ice at the earth's poles. Depletion of soil minerals will cause forest and agricultural plants to die. We think their forecast is very frightening so we suggest those who care about coming generations should write to: Hamaker-Weaver Publishers, Box 1961, Burlingame, California 94010 for more information.

Indeed the message is frightening. Since our prophecy is

closely related to the above theory, we read their message with interest. We are also pleased that in the past several years our prophecies have drawn much interest and have aroused much attention from the outside world. **Right or wrong, we believe another Ice Age is in the making. However, we also believe this disastrous event can be averted** when all Mankind returns to the original divine laws of the Great Creator . . . There is often the question of why the Hopi are so positive in their prophecies and claims of fulfillment. What proof do they have? How do they see these things?

I think it is usual to couple global warming with melting ice and floods. It is interesting then to read that some scientists say that the massive recent eastern United States snow storm may have been caused by global warming. The New York Times News Service reported on January 14, 1996, that "Just four days after scientists announced on Jan. 3 that the average surface temperature of the globe had crept to a recorded high of nearly 60 degrees in 1995, the blizzard of 1996 dropped . . . the third deepest snowfall ever measured there. A warming atmosphere causes more evaporation of water from the ocean, which means more rain, snow or sleet. The conversion of more water from vapor to precipitation also releases more energy into the atmosphere, making storms more powerful. . . . A warming climate is expected to produce hotter heat waves and more severe droughts."

- **The time will come when from the earth will arise a mystic fog which will dilute the minds and hearts of all people.** Their guidelines of wisdom and knowledge will falter, the Great Laws of our Creator will dissolve in the minds of people. Children will be out of control and will no longer obey the leaders, immorality and the competitive war of greed will flourish.

  Few will abide by their beliefs and their attempts to transform darkness into light will be in vain. **A sudden eruption** will explode within the midst of their follies, this will be within or of other lands and will creep over the earth. Then men will destroy each other savagely. **The period of this age will close by the gourd of ashes which will glow brighter than the Sun. The earth will turn over four times and mankind will end up in the lowest level of darkness where they will crawl on all fours forever.** Then the spirits of our Ancient Fathers will return to reclaim the land, they will mock the lowly man for he will no longer deserve or be worthy of the land. Only those who are obedient to the guidance of the Great Creator's laws will survive. If it is the will of the Creator, if the earth is totally destroyed by the willfulness of man, the true sister and brother will give a rebirth to recycle the earth and renew its life.

- According to prophecy, **the day will come when people in high places will be hunted and vice versa** the lowly hunters will be hunted. This will get out of control. The hunting will gather strength and spread far and wide. This situation might even erupt on our land. Finally, this will lead us to a Biblical version of **Armageddon** (the Hopi version is closely related). A final decisive battle between good and evil. This will occur under one God or Chief. They dare say (the prophets) we will speak one language and that this will happen in Hopi land, in the village of Oraibi. This will be where the new life plan will be drawn, in the pattern and cycle of religion. Here also a final decision will be made for the wicked. They will be beheaded and speak no more. If this does not materialize, there will be total destruction through the acts of man or nature. Then new life will begin from a girl and a boy. This is a frightening prophecy and will not be supported by many, but one can always take it as a theory.

- What about a coming ice age and other frightful prophecies? It may be possible, but at least we can hope and pray that our mother nature's computer is wrong. What about Bahanna's nuclear bomb Armageddon ideology? It is possible this also depends on Bahanna Chiefs pressing the button. **Do not worry, this might not happen in your lifetime. Hopi believe the Creator with Nature will decide the course. Keep strong.**

- Surely there is something wrong. We must look within ourselves and take care in our movements. We seem to be in doubt of the Great Laws that govern the earth. We are in doubt of the words of old. It has been said that there are two water serpents coiling the earth, from North to South pole. On each of the poles sits a warrior god on the serpents' head and tail, now and then communicating messages of our conduct and behavior toward each other; now and then releasing light pressure which causes the great serpents to move, resetting earth movements—a message also commanding nature to warn us by her actions that time is getting short and so we must correct ourselves. If we refuse to heed the warning, the warrior gods will let go of the serpents and we will all perish. They will say we do not deserve the land given to us because we are careless.

- We have a coil basket symbolizing the road of life. It is called *"Boo-da,"* meaning some great test which we will experience during our journey.

  Hopi tradition says we started our travel from the center or beginning of life, when life was perfect. But soon we began to face new obstacles. Small groups of ambitious minded men wanted to change their ways away from the original path. There were only small groups at first, but with time they increased to great numbers. Those who wanted to keep to their original ways became fewer and fewer. **Since mankind has**

lost peace with one another through the conflict because of the new ways, the Great Spirit, the Great Creator has punished the people in many ways. Through all of this there was always a small group who survived to keep the original ways of life alive. This small group are those who adhere to the laws of the Creator, who keep the spiritual path open, out from the circle of evil. According to our knowledge we are not quite out of the circle.

The men with ambitious minds will decrease, while the people of good hearts, who live in harmony with the earth, will increase until the earth is rid of evil. If the Hopi are right this will be accomplished and the earth will bloom again. The spiritual door is open, why not join the righteous people.

- The Hornytoad Woman gave Maasaw a promise that she would help him in time of need, saying she too had a metal helmet, possibly meaning that certain **people with metal helmets will help the Hopi when they get into difficulty** [in the final stage of the Fourth Cycle].

- **After the Hopi have fulfilled their pattern of life [when there are no more Traditionalists left and thus at the closing of the Fourth Cycle], Maasaw will be the leader, but not before, for He is the first and He shall be the last.**

- **At time's end, a new age will appear.**

- **There will be a new dawn of time when the world will bloom into peacefulness.**

People are lost and looking for direction. The Creator has known that this time would come, and uses the prophecies to get our attention. Then He calms our fears as He presents us with the way to handle whatever comes. His way even leads

to moral and unselfish lives. Plainly then, He wants us to survive in the fullest sense of the word.

But the solutions revealed to us in the secret have an innocence that is deceptive. On the surface, they will not seem to be enough to do the job. How else, though, we must ask ourselves, would we have the Creator do this? What other and better way would we choose for Him? What ways have we chosen for ourselves that have solved the accumulating problems thus far? We see in history that He does not approach things in the same way fallible human beings do. He approaches problems from vantage points that seldom occur to us. He places the Christ child in obscure Bethlehem. He chooses the unpretentious Hopi to carry a vital message to the world. He uses a frightening Maasaw to deliver his message to the Hopi and ourselves. Innocence is something that captivates us. Beginning in such simple and unexpected ways as these, He accomplishes the seemingly impossible.

The INSTRUCTIONS that follow have within them a hidden power that can accomplish what supposedly greater forces never could. Yet success hinges on our following the Hopi Pattern of Life. We should do this in the knowledge that through this opportunity the Creator has promised to bestow his greatest blessings. He knows that those of us who will take a chance on the seemingly impossible are those who, given help, can reach their goals. When He sees that we entrust ourselves to Him and trust Him to take us where He says He will, He does it!

Chapter 8

The Ark's Instructions

The survival record of the Traditionalist Hopi is a remarkable one. Even more remarkable is how well they managed it, how they have found fulfillment and happiness in the midst of the worst possible tragedies. This, of course, is the essence of the secret that Maasaw gave to the Hopi at Oraibi, and which is being passed on to you right now. This great secret of survival is a surpassing gift, both in its effect and amazing simplicity. This last is a factor of immeasurable worth, for it is a secret whose parts can be understood and followed by every person in the world, rich or poor, and regardless of education. There are no complex philosophies to ponder here. It is a plain, warm and gentle way to live that, in a personal sense, accomplishes everything anyone could possibly hope for, and at the same time triumphs over our every foe. And, it is a secret that can be put to work immediately to draw together and rescue the entire world.

You will recall however that *The Hopi Survival Kit* did not step easily into this bright light that I shine upon it. Perhaps this is because Maasaw knows human nature, and is reluctant to offer a precious gift to people who are likely to spurn it. He knows that some people—perhaps most—will reject him. And he knows that some who come aboard the Spiritual Ark now will later tire of the effort and want to return to the shore. If history follows its ordinary course in the days ahead, they can do this and not be concerned. If it does not, that is another boat ride entirely. Thus far, our optimistic nature has justified itself and each time held sway. Our country in particular has been in stormy seas galore, yet always docked safely. All things considered, life here in America has, until recently, worked out spectacularly well.

But the prophecies indicate that before long we will be dealing with changed and unusual circumstances. If we do not adopt a different way of life than the one we are presently pursuing, we may not survive. So far, too many of us have chosen comfort, convenience, and pleasure over responsibility and consequences. The situation has to be reversed. The time has come when the most important choices of our lives must be made. They can no longer be delayed or avoided.

In order to embrace Maasaw's way of survival, it is necessary to understand it correctly. Our tendency has been to focus upon prophesied events and to think that our only recourse is to deal with them when they occur. We sometimes refer to this kind of action as "closing the barn door after the horse is gone." In this approach, future problems are a secondary concern.

Maasaw's strategy is broader and smarter than that. He immerses us in a kind of life that prepares us in the way we condition our bodies and tone our minds in fitness centers. He not only equips us to run in the big events, he teaches us how to deal on a daily basis with the little ones, even with circumstances that will, in the end, cause a given prophesied event to happen. In other words, his way prepares us to meet daily challenges as they come. From the time we get up in the morning until we go to bed at night, we are in training. We are shaped and we are toughened, so that in the end we become hardened roots like the Elderly Elders are. Doing what Maasaw tells us to do creates a cumulative strength that brings comfort and understanding. It accomplishes its purposes as time passes, so that we can cope with what is happening now as well as with what the prophecies tell us will happen tomorrow.

The benefits and effectiveness of this approach are demonstrated by the Traditionalist Hopi who have followed the instructions for their entire lives. In Dan's case this is an impressive 102 years. A few weeks ago he went to a doctor, who, as he was leaving, told him that he was actually 108 years old. Dan must have wondered how the doctor arrived at that number, for no birth records were kept in Oraibi, or for that matter anywhere on the reservation for the next thirty years. Nor does that age fit what Dan has told me about himself. For example, it would move his birth date back six years to 1887. This would make him 19 at the time of the Oraibi split, and in Hopi eyes a man. He would hardly have been ordered by his father to stay home while the struggle for control of the village was going on. In addition, he would have been much older than the other boys who together formed the Men's Society, and would probably have been thrown in prison along with the other men from Hotevilla. In any event, 102 is a significant achievement, and I don't know why the doctor was not willing to just praise that.

By following the instructions, the Elderly Elders as a group have lived long and productive lives, and they have been blessed with wisdom, identity, security, satisfaction, and fulfillment. As a whole, these attributes have given them an inner peace that is rare among human beings. Don't let their references to constant problems mislead you into thinking that they have been always depressed and afraid. They have experienced these things at various times, but they have for amazing periods of time also triumphed over them.

Like the prophecies, the instructions and warnings are scattered throughout the pages of the *Techqua Ikachi* newsletters. So to serve our purposes, I have done with them here what I did with the prophecies. I have extracted them from the other material and drawn them together for our use. Since the instructions are intended for us as well as the Hopi, we need to have them in a form we can utilize.

The Tribal Council and the Hopi Office of Cultural Preservation would not agree with this. They would say that everything Maasaw said and did is intended for Hopi only. But few of them who have been in office over the years have practiced tradition, let alone Traditionalism. It is said that Leigh Jenkins is a Christian, and that he does not participate in the ceremonies. What he is and what he does I really do not know. But I do know that he regularly criticizes the Elderly Elders, and that any traditionalism he professes is only a cloak to hide his politics. For all of its existence, the Council has claimed to be the savior of something they have been only a marginal part of. In referring to the theft of the *Taalawtumsi,* Jenkins is quoted in a newspaper article as saying, "Hopi law is simple: Do a wrong against someone, and you will eventually pay for it." In terms of what he has done and is doing to the Traditionalists, he had better hope that he is wrong; else he is going to pay a ton.

The Council's own words and actions betray it. Even the way in which the prophecies, instructions, and warnings were given at Oraibi proves this. The urgent message is for everyone in the world. The Elderly Elders have stated that all along. Why would it take the form it did, if it was meant only for the Hopi? It is to be passed on to us, and that is what *The Hopi Survival Kit* is about. Although we are not called upon to live as Hopi, we are exhorted to employ the Hopi understandings of the prophecies, instructions, and warnings within the context of our own lifestyles. As we do this we are bound to become more Hopi-like in our thoughts and feelings, so that, as time passes, our person and world are reshaped. But our individualities are maintained, and that is what is intended. We are not called upon to be invasive, or to share sacred places with the Traditionalists or any other Hopi. They do not want outsiders at their shrines or in their Kivas. This is a condition everyone must respect.

How then, do we go about accomplishing what we are called to do?

One of the special values of the secret is found in its deeply personal revelations. In a surprisingly open manner, the Traditionalist Hopi tell how they think and feel as they follow the Maasaw-given Road Plan and Pattern of Life. This part of what they do is just as important as the physical acts involved in their rituals and farming. In the Plan and Pattern, **attitude is an equal partner of application**. Maasaw taught the founders of Oraibi that what we think and feel about any task we are performing has everything to do with its failure or its success. This aspect of Traditionalist Hopi life is missing from most books written by outsiders about the Hopi life way, but it is central to the newsletters!

A surprising number of books deal with only the material life of the Hopi. They say nothing about Hopi thoughts and feelings. It is as though these things either do not matter, or the authors believe the Hopi are incapable of emotion. When sensitivity is considered, and with a few exceptions where perceptive authors such as Frank Waters, Tony Hillerman, and Barton Wright are concerned, White writers sometimes tell us what they think the Hopi are thinking and feeling. They make assumptions as they watch the people respond to intrusion, perform a certain dance, share home life, or do a certain task. But *Techqua Ikachi* newsletters tell us that these are guesses that rarely connect because they come from the wrong direction. It is seldom what was actually going on in the minds of the Hopi. Our problem is that in describing a Native American event or reaction we look at it through White educated eyes and forget that there are important differences between our cultures. We ascribe to Native Americans what we would be thinking if we were doing the same thing. Worst of all, Native feelings are seldom given the credence they deserve. Naturally, the approach doesn't work. And, it falls far short of giving the natives the status they deserve.

When we consider the instructions in the pages ahead you will see how important it is that we have correct understandings where true Hopi attitudes are concerned. The Hopi have deep and profound feelings about everything. Moreover, these attitudes are so splendid that you will love them when you see how they are applied. Better still, it will not be long now before these attitudes are a part of you as well.

THE SPIRITUAL ARK

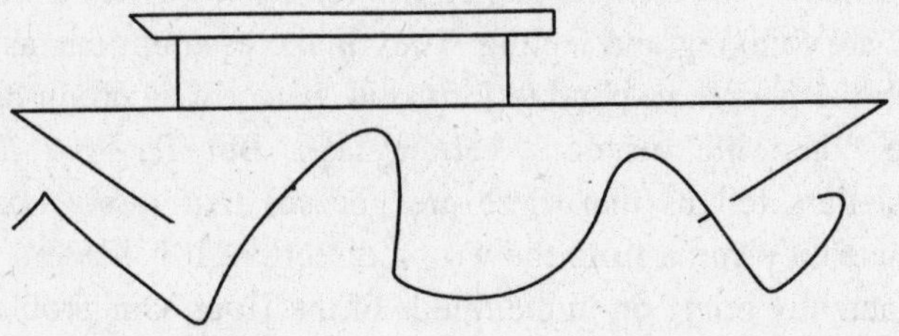

God told Noah that it would rain for forty days and forty nights, and then said that the earth would be covered with water. Everyone and everything on it would be drowned. Then he told Noah to build a huge Ark to save the faithful humans and other creatures that would be needed to start a new world once the flood waters receded. The Hopi say it was this flood that brought the Third Cycle of the world to a close.

The Bible story of the flood is an apt metaphor for those of us who wish to survive the closing phase of the Fourth Cycle, and who hope that we, or our descendants, will be around to enter the Fifth one. How wonderful then that, for the Hopi and us, the Creator and Maasaw have provided A SPIRITUAL ARK that consists of carefully chosen thoughts, words, deeds, and promises. Together, these make up the manner of life that will be led on the Ark. The existence of this Ark is what makes the giving of the prophecies understandable, and with the exception of the Biblical prophecies, it elevates the Hopi prophecies far above the rest of the prophetic field.

The whole of this magnificent Ark is found in the detailed instructions and warnings that Maasaw gave the Hopi at the same time he gave them the prophecies. Since the prophecies point to the instructions and warnings, they are beneficial things and a part of the spiritual Ark too. While the Hopi accounts do not tell us is how long Maasaw stayed with the people to give them this "Ark," from the volume of material involved, it appears that he remained with them for a prolonged period of time. That would seem logical, for they would not otherwise have been able to absorb and commit to memory the abundance of information he gave them. Not long ago, I read an article in a magazine that quoted a Hopi as saying a person could not look upon Maasaw for long without losing consciousness. If this is true, it leaves me wondering how the Hopi at Oraibi managed to collect all of the information they did from him. He would have spent all of his time reviving them. In their newsletters, the Elders say nothing about the fainting.

Before we move on, we need to ask ourselves some basic questions about prophecies: Assuming for the moment that the predictions are true, what will we do when the worst of them are fulfilled? Will we be ready? How will we conquer our fear, and how will we maintain our sanity, as we wait for them to take place and then experience them? How can our children and other loved ones be protected? When the world is shattered and in turmoil, and if we have experienced this also, how will we muster the strength to go on?

When we answer these questions honestly, we realize how inadequately prepared most of us are. Then we are at least open to considering the INSTRUCTIONS that guide life in the Ark. Even knowing what human nature is like, Maasaw presented the Hopi at Oraibi with these instructions. This means he also knew that when at last the instructions are passed on to us, some of us will listen, even though some of us will not. He took the time for those of us who will tune in. Jesus Christ and the leaders of all great faiths do the same thing.

I emphasize again that while the instructions and warnings were given first to the Hopi, they were also meant for us.

Maasaw would not have told them to pass on the prophecies if he had not wanted the instructions and warnings to be passed on as well. The Traditionalist Elders of every generation have recognized this truth, and have faithfully fulfilled Maasaw's request that they pass the information on. In fact, they tell us they would rather be put to death than give up this mandate:

> "The vow which we made with Maasaw obligated us to follow his way of life. He gave the land to us to use and to care for through our ceremonial duties. He instructed us and showed us the Road Plan by which we must govern our lives. We wrote this pattern on a rock so that we would always be reminded to follow the straight road. And we would rather die than give up this promise."

Maasaw opened his instruction sessions at Oraibi by talking about the kinds of things we who live in the outside world ordinarily reject. For example, he started with something that will make those of us who live comfortably today blink our eyes and clear our throats, even though our acceptance of it will put us well on our way to survival.

When the Hopi at Oraibi asked Maasaw if he would remain with them and watch over them, he pointed out that he had only his digging stick, his seeds, his water, and his cloak. It wasn't much, but he added, "If you will live as I live, you can come and live with me."

Compared to our standards, the Hopi already lived simply. And since they had no comprehension of what lay ahead, they decided to accept the offer. So long as they had no other choices they kept their promise. Later on, however, the lure of White amenities caused most of them to change their minds. While pressures were applied in the beginning to bring this to pass, a time came when the Hopi made these choices on their own just as prophecy said they would. We do not blame the Hopi for this as though they were the only culprits, for we do the same thing. But we must also take a good look at the price they have paid for it and ask ourselves what price we pay as well.

Maasaw's statement ends with the words, "If you will live as I live." He does not ask us to do anything he does not do himself. As a deity, he could have anything he wants, save that he chooses to live simply. Those who wish to live with him on the Ark must accept this same condition, which probably means that the population on the Ark may be smaller than we would hope. If so, prophecies will be affected accordingly. The world will reap what it sows.

In the amazing story of the Hopi we have learned that soon after they settled down in Oraibi, other Pueblo peoples began to arrive. When each of these asked permission to remain in the village, the Oraibi leaders remembered Maasaw's warnings. They were careful to admit only people of like minds, so they would blend into what was already a harmonious community with a primary purpose. **Boastful people** were sure to interfere with the keeping of the Covenant. They would hurt the prayers. These self-centered individuals were told to settle in villages where their own kinds already were. We sympathize with those who were shut out of Oraibi. But they would have an opportunity to change, and if the Oraibi leaders thought someone deserved a second chance, it was given to them. Was this choice by the Oraibi elders a wise one? Eight hundred years of relative peace seems to be a good recommendation. Perhaps some of us would benefit from a wiser choice of friends.

The simple life advocated by Maasaw bears a kind of fruit that we seldom acknowledge. It avoids waste and misuse. It is a great equalizer. It does not take more for itself than is required, or more than its share. There is nothing self-serving or selfish about it. A simple life style will go a long way toward assuring harmony in the Ark.

Have you begun to blink and clear your throat yet?

We also need to think about working tools that do not lend themselves to overproduction or pollution. In the First World countries, we could get by with a lot less if we wanted to. And, when the time comes that our lives depend on it, we may give up more than we expect we will. In a dire emergency, people jettison anything that might slow them down. With the earthquakes, fires and floods we have here in California, it happens all the time. On TV we see people dashing out of perishing buildings with very little in their arms.

Our family experienced this twice with forest fires. The first time we loaded what we could in a van. The second time we left virtually everything behind. What we could have taken was so little compared with what was left that it hardly mattered. Thanks to fire crews, we fortunately didn't lose anything in the house. But we sat at a safe distance from the house and watched the flames burn up to every side of it. As time passed, our conversations turned to wondering where we would live next. Clothing? Books? Working tools? Paintings? Furniture? Toys? Sculptures? Memorabilia? Tapes? Photographs? By the time it was over we really did not care what was left. All that mattered was that we were together and alive. These are lessons that remain with us, and possessions are not the focus of our lives. We can handle this part of life on the Spiritual Ark.

Where we are concerned, the matter of planting, cultivating, harvesting and thanksgiving has to do with **self-sufficiency,** so that no matter how the world goes in the years ahead, each of us will have enough to get by.

Maasaw is not suggesting that we here in the outside world

limit ourselves to a digging stick and some seeds. He knows full well that the world must have the industrial capacity to serve everyone. What he is aiming for is the development of an attitude among us that will lead to the kind of heartfelt relationship the Traditionalists have with Mother Earth. From this intertwined relationship will come the motivation to see that our brothers and sisters the world over get their rightful portion of whatever we have. We will not let them starve without sacrificing whatever we must to do something about it.

Some will say this is a foolish position to take, and that it is not realistic. On the contrary, and with the exception of a qualification that follows, there is really no alternative to it. If, as so many experts think it will, the population spirals upward by billions in the years immediately ahead—threatening to double within the next 50 years—the survival of everyone, including ourselves, will depend upon how well we carry out this particular instruction. If we do not willingly share, desperate people will seek to get what they can by whatever means they can. They will go after our water supply and grain sources, and they will do the kind of thing the Aum Shinri Kyo cult recently did when it placed poisonous chemicals in the subway trains of Japan. Poor people who are going to go down anyway, might soon come to the point where they think it is fair to take some of us down with them. As you have seen, the Hopi prophecies include that kind of promise. Nuclear, bacteriological and chemical proliferation being what they are, how will we stop millions of them if they try? How long does it take by air or missile to get here from anywhere else?

Through legal and illegal immigration, and by killing one another off, the Second and Third World peoples are already struggling desperately to stay alive. At this very moment there are twenty-four national conflicts going on, and the savagery of them defies belief. Politics may be the excuse, but survival is the real motivator. With the population explosion and other problems underway, the worst of what can happen may be yet to come. A proliferation of terrible weapons makes this frightening scenario more than likely.

The qualification "may" just given is deliberate. I find it interesting that the Hopi prophecies pay limited attention to the population problem. Perhaps this is because Maasaw knew that warfare, environmental changes, birth control, starvation, and rampant diseases could easily reduce the population to where it never becomes a problem. Most certainly, an Armageddon type of World War III would play an effective part in accomplishing this. Looking at what is portended by world developments, it is possible that world population will never reach the levels that are forecast. By the turn of the century, population numbers may in fact begin to diminish. Many of the prophets who forecast future problems and a great "war to end all wars" say that only one-third of humanity will survive these. The Hopi attach no numbers to their predictions, but the general terms they use to describe them seem to agree with the estimate. They even pose the possibility that virtually no one will survive. It all depends on how the "ifs" work out.

Sharing is part of the instructions and a Hopi tenet. The Elders tell us that the home that is beautiful is the one where visitors are invited to share whatever it has in the way of food, even if water is all there is. It is a way they have honored for thousands of years, and a way we have to admire.

Notice, too, that like Jesus, Maasaw had only **one garment** to cover him. In Massaw's case it was a simple, black-colored rabbitskin cloak. Why would he recommend such an outlandish thing to us? Next to sex and violence, fashion has become the holy grail of our lives. Will we follow his advice here? Probably not—at least most of us won't—until the day comes when we are walking around in a daze in the midst of smoking rubble. I suspect that the survivors of earthquake-stricken Kobe, Japan, and of Russia, or the bomb in Oklahoma City, of the flooded areas of Europe, China and the United States, or of the wars in Bosnia and in Ziare, are not nearly so clothes conscious as they were before these things hit. Perhaps this is even true of Chicago, Illinois, where suffocating heat has in the past five days sent almost 500 people to the morgues. In time the views of all who are suffering in these places may return to the mind-set of the pre-disaster stage, but for the moment they have more important priorities than an outfit for every occasion.

The Creator admires beauty. Look at the world and the universe he has created. Maasaw admires beauty. All that he teaches leads to a beautiful life. The Elders admire beauty. Anyone who has seen a Kachina dance, a splendidly painted pot, an intricately carved Kachina doll, an elaborately woven garment, or a sophisticated woven basket or plaque, will testify to this. Prior to White intrusion, their entire life was a walk in beauty. But they didn't, as too many of us do, flaunt it or make a fetish of it.

Some of the things Maasaw recommends will not please us. But for those of us who are looking for ways to survive, everything he advises makes sense. It guarantees a balance and harmony that is missing in much of the world today. Do not listen to financial interests who have only one goal in mind. We are already on our way down. What baggage do we want to carry with us as we fight to turn the tide? History demonstrates that the warrior who is overburdened is not able to maneuver well.

Until Bahanna came and Hopi adopted his ways, they followed Maasaw's instructions and limited themselves to a simple lifestyle. There were problems, naturally. But all of these were handled, and compared to the good things of life were of little consequence. There was love, there was peace, and there was unity. Wants were few, and people were seldom worried. Everything they needed was either readily at hand, or could be produced with the aid of a few simple tools. They felt no urge to be markedly different from one another. The pace of life was relaxed, and family ties were strong. The cycle of life was carried out in concert with Mother Earth, and everything was a celebration. Food was plentiful, and water was sufficient. Those who have lived long enough to make comparisons with the way it was and the way it is now wish it had never changed.

What a privilege it has been to look at Dan as an example of the truth of this. To see him and be with him is to be with the way it was. He fits into life as a hand does a glove. It is not hard to imagine what life was like there on the mesas when there were a thousand or more just like him. Sometimes I fear that in laying out for you in the amazing story the long struggle the Traditionalists have gone through, I have given you a different picture; one that is splattered with tragedy and always decomposing. I am not able to avoid showing you what the forces of evil can accomplish, lest in selling them short you will not prepare adequately to defeat them when they come. But you must know also that while the road we travel is as bone-jarring as the one that leads from Kykotsmovi to Dan's house, on arrival we always find an oasis of gentleness and peace.

"Before Bahanna came," the Elders say,
"we had plenty of food, and were happy together.
At that time everything was in balance,
we had rain and flowers,
we loved each other and lived in peace.
No one was anxious about losing his land,
no thoughts about the Bahannas troubled us."

And so, the Traditionalist Hopi are satisfied to let us live the way we want to, while they live the proven way. They get along fine without indoor plumbing, electricity, central heating, air conditioning, a telephone in every house, paved roads, sanitized garbage dumps, and all the rest. While they are very interested in what is going on in the outside world, they don't need a television set running most of the day. They don't need banks, and they don't want an endless number of bills to pay at the end of every month. They see what it costs people if bills are not paid, how homes and farming lands are lost to creditors and mortgage holders, including the Tribal Council. They observe how the destitute and untrained are shunned and have nowhere to turn. They have talked with embittered Hopi who wandered away into Bahanna's world, learned that they do not fit in, and have returned home worse off than before. They know that being on-the-fence can lead to razor-sharp cuts that are soon inflamed and cause high fevers. They have seen that since there is no doctor or medicine for this kind of ailment, death becomes a welcome guest.

The Tribal Council is seeking to put into effect at Hotevilla Village a trash-hauling fee of $10 a month per residence. It is an interesting fact that for ninety years in the case of Hotevilla, and hundreds of years in the cases of older villages, the simple lifeway never resulted in enough trash or the right kinds of trash to cause a problem. It is only as Bahanna ways are adopted that sufficient trash piles up to make removal by trucks necessary. Likewise, a bush to step behind, or the present wooden outhouse, never led to a need for expensive sewer lines and the necessity of maintaining them.

As we would expect, the Progressive Hopi, most of whom have been rewarded with government jobs while the Traditionalists get none, will enjoy the upgrading at Hopi Land. That is, they will enjoy it until Peabody depletes the water table, or until the Government funding ceases and the Hopi are unable to pay the bills, which, of course, is what the government has had in mind from the beginning. It wants all of the farming land for exploration purposes. As prophecy states, the day will come when all of the Progressive Hopi will learn a bitter lesson. No matter how well they think they have adapted to the Bahanna way of life, when the time arrives that the Bahanna wants what they have, they will be treated just like the Traditionalists. (This assumes, of course, that the closing of the Fourth Cycle is delayed, otherwise there will not be time for regrets.)

The Cherokees are a good example of this truth. They learned this lesson in a way they have not forgotten. Those who intermarried with Whites and were following the White lifestyle knew that removal was coming. But they assumed that their altered state would rescue them. They would continue on with their black slaves, White-run schools, and in their colonial homes. The full bloods might be removed, but they would not. On the contrary, when the blow fell, it fell equally on every Cherokee. In White eyes, to have even a tiny fraction of native blood made that person a Native. Off to Oklahoma, or into hiding in the North Carolina hills, every last Cherokee went. So too, even the Hopi Tribal Council will go if it ever gets in the Government's way.

"The time will come," the prophecies say, "when one will pay, and one will not." This points to the exodus of the Hopi to White ways that is presently taking place, and which is indicated by the vertical line on the Road Plan that is illustrated in Chapter 10. It also points to the Vs on the sacred tablet that foretell a divided people.

To avoid having this kind of thing happen to us, and to make life harmonious on the Ark, Maasaw tells us to move toward simplifying whatever we can. Instead of wanting more, we should concentrate on wanting less. Then losses will be less traumatic, minimal insurance will be required, taxes will be lower, and security devices will be a needless commodity. The time formerly spent in acquiring and hoarding things can then be spent with those we love, who will value the sharing for the rest of their lives.

Just think what we could accomplish if we did as Maasaw recommends when he advises us to make the right choices and change our priorities. Some people may think this is not necessary, or that we can't really do it. On the contrary, we won't know until we try. Maasaw would not suggest it if he did not believe we can measure up to the challenge. Yet the prophecies indicate that the opportunity to do this grows shorter every day. Even the Elders note that everything is speeding up. As actors in the great play of life we are encouraged to choose wisely and soon in the belief that we will be blessed if we do. In looking honestly at the world today, would anyone say that the kinds of choices we have been making have brought us even close to where we ought to be or would like to be? It has been said that the coming Fifth Cycle of the world will be an opportunity to make a fresh new start. Is it not more sensible to do what we can to make that new start now, so as to avoid having to pass through Armageddon on the way there? And yes, we can avoid it in the sense that the cataclysmic Third World War can be moved back, and moved back for a long time to come. It is not—virtually all of the experts who decode prophecies admit this—inevitable that we will go down the tubes on any given month or day that is predicted. That is precisely where the Hopi prophecies, instructions and warnings enter the picture. They were given to us by the Creator to show us how to disarm nearly everything that is predicted.

Nor do the Elders take anything for granted, especially their relationship with the Creator. They never assume they have it made. They know from experience that life aboard the Ark requires diligent regular, and continuing labor. Regarding his return, Jesus said, "No one knows the day or the hour." Not even he knew when this would be. Whenever the leader of some cult declares that Jesus is coming back on a certain day or night, that is the day I nap and the night I sleep the best. There is no need to get ready or to arrange for anything. It can be taken care of the next day. As for the Rapture referred to in the Bible, I am not sure how this stunning moment in time is to be correctly understood, and I doubt that many others understand it either. So far, Theologians are as varied in their opinions about this as a patchwork quilt is in its design.

We have not yet come to the fun part of the INSTRUCTIONS, but the following is a summary of what we have been given so far regarding the activities of life on the Spiritual Ark. To escape the wrath indicated by the prophecies, begin by:

1. **Making your own Covenant with Maasaw.**
2. **Living simply, as Maasaw himself lives.**
3. **Practicing self-denial.**
4. **Practicing self-sufficiency.**
5. **Changing your priorities.**
6. **Recognizing that it is the Creator's wish to rescue us, and that, together with the Hopi, we can rescue the world.**

Concerned people have already undertaken countless individual projects to save the world. They deserve our heartfelt thanks. Yet it is clear that something more is needed to do the job. We can recycle, flush out waterways, save forests, conserve water, shut down chlorofluorocarbons, cut down on other chemicals, stop nuclear testing, save endangered species, control pollution, do all of the rest that is needed, and it still will not be enough. We cannot save the world by simply plugging holes in the dike.

What the Creator and Maasaw tell us is that human beings the world over must undergo a total change in attitude regarding life and the environment. From the cradle to the grave, we must, as the Hopi Traditionalists do, immerse ourselves in Mother Earth. To put this succinctly, we need to blend with her so that we can celebrate life.

Seems simple enough to do, doesn't it? And yet it is not something we have done so far. The justifications for blending are ample. When we continue with the instructions, and when we adapt new thoughts that accompany new actions to our new lives, the qualities that have enabled the Elders to survive the vicissitudes of life will merge with ours. As a result of this blending with Mother Earth, which includes in fact a blending with ourselves, we will become calmer, more serene, less argumentative, and more secure. No matter what developments take place in the world, our oneness with others will deepen. There will be no need for selfishness or acquisitiveness. We will know who we are and where our loyalties lie. Right choices will come easier to us, and temptations will be less of a problem. We will work harder and enjoy it. We will live longer. It is no accident that Traditionalists surpass the average life span of forty-two years for reservation Native Americans. Traditionalists commonly live into their 90s, and in the case of the most deeply committed and spiritual, past 100. In sum, we find here the real Fountain of Youth.

The development of this kind of attitude will promote a deeper respect for the rest of creation. When it comes to saving the earth we will automatically do the individual things that need to be done. We will continue to practice such things as recycling and environmental control, but not because we are forced to. We will do it as a result of our new attitude regarding life. We will see ourselves as a part of a living whole, and not as someone put here on earth to dominate, use and abuse the rest. If children grow up in this truly natural way, respecting their one-ness with the earth and its creatures, we will not need to ask them to stop littering, wasting, overconsuming, and abusing. They will do this on their own, and in this wise will be following in the footsteps of the ancient Native Americans. It is something that parents and schoolteachers need to teach kids from the very first moment they have them at home and in their classrooms.

I am well aware of recently published statements citing proofs that Native Americans were not ecologists by choice; there simply weren't enough of them to impact heavily upon the territories where they lived. Some researchers, as do those who seek to debunk the Bible, take particular delight in revealing that this is the way it "really" was. Let us be honest, they say, and tell how things actually were. The realities of this position are both interesting and portentous. If advanced technologies have only now come to the point where these truths can be known, future technological developments will surely override the present discoveries. This means we are not likely to ever know the real truth. So present speculations should be taken as such, and nothing more. We are caught in the trap of never knowing anything for certain.

Still, there are precious few evidences that the Natives were deliberately careless about their environments. Even though we now know there were at least twenty million natives in south and middle America, and ten million in North America—surely enough to make a mess somewhere—when the first explorers arrived here they marvelled at how pristine everything was. This was due to the Native attitude regarding the rest of creation.

They saw themselves as a part of it, as blended with it, and not as something separate and superior. Under these circumstances one does not wantonly litter or destroy. Europeans had, and still have, trouble coming to grips with this kind of behavior. Odes to Longfellow and John Muir aside, where conquests are concerned, we have not been able to identify ourselves with a people who would by nature treat nature as an equal.

Attitude: According to the American Heritage Dictionary it is "a state of mind or feeling with regard for a person or thing."

As we do all of these things the Creator advises us to, we will gain from them the wisdom, strength and assurance we need to survive—especially to survive the ending, which so far promises to be cataclysmic, and will be, unless we change it. With what is portended, some of us will also be casualties. But so long as we live, we can work to make our present and coming worlds the best they can be for our children and grandchildren. I say again that, by becoming what the Hopi Elders are and making the right choices, we can influence the pace of the world's decline, the intensity of things that happen, and we can shape the cycle's ending.

If you find it difficult to believe we can really do these things, it is because you have not yet come to the point where you recognize how simply and gently it is done.

THIS IS OUR OPTION: As we join together with a new attitude in following the instructions, the mood of the world will change with us. Without a single overt thing taking place, the transformation will be underway. At first, no one will even know it is happening. In the midst of clouds of recurring problems, every now and then the result will be sufficient for someone to see that a problem that existed before has disappeared. It will be gone. The population boom will subside. People will become more caring and sharing. One day we will awake to the news that the fires in the Brazilian jungle are no longer burning. Or a scientist measuring the ozone hole will enthusiastically report that it is shrinking in size. Without a single formal meeting, divided peoples will lay down their guns and begin to cooperate. Drive by shootings will become a thing of the past.

Therefore, even in the midst of chaos there is hope and encouragement. The Hopi prophecies themselves tell us that there can be a new dawn. Even Nostradamus, after posing the specter of a devastating war to come in July of 1999, holds open the probability of worthwhile life continuing on after it. And if you or I do become casualties in war, we will move to the other-side world in the security of knowing we will be eternally with the Creator. That is a finer Ark than the one that is available to us down here.

I trust I have made it clear that in all of this I am not discounting the fact that the two-hearteds will continue their attempt to do us harm. But I am not forgetting either that they did not keep Hotevilla Village, the Elders, and especially Dan, from delivering this superb secret to us, and from delivering a secret challenge you are yet to learn about. Surely, Noah must have had a stormy time as the rain fell. He must have had many a sleepless night as the waters rose and the winds blew. But just as the Creator promised he would, he made it through unscathed. One day his scouting dove returned with a twig from dry land. And if we remain in the Spiritual Ark, the storms will not submerge us or keep us from dry land either.

In the Ceremonial Cycle we will be following, there will be dancing in the Ark. This raises a question. Is it the dancing, or the way that we feel when we are dancing, that counts most? From what I learn from the Elders, it appears they count equally; or if one is actually more important than the other, it is feelings. This is why the Elders say photographs, tapes, and videotapes cannot supplant tradition as a way of recording events. The sounds, words, gestures, and paraphernalia can be captured, but how does someone record the feelings and attitudes that are so vital to successful blending?

Whenever I met with Dan Evehema in Flagstaff to continue our interviews, in no time at all he was anxious as could be to get back to his house and fields. Why was this, I wondered, since the restaurant meals were superb, and his motel room was posh by comparison? His every need was catered to. Only in time did I realize that it was because he, his home, and his fields, were one. The years of cycles have blended them together, and when they are separated each of them feels the estrangement. He was more than a hundred years old, far beyond the age where most men retire from their jobs. Yet he would say as he paced the motel room, "Got to get back, work to do." Eventually, I recognized that what he did was not work to him. It was the carrying out of a love affair. If you come aboard the Spiritual Ark, life can be like that for you.

If we were going to follow the usual interests where Hopi ceremonies are concerned, we would at this point focus on the resplendent rituals and the Kachinas who participate in them. But the Creator told them and tells us to pursue something else, something that is vastly more important. Not surprisingly then, the newsletters do not focus on the Kachinas when they refer to the cycle of rituals. They center themselves in the attitudes that are involved as the ceremonies are done. And, we must learn to think and feel as the Traditionalists do when our seasons pass by. Once we have become through this means a part of the greater life, our own rituals and plantings will bear wonderful fruit.

Above all, we learn that the cycle of rituals is done in concert with Mother Earth herself. They are celebrated with her. The sense is that of walking side by side with our dearest friend, moving in the same direction, and with the same thoughts and the same goals in mind.

The annual Hopi religious cycle consists of two seasons, each of which is about six months in length. And when the Kachinas come to dance in the first season, there are four parts: PREPARATION, PURIFICATION, CONSECRATION, and THANKSGIVING.

The four parts of the second season, which is the annual subsistence cycle, are: PLANTING, CULTIVATING, HARVESTING, and THANKSGIVING. If the subsistence names sound ordinary to you, you will find that, as they are performed, they are more like a mother's involved love relationship with her child, for they are the steps needed to build a powerful bond between Mother Earth and ourselves.

BLENDING: SOYAL AND SETTING THE MOOD

The ceremonial season at Hotevilla Village gets underway with Soyal, which is the first Preparatory Ceremony. In some years, the season begins earlier when young adults pass through **initiation rites** that make them men. After this, the elders can begin to teach them the things they must know about Kiva rituals, and about Maasaw's challenges and blessings.

The Government Agents learned about this when they were looking for ways to break up the villages. As explained in "The Amazing Story," they determined that if the children were away at boarding schools, the initiations could not happen. So they took every one of them away for four years and more.

Under normal circumstances, the first thing that is done each year is the making of certain kinds of prayer feathers. Hundreds of them are fashioned in the Kivas of the clans who are appointed for the honor, but only by men who are properly qualified for the task. Dan Evehema is one of them. **These particular prayer feathers become actual prayers for the well-being of the entire world.** Once the spoken prayers and proper gestures enter into them, the feathers are placed out in shrines that are open to Sun. As he passes over each day, he picks up the spirit of the prayers and carries it to the deities. This continues until the feathers disintegrate and return to Mother Earth.

We can easily see why the cycle begins this way at Hotevilla. It creates an atmosphere of goodwill for each of the rituals to bask in as it is performed. Whenever a village closes all of its major dances to outsiders, we can be certain that no goodwill has been expressed there.

It takes sixteen days to establish this mood for the year. All major ceremonials, in fact, last for 16 days, and follow a similar pattern. Other ceremonials last for 9 days. They begin with an expression of assurance that the ceremony will accomplish its purposes, and end with a feast of celebration and a public Kachina dance. The dance acknowledges the success of the ritual and shares its blessings with the other members of the village.

As we follow what the Traditionalists have done for all of their years, we come immediately to **attitudes and feelings**.

The Elders describe December as the time when Sun has reached his winter home and begun his journey back to his summer home.

Since the month of December requires respect and happiness for its success, only cheerful and **wholesome words** are to be spoken to one another. And what are wholesome words? They are words that brighten another person's day, especially when they have experienced something hurtful in their lives. Such words will be appreciated, and what you have said will establish a warm relationship between the two of you. When you are hurting on another day, your gift will be returned to you.

There are those among us who only appreciate what they initiate themselves and who believe heady psychological stuff is all that can solve the problems of the world. They talk of mind expansion and of altered levels of existence, ignoring the fact that the level of educated intelligence in the world will not be able to make use of these ideas. They will scoff at simple actions like these you will find here. But many who have tried doing it their own way have discovered that it does not lead to warm relationships. Nor will it work for everyone as Maasaw's way does. No one at Oraibi had a college degree. They did not even have a certificate of graduation from kindergarten. But we soon see that the Creator can use anyone to carry His message to everyone. He knows that education is a wonderful thing, but it can sometimes get in the way of faith. At Oraibi, He chose to work with people who were incapable of forgery and plotting.

After the dreadful bombing in Oklahoma City on April 19, 1995, I talked with a friend who lives in Tulsa. Her father has a business building two blocks from where the blast took place, and its front was badly damaged. She was devastated by the catastrophe, but said, "I hope it will change the way people behave. So many of them are so self-centered and angry at one another that there is little shared happiness or peace."

Things have changed there now, even to the point where the people she refers to are speaking wholesome words to one another. And what else exactly are wholesome words? They are words that uplift rather than tear down. Words that encourage rather than destroy. Words that seek harmony rather than dissent. Words that are conducive to physical and mental well-being.

In describing Soyal, the Elders say, "In this sacred season, ceremonies begin, and the germs of seeds are planted within

Mother Earth's womb, the Kiva." These are real seeds, but the reference is also to special thoughts. "The Hopi," they continue, "believe that the Earth is a living Mother to all life and nourishes all of her living children. We must prepare quietly for the coming year, and it is a time for storytelling. The time is sacred. All motions must be slow and silent as possible, because all life is germinating in the Mother's womb, and nothing must disturb her. Doing this leads to a healthy village as well as a healthy body. We must retrace our steps to see how we came into the cycle of life with our father Sun, our Mother Earth, and all children of nature. If we forget these things, we will lose our way of life, which will affect our future children."

"The priests in the Kivas pray for prosperity in food, health, happiness, and for protection against evil for all land and life. The Kachinas visit to bring happiness and joy for young and old. They bring **the rain of loving care** upon the corn fields, and deliver our messages of desire to the Rain Gods.

"There must be **no disturbing loud behavior** or running during Soyal." Why not? Because loud behavior is self-centered. It interrupts others, and it disturbs the deities who are involved in the cycle as well.

"Soyal time," the Elders say, "is a good time to **teach children to respect others,** so that they will continue to practice it throughout their lives."

We need to recognize, too, that just as Soyal at Hotevilla does not last all year, Soyal on the Ark will only last 16 days. There is plenty of time to break the silence and enjoy ourselves when it is over. But these 16 days have been enough for the Hopi to establish a reverential pace and mood that lowers intensities and gives them an opportunity to think. When the tenets of Soyal had been observed year after year, they affected everyone, and they affected nature too. She felt the respect, and she quieted down.

Those who learn to think of the earth as a living organism accept that she responds to everything that is done to her. They believe that when you hurt her enough, she strikes back to let you know how she feels, and that when you treat her lovingly, she shows her love for you in return. Considering what has been done to her over the past century, and laying this alongside the natural catastrophes that have occurred during the last few years, this observation appears to be a more scientific one than we are ordinarily willing to admit. If enough people were to caress and talk with Mother Earth, harmony and balance might be maintained far longer than we can otherwise hope.

At Hotevilla, **no digging** in the ground is permitted during Soyal. Doing this would be disturbing to Mother Earth. Notice that the Elders do not say anything against digging at other times. I have a reason for bringing this up, and I tell you what it is in Chapter 11.

So what have the Traditionalists done instead?

They have followed the instructions, gathering family and friends around them and sitting together while they **talked of the past, the present, and the future**. Topics like these drew family and friends closer together, and refreshed memories of times that made them appreciate one another. A special strength and changed attitude came from this alone as they recognized they had a warm bond and someone they could depend upon.

Next, they **reviewed the Divine laws** the Great Creator had given them.

Soyal was a time when they were instructed to **review their own conduct, and the conduct and attitudes of people as a whole.**

The instructions included **making plans** during Soyal for the coming year, so as not to be caught unprepared. The Elders tell us, "The Creator, nature, and Spirits, **controllers of movement,** plan both good and bad for the coming year. All plans depend upon the behavior of mankind. Even the wicked and the witches devise a scheme to destroy the morals of people, and to separate them from the Creator's divine laws, leading them to self- destruction."

Remember that the mood of Soyal carries over into the rest of the year. It affects everything the Hopi do, and it will affect us as well. As I said earlier, it is why Hopi Land is such a quiet place.

BLENDING: PA-MU-YA—PURIFICATION

This is a phase of the cycle we can understand best by reading the Elderly Elders' own words. Having established the mood for the year in Soyal, the instructions tell the people to make themselves fit for communion with the Creator and His helpers. It is a time of washing off the old and corrupt and becoming clean. It is a time to dress up in new garments and new thoughts. Pa-mu-ya is a time of establishing a healthy environment for all things, for as the humans cleanse themselves, the impurities are also cleansed from Mother Earth. This is an entirely new approach to environmentalism. Because of what is being accomplished, the purification is a happy and social time, a prelude to a period of celebration.

"In Pa-mu-ya, the water month (February), the Kachinas, the messengers between the Hopi and the cloud spirits, come to bring food and happiness to both young and old. This part is activated by the religious groups and by the religious and spiritual leaders of every phase of the ceremonials. No ceremonial is complete without the proper leaders—the religious priests. This **purification** month has an important part in our yearly cycle. There are many parts and dramas which are spiritually meaningful and complete the ceremonial. We need not explain much of it because the word itself, purification, is clearly explanatory to those with an open mind.

"Not all the village members can participate. Only those who are members of the sacred Po-wa-mu-ya Society. This ritual takes all day with the songs or chants, praying, blessing and the purification of the land all life on it. It includes **praying** they may be successful so men on earth will improve their conduct and behavior, that they will improve to the very best from the past year toward good health and happiness.

"The deeper thoughts in the prayers are that purification must be fulfilled as prophesied *to a new dawn of time so the world will bloom into peacefulness.*

"If one is fortunate enough to be in one of the villages, one can hear the boom, boom of the drums, the sound of rattles and turtle shells throughout the kivas. Now the seeds within our Mother Earth begin to stir into life with the blessings of the people and the Kachinas. This is a time of social dancing for both sexes, singing and dancing for happiness and prosperity.

"Po-wa-mu, the purification, will now put things in order. A perfectly healthy environment is required in order to receive the new life seed into the world. **The purification ceremony is performed which cleanses away the impurities upon Mother Earth.**

"The rest is very complex and sacred and also closely guarded. We hope you have followed us up to this point through your own spiritual guidance.

"On the 16th day the new life comes into our world, it comes in the form of food (bean sprouts) which symbolize that our labor and prayers have borne fruit. From each kiva the Kachinas deliver the new food to each household. For the boys, there are gifts of bows and arrows and rattles. For the girls, there are Kachina dolls and rattles to bring joy and happiness. During the day many visiting Kachinas go through the village repeatedly to bring more gifts and spread happiness among the children. This continues until sundown. This is not the end of the ceremonial. More singing and dancing follows from midnight until dawn. These dances are different and unique. The dancers are lined up according to age. The youngest are the beginning of the movement from the center, from there it proceeds through the middle of the dancers to those at the end. The movements, which are repeated until the song ends, symbolize the life cycles of Life and Earth. **The rebirth of new age to old age. That this life must continue on the Earth, continue its cycle from season to season. Should we forget and stray from the great laws of the Creator we all will face the end of time. A New Age will appear as all civilizations disappear.** This will be the consequence if, through our recklessness, we continue to abuse the Earth and so do not deserve to have the use of it. Then a new age and new life forms will appear to make the Earth bloom once more.

It is the duty of the Hopi to keep all cycles continuing. Would any open-minded thinking person permit our way of life to die in the midst of civilization? Does anyone know how our way of life may be saved and protected from harm?"

But there are more instructions, many more, and as we learn them the wonder of it all grows with them. This secret the Traditionalists pass on to us is simply magnificent!

CHAPTER 9

The Ark's Instructions
Part Two

While you read this part of the instructions, hold three words firmly in your mind—**attitude, feelings,** and **rhythm**. Then as you put the secret to work where you live, where you work, where you travel, and where you play, these attributes will give you a new, improved attitude. It will become one of love and peace, with new, improved feelings about life, and people, and the things you do. You will be caught up in a new, improved rhythm of synchronization with Mother Earth, the planet, the universe, and others. You will have more energy, move differently, feel differently, and have a sense of fulfillment.

Are these idle promises? They haven't been for the Traditionalists. They are the gifts that came to them from the Creator as they continued to keep their Covenant vows. Why would they not come to us as well, especially as we take up our roles in the final act of the Great Play of life?

Notice that there is no call here to join in protest marches or to go out in boats to save the whales or stop pollution practices. As we follow the instructions and the warnings, these things and more will be taken care of automatically. Our attitudes, feelings, and rhythms will reach out to those who are causing problems and get them to change their minds and practices. I know this sounds foolish, but remember that it is the Creator, and not I, who makes this promise. I think we can rely on Him. It will not turn out perfectly, but enormous changes can still be made, if we start now. In the last chapter you will see that we have to become what the Hopi Elders have been, so that, as they say, "They will not have worked and died in vain."

The subsistence cycle consists of four phases: planting, cultivating, harvesting, and thanksgiving. This, too, is part of life on the Spiritual Ark. For the first of what we need to learn here, we will turn to the words of the newsletters themselves, and then to an evaluation of how we will fit this into our lives, as we survive here in the outside world.

"This life cycle," the Elders say, referring to the entire year of cyclical events that together make up one great cycle, "is also known as the ceremonial cycle. An ending and beginning, an ending of a time and a new life." What they are telling us is that the life cycle is followed year after year. The ceremonies and the subsistence routine are performed over and over again. As soon as they reach the end of one cycle, they start all over again. Someone might decide that for us this could be boring, but we need to recognize that while the same routine is followed, the world around us is changing. We must constantly shape what we do to meet the world where it is. Also, our choices and behavior will affect the results of what we do. We will not know how any cycle is going to turn out until we have finished it. So we have every reason to keep alert. There will always be expectation, anxiety, surprises. No one can read the Amazing Story of the Traditionalists and say they have lived boring lives.

As they have planted, cultivated, harvested, and offered thanks, they have been in training and getting ready. That is what counted. Nothing hit them that those who held on could not meet head on and triumph over.

And so those Hopi who are already in the Spiritual Ark send us an important message about blending with the land and celebrating life:

"The Great Spirit has marked out this part of the land for the Hopi to live upon. We will not forget His spiritual knowledge and wisdom by which the Hopi are to take care of the land and feed His children while communicating with the natural forces for their health. The Hopi must plant his seeds and watch them grow, he must pay attention to the signs of change in natural order. He must watch with close attention the behavior of all life on earth. Any change or odd behavior will be the sign that the natural order of the earth is getting out of balance. <u>Hopi believe that Hopi Land is the Spiritual Center where changes will be visible to the trained mind and sight</u>."

The Elders underlined this last sentence. They want to make certain we notice that there are reasons why some people do not see things that ought to be obvious to them. It is because they have not been properly trained in what they think about, see, and then do. Training comes automatically as we follow the prophecies, instructions and warnings. As we do what the Elders tell us to, we come eventually to a place where we too see things about Mother Earth that others miss. We will also see things past, present, and future from the Creator's perspective, which is a tall step up from the vantage points available to us now.

We are told that only those who use the proper ways of access can commune effectively with Mother Earth. This means we cannot do it by wishful thinking, or casually. If we want to learn things that will take us where the Elders are, we must make the same kind of concerted effort they have.

It all begins with a moment of wide-eyed wonder, a spirit of stepping into something new and glorious, a spirit of being a partner in a grand miracle!

"Meanwhile, we here in Hopi Land," the Elders continue, "wonder how our crops will be this year. Will there be enough moisture in the soil to bring the young plants to the surface? Will it rain so the plants will grow strong and healthy for a good harvest? These are our main concerns because we live in an arid land. No matter, the Hopi will plant to keep culture and tradition alive. Sadly, up to this time, Hopi life in many ways has been hooked into the materialistic society along with the rest of the Bahanna countries. Those who have adopted materialistic ways desire a cash income in order to 'keep up with the Joneses.' This attitude also robs most Hopi of the ambition needed to farm. So also goes the educated Hopi who is not willing to help the traditional Hopi without cash payment. If this situation continues, the fields will lie idle when the devoted traditionals pass on.

"Some of us like to raise our own food. It gives one great pride just to see the seed you put into the soft which comes up. 'Miracle,' you whisper to yourself. Then you feel even more delighted when you get a meal from it.

"Here is another subject often asked about. When is the right time for Hopi to plant? Now-a-days most people plant by a calendar or almanac. Hopi use their own system, a wisdom that all things are activated and stir to life through space and time upon times of their own. It is a knowledge to be aware of, a sign will show when Natural Order is out of balance.

"As spring approaches, the time markers are closely watched, which can be any landmark which is stationary. As the sun travels along to his summer house (summer solstice), the sun will rise from a certain landmark that means the beginning of spring. Hopi then begin to plant. Sweet corn first, which is fast growing for special purposes. Next come the slower plants such as lima beans and melons. From there on the other crops are planted. The main crop of corn follows in bigger fields. Then once again the sweet corn is planted. This doses the planting season. By this time the sun will reach his summer home.

"Hopi also watch and observe the flowering of certain desert plants which bloom according to their own timetable. By giving attention to all these the Hopi know the earth is still stable and in balance. They say each marker represents where certain things will occur or begin to show itself according to the timing of nature. Knowing this, we know if the clock is ticking awkwardly. Our ceremonial cycle also serves other purposes. Sadly it is waning. This may mean something.

"Why all this hocus-pocus raising our corn? Our concepts may not mean much of value to most people. But Hopi are proud to have a spiritual guide to lead them on. In addition, especially during the fall and winter months, the ceremonial is a must and must be honored in the proper order so that it will be effective in keeping the world and natural order in balance.

"Often we receive letters regarding the Hopi farming methods of raising Hopi corn. There are no ready answers as to how it is done. The Traditional way we do our planting is very complicated. Much of it is connected to the concepts of spiritual bases and our ceremonials. This we feel would not be understandable to non-Hopi. However, we can say freely that corn can be grown almost anywhere that the climate and soil is right. Since Hopi land is arid, we neither irrigate or fertilize our fields. The fact is that Hopi land is like anywhere else. There are some differences, but by long experience the Hopi are able to find fertile land which can best be suited to each crop."

In considering the Hopi dry-farming methods, it is worth noting that our Department of Agriculture has just estimated that 2 billion tons of topsoil are lost from United States croplands each year. It appears that the use of the steel plow has irrevocably damaged much of the nation's arable land, especially in the Great Plains area. No-till farming like that employed by the Hopi, combined with careful crop rotation and other practices currently regarded as alternatives, would reduce soil loss. It would also increase fertility and lessen the need for pesticides.

In 1960, I visited a family in North Dakota. On the way to their house, the wind was blowing so hard that the swirling brown dust it churned up nearly blotted out the road. When I mentioned the driving conditions to my hosts, they said it was fairly common for nearly all of one farm's plowed topsoil to blow onto a neighbor's place within the space of a few days. This kind of wind always came from the north, so what was removed did not blow back. The restoration had to be done with trucks and dozing equipment, which was a terribly expensive operation. Sometimes, people who were short of funds had to do without topsoil to plant in. The Hopi farming methods are simple, but they do not create this kind of problem.

"Since not all Hopi know the traditional ways of growing things, especially younger Hopi, it is now up to the elders to teach them some wisdom in growing corn and other crops. Herein is a brief view. The Elders would say that growing things is important and sacred. It holds the significance of many things, that without food there would be no life. Someone must provide food so that all life will continue on with good health and happiness. One must be willing and put his heart into it. That way, one will gradually blend with the fields so that he will work in harmony. When planting one must be in a good humor, no anger or sad thoughts. One must sing and talk to the seeds, encourage them to come to the surface with joy. When they surface, thank them and encourage them to keep strong. As they grow, you thank them and also the unseen spirits who helped make it possible for the harvest which will provide food. These are a few sides of the wisdom for growing crops.

"The Traditional way of planting is unique. The environment and Natural Order must be considered. Seeds are planted in rows, at least four or five steps apart. The same distance apart for corn and melons, two steps for beans and other crops.

"Since no source of water is available for irrigation, this method lets moisture in the soil equalize to reach each plant for growing and rooting deeper until the rain comes. A planting stick of wild desert oak is used in making the holes by hand for the seed. A large field is finished in a week or more. At least eight to twelve kernels are planted so that the plants will surface with strong energy. Later they will be thinned to four or five stalks depending on whether pests are more or less bothersome. The task can be easier if it is a wet spring, the moist soil is near the top. A foot or more down is dug during a dry spring. The pests, wind, and drought are considered for protection of the plants. Our prayers and ceremonials are important in helping our plants to grow."

BLENDING WITH THE LAND: SPRING

"Spring is here. The time for hard work is fast approaching. It will be a relief to go out into the wide open spaces, surrounded by the mesas, hills, and mountains after the long winter months.

We missed our fields and are anxious to once again work the land and plant. Other people around the country with green thumbs will be turning their best efforts toward self-sufficiency. The right direction, we say. We wish them luck.

"This is a good time to pass on our greetings to our loved ones with thoughts of good health and happiness. It is a time which gives us good feelings of strength, so we hustle around readying our gardens and fields for planting. With our blessings, the seeds are put into the soil, the womb of our Mother Earth. She too feels the warmth of our Father Sun. She begins to stir, with the power of her kindness, she commences her duty of glorifying the land with a green coating of meadows and flowers. Let us be in harmony, for we are one. We have called to Mother Nature with our prayers. 'May your Creations come up strong and healthy so there will be an abundance of food for us and for all.'

"Some of us will be busy working our fields, planting, blending with nature, putting in our seeds, watching them appear. It makes us proud that we too are creators. **We pamper our plants, sing and pray so they will grow healthy and strong.** They will grow to produce food for our nourishment in return for our kindness and care so that we will stay strong and healthy. The plants will be happy for the duty they have done, both we and the plants will be happy to be part of nature."

BLENDING WITH THE LAND: SUMMER

"So the time passes on into summer and men tend their plants like newly born infants. We will face all the challenges of nature, wind, animals, and insects, plus keep the weeds removed, or the soil will be sucked bone dry.

"Now is the time for Kachina Ceremonial dances, for rain and blessings, for people's happiness. Clowns usually participate, not only filling the people with laughter, but also to imitate people's behavior, so they can correct their ways. This sacred drama is not understood by many.

"As the day nears its end, warrior Kachinas of different characteristics signifying different races of people appear as clowns to check if there are any corruptions. Very near the end of the ceremony the clown chief will admit the wrongdoings and request that this be accepted as purification for his children by the warriors, who will return to whip and dowse the clowns with water. The clowns then have to sing and dance of their sins or wrong-doings, clowning in the opposite meaning while under the watchful eye of the warrior kachinas. Someday we will all have to do this clowning, for it is prophesied, and it will be up to the purifier what is to be done with those of us who have become traitors to our beliefs. We might have our ears boxed, or even lose our right to the land.

"Summer is here, the fields are green with growing crops. Ears of corn begin to appear on the stalks. Melons and beans appear on the vines. As you walk among the plants talking and singing, a good feeling of pride and happiness fills your heart. You can now say the labor you put into it will produce some harvest which will keep the wolf away from your door.

CELEBRATING LIFE

"There is the sweet corn that was planted earlier which is ready for a good meal, but you don't dare touch it yet because you know this is for a special occasion which is only a few days away. Everyone hustles around preparing for the Niman Ceremonial (home dance). Women are readying the food to feed the guests. Maybe for relations or friends from neighboring villages, maybe even from far away cities. The men folk spend much of their time in Kivas, smoking and praying for success (that their efforts are) not in vain.

"Both young and old are waiting anxiously, especially the children. They were told that if their behavior is good the Kachina friends will bring them gifts of melon, fresh corn, dolls, or bows and arrows.

"Finally the day has arrived. Kachinas come in with beauty. The children receive their gifts with joy and happiness. In like manner the grown ups are happy to enjoy the day watching and listening to songs. This is the time when all hateful moods and attitudes are forgotten. Time to turn to love one another. This closes the Kachina dances for the summer.

"Let us talk of happiness. The Hopi still practice many things which bring happiness to people. Hopi have not yet commercialized the native dances, so anyone who is fortunate enough to be in Hopi Land at the right moment can share with us our joy. An exception is during the Sacred Ceremonial, most of it is barred to outsiders. Most dances are in the summer months. These dances bring together our relatives and friends from neighboring villages and from distant places. We also get to see our youngsters from far away schools whom we may not have seen for months, even years. We laugh with joy to see how our children and grandchildren have grown. We, the elders, tease one another about our age. We look back over our younger days and on to our long gone grandmas and grandpas in an effort to find our family tree. There may be a new addition in our relatives who have been away a long time. In this case a small Hopi naming ceremonial is done by the women folks. This is done so our relationship and identity may be closely knitted. At this time our corn, melons and other things are ready to eat so there is lots of food. People sit by the open fire outdoors, roasting their corn during the evening hours. Passersby are invited to share, or relatives will get together to enjoy their meal and exchange the latest news and stories."

CELEBRATING LIFE: FALL—HARVEST

"The summer growing months and harvesting took most of our time. Farming is hard work, but as usual we enjoyed our days in the fields. In caring for our crops we talk and sing to them so they can grow healthy and strong. When harvest time comes, harvesting is hard work but can be fun. If the harvest is good, one can be eager. A satisfying reward for the relatives who help with the harvest is a meal of good stew and corn bread (piki). This is our thanksgiving to them for the reward we have received for our labor from our Mother Earth and the other unseen Spirits who made this possible. The harvest time is important, this is the time when we look within the hearts and thoughts of ourselves and others. If the harvest is good, we are happy that our prayers are successful, but if the harvest is poor, something is very wrong with us.

"We are now into Harvest Season. Our youngsters and adults take it just like any other season, but it has some important meaning. It changes the life pattern of all land and life.

"We Hopi are enabled to look at ourselves as we are. The amount and quality we harvest reflect our ways of life in the past years. If the harvest is good, our mind power was strong and clear and in harmony with nature and spirit through prayers. This is faithfulness and happiness. If the harvest is poor, our power of mind strayed because it was not clear, and the prayers did not connect to accomplish the desire. This is sadness and a reason to worry.

"This season is also a harvest of unknown mystery. Only nature and spirit know what kind of life we did harvest, what they store away for us for the coming year, what most of us will see as we move ahead.

"This is the season of happiness and joy, abundance of food, and no lack of appetite. There is hard work for men and women, as well as children old enough to help their parents. Each boy also helps his uncle who will in turn help him when he is old enough to become a man. Each girl helps her clan relations and aunts with the same hope for the time she enters marriage.

"First peaches must be brought in, split and dried on the housetops or on rocky places. Some people even build small sheds of stone where they stay to look after their fruit in case it rains. Men bring muskmelons and watermelons on their backs or on donkeys and nowadays on trucks or wagons. Beans are gathered, winnowed, and cleaned.

"Navajos come to the villages with mutton for trade, and the Hopi go into Navajo country to trade for mutton or even live sheep. Three or four melons will get a head, including free fresh mutton roasts at every hogan they visit. Everyone has a good time, happy to share their harvest again. Corn harvesting begins, with many people living by their fields until it is finished. Some will bring their corn on donkeys and wagons and even on their backs for many miles. When everything is gathered the housetops and yards look colorful beyond description, outer walls covered with drying food such as roasted sweet corn, muskmelon, and beans, even jerky meat from the Navajos, for use during winter. These are just a few glimpses of yesteryear, when our thoughts were one.

"'That's past, why talk about it! Today is today!' the younger set would reply with a frown. 'Yes,' we agree, 'but we are only humans like anybody else. Memories often drift back of the beautiful things as well as bad experiences of the past. Perhaps we would still walk in beauty if we had not made mistakes.'

"We don't have to look far to find it within us. It might not be too late. Beauty and happiness can be renewed when we find our way and abide as closely as possible to the Great Creator's laws. Harvest time is very sacred. There is not only food for thought, but a blessing for the coming year. What we harvest is also a spiritual matter. Will we reap obstacles in the coming year, or perhaps some advantage by which to survive? No one knows but the Creator. Let us all pray that today's harvest is good health and happiness to all people on earth."

CELEBRATING LIFE: THANKSGIVING

"We know that most Indian tribes have some form of celebrating the Thanksgiving day with dances and feasts in traditional ways to give thanks for abundant harvest. Hopi have our own way of Thanksgiving during this time of the year. It is based on ancient concepts. Hopi believe all life on our earth lives and goes by life cycles. Therefore, all must rest and renew for the coming cycle. Whatever it may bring, either good or bad, in some part depends on man's behavior.

"When this cycle ends, we give thanks to our guiding spirits and Mother Earth for their care. We give thanks for our health and nourishment, for completing the cycle with all life, and we pray and ask for the same during the coming new cycle. We often hear our Grandmothers and Grandfathers saying, 'Thank you. Thank you, my guiding spirit for the care in making it possible for me to complete this cycle. I wish to be here next year.' This Thanksgiving is not only for ourselves, it includes all life. We must all keep strong and pray that we all reach the end of this year's cycle with good health and peace. Happy Thanksgiving.

"Now it is up to us to make this real. We must perform self-analysis and change our behavior and character. We must not pretend to be something which we are not, which results in friction. We must not deceive our fellow men. Let us become realistic and establish a goal to have faith in the All-Powerful Creator, for we are not above His laws. Let Him be the Judge according to His plan. Let us establish a goal of happiness and love. We must ready ourselves to serve and work for the Great Spirit, not in search of supremacy or superiority as a goal. That aim is not successful in reaching the purpose which we set out to do."

PRAYERS ARE A REGULAR PART OF EVERYTHING THE TRADITIONALIST HOPI DO.

The following prayer was read to the UN General Assembly and to the UN Peoples Assembly. By examining it, you will see what kinds of things they focus on when they turn to the Creator. If you have difficulty deciding what to pray about, or how to go about prayer, this prayer and the following supplications should help you.

"Great Spirit and all unseen, this day we pray and ask You for guidance, humbly we ask You to help us and fellowmen to have recourse to peaceful ways of life, because of uncontrolled deceitfulness by humankind.
Help us all to love, not hate one another.
We ask you to be seen in an image of Love and Peace.
Let us be seen in beauty, the colors of the rainbow.
We respect our Mother, the plant, with our loving care,
for from Her breast we receive our nourishment.
Let us not listen to the voices of the two-hearteds,
the destroyers of mind, the haters and self-made leaders,
whose lusts for power and wealth will lead us into confusion and darkness.
Seek visions always of world beauty, not violence nor battlefield. It is our duty to pray always for harmony between man and earth, so that the earth will bloom once more.
Let us show our emblem of love and good will for all life and land. Pray for the House of Glass, for within it are minds clear and pure as ice and mountain streams.

Pray for the great leaders of nations in the House of Mica who in their own quiet ways help keep the earth in balance.
We pray the Great Spirit that one day our Mother Earth will be purified into a healthy peaceful one.
Let us sing for strength of wisdom with all nations for the good of the people.
Our hope is not yet lost, purification must occur to restore the health of our Mother Earth for lasting peace and happiness.
Techqua Ikachi."

This is an Elder's prayer to Maasaw:

"Here I am asking you,
You who own the world,
There are two of you.
It is you with the simple way of life
which is everlasting that we follow.
You have the whole universe,
we do not follow the materialistic God.
We ask you, with your strength, to speak through us.
With the prayers of all the people here
we shall reclaim the land for you."

In the first chapter, I said that Dan Evehema's manner of life had sustained him in "Fountain of Youth" fashion in a remarkable way. He is a realist, He knows how old he is and that the time has come for him to begin to think about going to join the Kachinas at the San Francisco Peaks. But he does not do this because of a failing mind or physical infirmities. He did have a bad bout of pneumonia this past winter, but that is fairly common for Natives who must heat their homes to the boiling point to withstand the severe cold, and then step outside into freezing temperatures to bring in wood or do various other tasks. It is the sharp contrast between temperatures that makes them sick. Fools Crow experienced this too. Yet he lived nearly 100 years, and even at 102 years, Dan thinks and acts like a man half his age. It is because he has for the whole of his life followed the INSTRUCTIONS and heeded the WARNINGS. Hard work helps, but attitudes, feelings, rhythm, and power help even more. They are a quartet of troubadours who join forces to increase fitness and longevity.

Sharing in miracles! That is what *The Hopi Survival Kit* is really all about. This does not mean that our problems will end. Far from it! The prophecies make this clear. But as we follow the INSTRUCTIONS and WARNINGS, resistance will spread out from us to meet them head-on and handle them better than anyone imagines. The Elderly Elders, Maasaw, and the Creator know this will happen. If this were not so, wouldn't they have told us? And, you can be sure that, as it does, they will be cheering us on. Think on this. It may be late in the day, but the revolution is about to begin, and it is exciting to know that we are being given an opportunity to be a vital part of it!

It is rewarding to find that the Traditionalist Hopi become deeply personal with us, telling us things they have never before told to outsiders. You will recall that, even though this was a message to be shared with the world, they did not see fit to share this precious information with the early scientists who so ruthlessly invaded their Kivas, or with the colonel and the Agent. Our relationship has changed, however, and now they have decided to reveal to us how they think and feel as they follow Maasaw's instructions. There is a particular reason for this that has been hinted at in previous chapters, but it is only spelled out in careful detail in Chapter 11.

The INSTRUCTIONS and WARNINGS became to the Traditionalists a "Pattern of Life."

The Pattern consists of the detailed way of daily life that Massaw laid out at Oraibi for the people to follow. It is an overall cycle of activities and thoughts that are to be repeated year after year. Carrying it out prepares the Traditionalist Hopi for dealing with life in the past, present, and future.

To join with the Traditionalist Hopi in this great adventure, we must choose to go aboard the Spiritual Ark they already live on, and let our lives be infused with the same wonderful thoughts and feelings they experience. None of these things have to do with Hopi rituals. Even though the rituals are intriguing, they belong to the Hopi, and Maasaw did not tell the Oraibi people to pass any of that information on to us. It is simply not pertinent to any of us who live and produce here in the huge world outside Hopi Land.

Just as the Traditionalist Hopi have been a people of peace, so too will peace and beauty come into our lives as we do these things. The Spiritual Ark is a spiritual flower garden, and at the same time a fortress. So long as we follow its rules, it will entrance us, and it will protect us. The boarding call is sounding from the stack of the Spiritual Ark. Do you hear it? Listen to it, and come aboard.

I repeat that there is no call here to join in protest marches or to go out in boats to save the whales or stop pollution practices. That does not mean we disagree with them. Until now it has been one of the only ways we have had to get the perpetrator's attention. But with the Ark the Traditionalists have given us a better way. As we follow the instructions and the warnings, these needs and more will be taken care of automatically. Our attitudes, feelings and rhythm will reach out to those whose are causing problems and get them to change their minds and practices. I know this sounds foolish, and if it were just the Hopi and I, as mere human beings, suggesting it, it would be. But remember that it is the Creator who makes this promise. He is putting Divine power to work through those who follow the instructions. If we start now, the prophecies make it clear that life will not turn out perfectly, but enormous changes and improvements can still be made.

You will notice that none of what is being advocated here intrudes upon Hopi religious life. With good justification, Native Americans are concerned about non-Indians who, without proper training, want to, and even seek too, duplicate their sacred rites such as the sweat lodge, sun dance, and vision questing. This objection is not so much aimed at serious individuals who have earned the trust of qualified instructors as it is at those who have let the situation get out of control.

So what do we do instead? How do we put the secret to work?

BLEND WITH THE LAND AND CELEBRATE LIFE. THERE IS A GENTLE WAY TO SURVIVAL

1. As you board the Ark, make your own Covenant with the Creator and Maasaw. That does not mean you will exchange what you are going to do on the Ark for your own religious faith. While the Ark does function in a relationship with the Creator, it is not a place of religion, nor does it recognize any religion as superior to others. Where the survival of the planet and living beings who live in this world of the Fourth Cycle is concerned, the Ark takes for granted that every person in the world has a stake in it. The Ark is a place where the recognition of a Divine Creator is involved, and anyone who boards it will need to have come at least that far where

> faith is concerned. That won't leave many standing on the dock. If the statistics I read are correct, only a small percentage of the people in the world do not believe there is a Creator.

So all who board will add what is being recommended to what they already believe. Your eternal relationship with the Creator is something you will continue to work out elsewhere. Be very clear about this: except for the Hopi themselves, the Pattern of Life is not a religion. The Traditionalists do not pass this information on to seek conversions. They do not want you to wish you could even become a Hopi. The newsletters make this exceedingly clear. As you follow this astonishing Pattern of Life that is aimed at surviving, you will be seeing things through His eyes and it will give you a priceless perspective, but it will be a perspective about survival here on earth. It will not deal with eternal matters. However beautiful and sublime it is, it is limited to accomplishing one, single thing—SURVIVAL!

2. Live simply, as Maasaw himself lives and don't let materialism control your life.

3. Practice self-denial.

4. Practice self-sufficiency. Each of us should possess whatever margin of preparation we need to get us over humps that may last for long periods of time. We who live in cities must ask ourselves what we would do if all of our food supply sources closed down tomorrow. By asking other Hopi this same question in the newsletters, the Elders confront Progressives who have either given up their farms in favor of wage work, or have forgotten how to farm. The Elders care about their fellow Hopi, and they worry about the prices that will be paid for poorly thought-out decisions.

We have made some choices that will not be easy to rectify either. Many of us who live in urban areas not only haven't gardens to tide us over, we don't have places to put them. In this regard, we have painted ourselves into a serious corner. Unless we begin to do something about it while the window of opportunity is still open, it will get worse. When the things that are prophesied do come to pass, we are going to be in far more trouble than we ever imagined. We can attempt to ease our way out of this dilemma by arguing that none of these things will actually happen, that the idea of prophetic fulfillment is really preposterous. On the other hand it is helpful to add to the Hopi prophecies the material that is included in the next chapter. Then you will see that attempts to pass these things off lightly won't wash. What I am saying is that the things that are happening in the world today give credence to the Hopi prophecies. They support one another. If we accept this and prepare for them in advance, we can meet anything that comes with resolution and inner peace.

Practicing self-sufficiency is something the Traditionalist Hopi do as a natural way of life, and it is one of the strategies that has enabled them to endure for thousands of years. Having learned from long experience that circumstances can change drastically from one year to the next, and on occasion even more quickly than that, they lay aside enough food each Fall to get them through the next year. If the worst happens, they are ready. We too are advised to stock our shelves with enough non-perishable foods to sustain our families when the prophesied emergencies strike. Fortunately, firms who offer such foodstuffs for sale are already in existence. Find those in your area, and begin to put aside, along with what other items you will need, enough to get you by until something akin to normalcy returns, which could easily be for several months or more.

We Californians are accustomed to earthquakes, and we have already been told to set aside sufficient provisions and emergency equipment to get us through what life will be like in the aftermath of a major shock, which we are repeatedly warned could come any day now. Some of us are paying attention, but most of us are not. After all, we have been through so many quakes without serious problems that we are jaded about them.

But the prophetic situation is another ball game entirely. In its light, ignoring the warnings is not smart. Delaying is equally foolish, since preparing in advance is not wasteful. Most non-perishable foods have a shelf life of a year or more. And when the expiration date arrives, if you haven't needed what you stored, it can be eaten and then replaced with fresh items. There is some time and inconvenience connected with this. But sooner or later, the day will come when those who are prepared will thank Maasaw for the warning and advice.

In the previous material the Hopi have shown us how marvelous the experience of planting, cultivating, harvesting and thanksgiving can be. Traditionalists like Dan would not trade what they do in the seasonal cycle for anything the outside world has to offer. And having learned how Dan farms, you know why he feels this way. What he does turns hard work into a beautiful experience.

We can share this wonder and joy, and we can do it as we continue to live and work here in the outside world. We simply need to allocate enough time from our busy schedules to accomplish it. The instructions tell us to do things that are so simple they are deceptive. Yet the simplicity is crucial, for they are things anyone can do anyplace in the world. Many will toss them aside as ridiculous ideas. But make your own decision, and do not be influenced by doubters.

5. Change your priorities. Make careful choices.

6. Recognize that it is the Creator's wish to rescue us, and that together with the Hopi we can rescue the world.

7. Think of attitude as being an equal partner of application. What you think about what you do may be even more important than what you do.

8. Make your attitude regarding life and the environment a reverent one.

9. Throughout the Ceremonial Cycle there will be dancing in the Ark. This pursuit we are following has a serious nature, but we know it will be successful. This awareness keeps us in a state of joy and fulfillment. So, except for the sixteen days of Soyal, listen to music and dance when you want to. Remember that it was the Creator who originated the Kachina and unmasked dances. The Hopi perform social dances throughout much of the year. The Creator made it possible for us to enjoy sex too, so long as we do this in a healthy way and with a sense of responsibility.

10. During the first part of December say prayers for the well-being of the entire world.

What is being done during this season is to set the stage, to prepare the atmosphere, for the coming year. During this period, you will be blending with the world, and your consciousness of this state will enfold you and affect everything else you do during the coming year. If people all over the world are doing this, think of what the effect will be.

11. On December 21, do initiations to bring others aboard the Spiritual Ark.

Follow this with your own SOYAL.

Make it a sixteen day period in January during which you will do the following things. While you are doing them, concentrate on attitudes and feelings that will bring you closer to loved ones and to the rest of the world. Remember that as you carry out these actions you will achieve a magnificent sense of inner peace.

As you work, your problems will either go away on their own, or solutions to them will come to you. You will fret less since everything is being taken care of. Beyond this, you will be building an inner strength that will shield you when future prophecies are fulfilled. Following the instructions will accomplish your survival in every way.

1. Use wholesome words when you talk to or describe people. Uplift, and do not hurt others.

2. Ask the Spirits to listen to you and to bring the rain of loving care down upon the whole world.

3. Guard against disturbing or loud behavior.

4. Teach children to respect others, and tell them why they should do this.

5. Think of the earth as Mother Earth or Earth Mother, a Spirit person who is a living organism who feels and responds.

6. During these sixteen days, do not dig in the earth, since Mother Earth is joining you in this Soyal period of peace and preparation.

7. Talk with those who are close to you of the past, the present, and the future. Discuss what is going on in the world, and try

to determine where it is heading. Do not postpone the strengthening of your bonds with family members. As Maasaw knew it would, this has become a neglected area in our way of life here in the United States, and it is something we need to correct. Recently, Henry Clark revealed in *The Los Angeles Times* how his receipt of an artificial heart has caused him to change his priorities. Business no longer comes first. He at last realizes the supreme value of elemental discourse with loved ones before it is too late. Heed his example.

8. Review with yourself and these same close ones the Divine laws. These laws will vary with different cultures and religions. But we all know, or at one time did know, our own, and we know the Hopi laws now. Talking about them will refresh our minds about what we were taught to do, and will expose how far we have strayed from these mandates. If we do not do well at this discussion, we will know that we need to return to our Sources so that we can do better next year.

9. Review your own conduct during the past year, and the conduct and attitudes of people as a whole.

10. Make an honest self-examination, and see where you can make improvements. This is a touchy topic, and one that can be easily ignored. We need to look together at the world around us, and attempt to make reasonable assessments of what is going on. During Soyal, self-examination is also in order. If we hope to do better than we have, we must take a good look at ourselves and be honest about what we find

11. Make plans for the forthcoming year. Prepare in advance for the known and the unknown. This will include a review of the prophecies, to see what they portend. Keep current with

what is going on at Hotevilla, for this microcosm of the world will continue to serve in this capacity. At the end of this book you are told how that can be done. Look back at what has happened, and see what of this will be duplicated. What you will be doing throughout the entire cycle will be preparing for the unexpected.

12. Remember that the Creator, Earth Mother, Father Sun, and the other Helper Spirits—the controllers of movement here and in the universe—are making their own plans, based upon the course the Great Play is following. Try to determine what this course might be, and prepare accordingly. Remember also that while we are doing our part, the Traditionalist Hopi who still remain will be doing the necessary things to keep the world and the universe in balance and harmony. Never forget to support them in this, and at the end of this book you are told how that can be done.

NEXT, DO YOUR OWN PA-MU-YA, OR PURIFICATION

1. Begin this important season in Ferbruary by thinking about purification—what it means to become fit to step into the presence of the Creator where you will seek his blessings. Ask yourself what you should put aside before you did that? Always begin what you do with a positive approach. Long before the Kachinas come they prepare the gifts that are given out to celebrate the fact that, having asked, the people will receive. Build in yourself the same attitude. I get goose-bumps whenever I think of the Elder's line, "Kachinas come to bring the rain of loving care."

2. Pray about purification for yourself and everyone else in the world. Try to connect with them to make this a common endeavor.

3. Use water and prayer to perform a purification ceremony that cleanses yourself, and also the impurities upon Mother Earth. When you do this, you will automatically share in the kinds of deeds that are being done by others, and which we realize need to be done. There will always be the need to clean up ourselves and preserve the planet and its creatures.

4. Remember that in this season the Traditionalist Hopi celebrate the rebirth of new age to old age. They acknowledge that this life must continue on the Earth, continuing its cycle from season to season. At the same time this is being done, they bear in mind that should we forget and stray from the great laws of the Creator, we will at the end of time all face a New Age that will appear as all civilizations disappear.

IN MAY, SHIFT INTO YOUR OWN SUBSISTENCE SEASON

The Elders tell us that this is a time when something especially beautiful begins to happen. It is the time when "changes become visible to the trained mind and sight." In other words, until now we will have thought about it and anticipated it. Only now though will the proofs come rushing in. Among these, as Mother Earth communes with us, we will hear Her actual voice speaking to us for the first time.

1. Enter this cycle with a feeling of wonder. I'm sure you noticed how the Elders say that, even though they had done it for centuries, a sense of wonder came over them as they began each planting season. It never got old. It was always new. There was the wonder of the Creators desire to go on doing this through them, the wonder of joining with Earth Mother as she began stirring to bring new life into the world, the wonder of becoming creators themselves as they planted and then saw the food the world needed to sustain its people

come to maturity. There was a rhythm of life attained.

2. Why all this "hocus-pocus, all these strange things we do to raise our corn," the Elders ask? Then they point out that while their concepts may not mean much of value to most people, and to a high-powered modern world, the Hopi are proud to have a spiritual guide to lead them on. They are profoundly grateful that they never walk alone. To celebrate this, "especially during the fall and winter months, the ceremonial is a must and must be honored in the proper order so that it will be effective in keeping the world and natural order in balance." In other words what is done in the fields as well as what is done in the Kivas is part of keeping the world and natural order in balance and harmony. Therefore, the entire life of the Traditionalist Hopi is involved in this enormous responsibility. We need to acknowledge our spiritual guide.

3. The Traditionalist farmer does not jump into his task with powerful machinery. He gradually blends with the fields so that everything will work in harmony. That is why Hopi are able to grow crops where no one else would even dare try. Still no Hopi farmer has ever been subsidized as are farmers in the outside world. Our Government has left them to sink or swim on their own.

4. Be in a good humor. Do not be angry or have sad thoughts. Won't it be magnificent to be on an Ark filled with people who are neither angry or sad? Instead one must sing and talk to the seeds, commune with them and encourage them to come to the surface with joy. When they surface thank them and encourage them to keep strong. As they grow you thank them and also the unseen spirits who helped make it possible for the harvest which will provide food.

Well and good, I hear someone saying, for people who live on an isolated reservation instead of in an industrial metropolis. How are we supposed to maintain these attitudes out here? To say this is to forget the Amazing Story, and what the Traditionalists have endured for so long a time.

5. Share your greetings with your loved ones, shower them with thoughts of good health and happiness.

PLANT SOMETHING!

6. When springtime comes next year and you are feeling the joy that has already come to you, plant a few seeds somewhere. Corn will even grow in a hot, dry apartment. If you have no dirt area, use a wooden or metal box. Do the planting the way Dan does his, and then treat the plants in the same fashion. When you plant, cultivate, harvest, and offer thanks as Maasaw taught the Hopi to do, the experience will bring you closer to Mother Earth and the rest of creation than you could ever come in another way. You will be able to communicate with Her, and you will have whole new understandings regarding Her. To plant, use a digging stick like that shown in the illustrations, and any kind of wood will do so long as it is a branch from a fruit bearing tree. That, your two hands, sensitivity, a handful of seeds, and some sunshine and water, are all you will need. A single ear of corn will be enough to share in the life that is beginning to stir all over the earth. What matters for us here in the outside world is what we are thinking, and not the amount produced. We must expand our vision, and think of what this will accomplish when people all over the world are doing it at the same time.

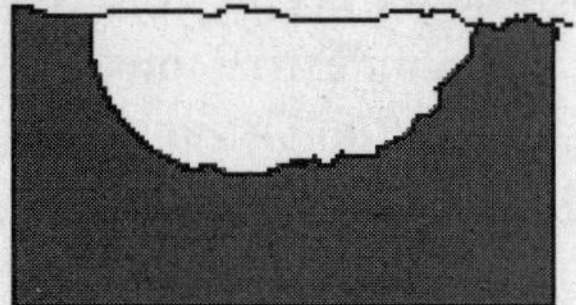

1. Dig an oval-shaped basin about 12 inches deep.

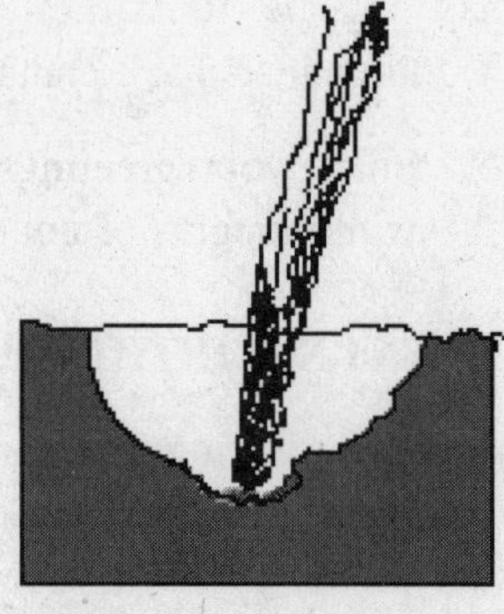

2. Use the digging stick to make a small hole to drop the seeds into

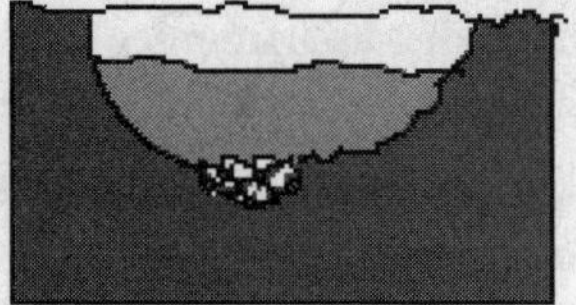

3. Fill the basin to within two inches of the top, leaving a shallow area to catch water.

Planting

What we see at Hopi Land during the farming season may look ordinary, but it is not. All kinds of things are going on that are not visible to the naked eye. Farming is a way of sinking roots into Mother Earth, and so long as the farmer has not fouled things up by making bad choices, She responds to this in wonderful and abundant ways, making planting a way of reaching out to the whole of creation. Think about this aspect of planting, and think about joining with the Traditionalists in making this gesture of love to the world. How splendidly the secret unfolds!

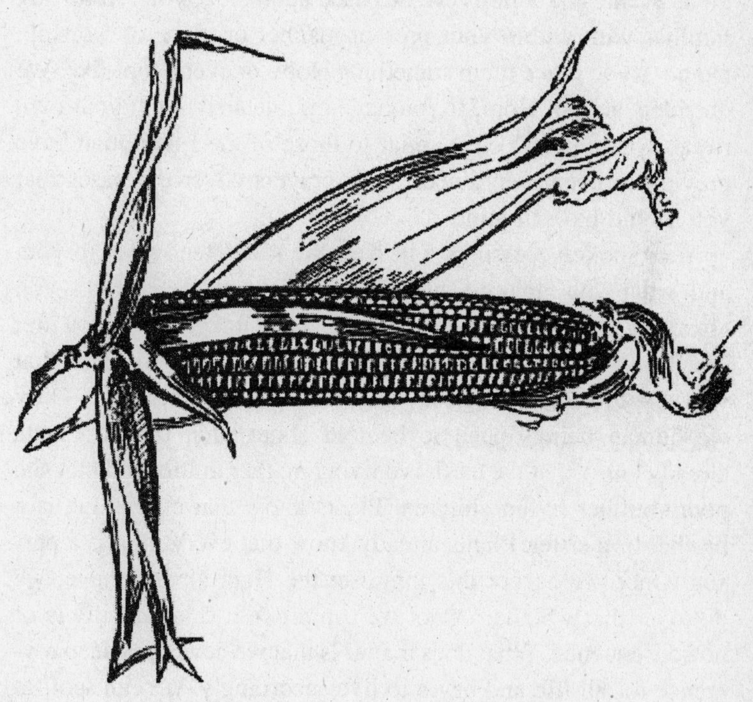

CULTIVATE WHAT YOU PLANT

You must do your planting in a ritual manner to make it a religious event. The actions can be based upon those you are already familiar with within your present manner or place of worship. Do not try to make them something Hopi, or even Hopi-like. We outsiders are not Hopi. If you have trouble arriving at your own ritual words, use words similar to those of the Elders that have previously been mentioned. Their prayers cover the bases that you should have in mind.

Your spoken blessings will help the seeds feel close to you, and what you imagine now is very important. Haven't you always wanted to be close to a seed? Then imagine that you are. The Traditionalists have learned that the seeds already know that you should do this, and they are waiting for it to happen. Only we human beings need to be told about such things. Plants already know that the earth is a living mother to life, and that she nourishes her living children. Plants know that everything is a brother or a sister. Plants already know that everything is a person. Once we accept this mind-set the Hopi already have, we discover that whether or not we can prove it scientifically is of no consequence. What does matter is that we develop a deep reverence for all life and begin to live accordingly. We can scoff at this idea, we can worry about what other people will think when they see us doing it, or we can just do it and let the chips fall where they may. Our choice depends upon what we want to happen in our life, and want to happen in the life of the world. We should let others worry about their own choices, and at the same time ask themselves what exactly they are doing to assure their survival and the survival of the rest of creation.

Once your plants are planted, you will spend part of each day or evening watching them grow and communing with them. A few minutes in the early morning, or even late at night will suffice to keep you involved in what is going on. We watch fish, insects, rodents, rabbits, and snakes; why not plants? When they sprout you will touch their leaves, speak to them, and sing to them. You read me correctly. I did say, "Sing to them." A good singing voice is not required, and you can do it when no one else is around to call 911. By doing these things you will share with them the happiness that is in your heart. Dan assures me that if you do this, the seeds will form normally and perfectly. The corn stalks will grow strong and tall. At harvest time, place some of your produce near other plants where they can share with each other the warm and encouraging feeling you have already shared with them. What's that? You didn't know plants visited together? Shame on you.

Ask yourself this: When two people are in love, must audible words always be spoken between them in order for them to communicate with one another? Answer—of course not! Is it then not possible that one plant can exude a chemical that can carry a message to another plant? If this is not so, what other possibilities for communication might there be?

Little things. Seemingly foolish things. But as the earth and we become one, out of them can come the greatest wonders of all time.

You've noticed that Dan even thinks the privilege of watching crops emerge from Mother Earth and grow is in itself a miracle. And beyond this, little individual miracles come to those who listen to Maasaw and follow his guidance. When Dan talks and sings to his plants, they respond. I don't know that they speak and sing to him, but they show they have heard him in the way they grow. This year, he is delighted because the corn that he planted last May is a foot taller than everyone else's. That's understandable. He can often be seen alone in his fields and lost in prayer for his plants. He told Katherine one day that when he sings to a plant, little clouds often come to where he is, and as they pass over him release tiny drops of water that fall on the plant. He also said that a little rainbow sometimes forms there. Later on, she took a photograph of him while he was singing to a stalk of his corn. She did not at the time see a rainbow, but when the picture was printed, there was the rainbow.

Begin your own actual blending with nature, putting in your seeds, and watching them appear. It will make you proud that you too are creators. Pamper your plants. Sing and pray to them so they will grow healthy and strong. Know in your hearts that they will grow and grow to produce food for your nourishment in return for your kindness and care so that everyone will stay strong and healthy. "The plants," the Elders say, "will be happy for the duty they have done, both we and the plants will be happy to be part of nature."

BLENDING: SUMMER

1. As the time passes on into summer, tend your plant or plants like newly born infants. Do this, and experience the miracle of how it affects everything else you do! The shared feelings carry over to everything else in life—at home, school, in the community, and on the job.

2. At Hopi Land, now will be the time for Kachina Ceremonial dances, for rain and blessings, for people's happiness. "Clowns usually participate, not only filling the people with laughter, but also to imitate people's behavior, so they can correct their ways. As you do your own correcting and walk around or among your plants talking and singing, a good feeling of pride and happiness will fill your heart."

3. Hopefully, at Hopi Land, the Niman, or Home Going

Ceremonial, will still be taking place at Hotevilla around the end of July. Whatever happens to the village, we should pray for the success of the Kachina season. After all, the Kachinas are praying for us.

4. If the Home Going Dance does continue, the Hopi people will see the Kachinas come in with beauty. The children will receive their gifts with joy and happiness. In like manner the grown-ups will enjoy the day watching and listening to songs. Until the Tribal Council and its Office of Cultural Preservation moved in, this was the time when all hateful moods and attitudes were forgotten. It was a time to turn to love one another. The Kachinas returned to their sacred home carrying with them the prayers and thanks of the people. This closed the Kachina dances for the summer. The Council intrusion has, however, significantly changed the mood.

Most social dances are held in the summer months. These dances are opportunities to bring together relatives and friends from neighboring villages and from distant places. It is also a time when our Spiritual Ark will be in a party mode.

CELEBRATING LIFE: FALL—HARVEST

Harvesting is hard work, but the Hopi tell us it can be fun. If the harvest is good, one can be eager about what it portends for the coming year. Depending on what we plant on the Ark, our harvest may not entail a lot of work. But since we have other foodstuffs to depend on, it is the thought and not the number of plants that matters. Even a single corn plant, one melon, a batch of beans, or a fruit tree can accomplish our purpose in the context of the way we are considering it.

The Elders say, "The harvest time is important, this is the time when we look within the hearts and thoughts of ourselves and others. If the harvest is good we are happy that our prayers are successful, but if the harvest is poor, something is very wrong with us."

1. As we move into the Harvest Season, our youngsters and some adults, as do many of the Hopi today, may treat it just like any other season. But the season has a special and important meaning, for if you think about it, it affects the life pattern of all land and life. In the crops that appear, the Traditionalist Hopi see themselves as they really are. We will receive the same messages too, and they may tell us more about ourselves than we want to know. If a warning message comes to you, take it as an opportunity to do better next time, and make sure to correct what there is about yourself that needs to be corrected. "We don't have to look far," the Elders say, "to find it within us. If this happens to you, take it as a warning. It might not be too late to change the situation. Beauty and happiness can be renewed when we find our way and abide as closely as possible to the Great Creator's laws. Harvest time is very sacred, for this season is also a harvest of unknown mystery.This is the season of happiness and joy, abundance of food, and no lack of appetite."

The Elders complete their subsistence accounts by pointing out that "these are just a few glimpses of yesteryear, when our thoughts were one." In other words, what we are being called to do comes from the ancient days. Except for the few Traditionalists who continue to follow the Pattern of Life, this is not what we will find at Hopi Land now. Job wages have replaced farming along with the ancient way of life generally. It follows also that the Hopi who no longer farm no longer experience these wonderful things.

CELEBRATING LIFE: THANKSGIVING— A TIME OF REST AND RENEWAL

The Elders tell us that "Hopi believe all life on our earth lives and goes by life cycles; therefore all must rest and renew for the coming cycle. Whatever it may bring, either good or bad, in some part depends on man's behavior. When this cycle ends, we give thanks to our guiding spirits and Mother Earth for their care. We give thanks for our health and nourishment, for completing the cycle with all life, and we pray and ask for the same during the coming new cycle. Now it is up to us to make this real. We must perform self analysis and change our behavior and character. We must not pretend to be something which we are not, which results in friction. We must not deceive our fellow men. Let us become realistic and establish a goal to have faith in the All-Powerful Creator, for we are not above His laws. Let him be the Judge according to His plan. Let us establish a goal of happiness and love. We must ready ourselves to serve and work for the Great Spirit, not in search of supremacy or superiority as a goal. That aim is not successful in reaching the purpose which we set out to do."

Never forget that Prayers are a regular part of everything the Traditionalist Hopi do in every season.

On December 21 of each year, you and I will start all over by praying again for everyone and everything in the whole world. We will think again about self-sufficiency, and take whatever steps are necessary to maintain it. To accomplish this, save a few seeds from your crop to plant next Spring.

Another reminder:

Life on the spiritual Ark can flow so smoothly we can easily be lulled into complacency. The two-hearteds know this, and wait for it to happen. When it does, they move swiftly to take advantage of our weakness. We need to remind ourselves that the going will never be easy, that life is filled with common problems that always lie ahead. In addition, there are the formidable prophecies that are yet to be fulfilled. When in A.D. 1100 they met at the sounding rock at Oraibi, Maasaw presented the people with a number of warnings that are still applicable to us today. We also need to take a somber look at the problems that are present in the world and are portended. Our place on the Ark will never be an absolutely secure one. We always have our natures and weaknesses to consider, for no one succumbs to temptation better than we do. We are masters at it. But temptation takes its toll. While in the last century the Traditionalists have kept their vow, experienced happiness, achieved satisfaction, and accomplished their purposes, their ranks have also suffered terrible losses. Only a handful of them are left today. In the same way, our best efforts will be required to survive the obstacles that lie ahead of us.

CHAPTER 10

The Ark's Warnings

"When a Hopi is ordained into the higher religious order, the Earth and all living things are placed upon his hands. He becomes a father to all. He is entitled to advise and correct his children in whatever way he can. Together with the other religious leaders they decide the destiny of their children."

Maasaw told the Hopi to be alert and watchful, and he named specific things they should do to protect themselves. As we consider these wise specifics, we will see that they are cautions that we should exercise too. So that you can scan it and commit it to memory, I present the warnings given to the Hopi with bold headings, and include for each of them what the Hopi say about them in the newsletters. Since they are quotes, I use quote marks to identify their statements.

Beyond these, we must be aware of awesome situations that are going on in the world, for with every passing day they will impinge in increasing measure upon our lives. These are warnings too, and balanced judgments about them must be made.

The warnings given to the Hopi are summed up in the famous Road Plan and stone tablet already mentioned. These are illustrated and the meanings of their symbols are explained at the end of this chapter. When we recognize that the stone writings consist of information the Hopi received nearly a thousand years ago, we have no option but to admit they are astounding in what they reveal.

Make careful Choices:

"Make careful Choices: When new opportunities are introduced and new advantages come, be cautious and accept the least harmful things. Choose which path you will follow—the materialistic way or the Creator's way. Do not get careless as time passes and forget your vows to the Creator and the spiritual laws. If you do, it will be a sign you have forsaken the Great Creator."

Avoid temptation:

"Recognize the form in which temptation comes, and how it works. Remember that there are two Maasaws, and know the characteristics of each. Temptation always wears a guise that is deceiving. It wants us to believe it is not what it actually is. This is but one aspect of its sly approach. Do not be tempted into anything that will harm your way of life, get you into trouble, or produce problems. Even though temptation is evil, desire is strong within us and hard to control. As we pass into the worlds of different ideas, temptation will weaken us. Avoiding temptation is a key to survival. If you cannot escape new changes, use them wisely. Don't let them destroy the valuable elements in your life.

"Temptation is dangerous. It can destroy. Each of the previous worlds was destroyed by temptation. It is this law that is producing the troubles and unrest throughout the world today. Anything that glitters with charm and lures one to promises and gain is temptation. It might not bring immediate harm, but it leads to slow decline and even death.

"The wisdom of Hopi tells us that **we are like a string of beads,** all united. As time passes people will begin to unstring themselves from this true life line. When they see or hear temptations of pleasure and gain, the beads on the string will decrease in numbers. The string will become shorter until only a few with strong wills will be left hanging onto the life line to pursue their destiny as laid out by Massau and the Great Spirit. There will be a great joy if they achieve this goal. This will purify the land to peaceful ways of life. But if they fail it will be up to the Great Creator through nature to do to us what we deserve."

Avoid Pitfalls:

"Avoid Pitfalls: We often step into these very traps because we think they will improve our lives. On the contrary, they can drain our mind and strength. Deceit is common among world leaders. Advantageous lifestyles often lead us astray. Modern concepts will not help balance the natural order on earth and in the universe. Pitfalls are experiences that teach us facts of life, such as that life is not always a path of roses."

Listen to your elders:

"Listen to your elders, and you will learn that Divine laws and religion are important. At one time Hopi learned wisdom, knowledge, and prophecy through their elders in order to live wisely. It is a pity in these changing times, that they hear no more, see no more, nor do they understand. Yet these wise teachings are the key to happiness and health.

"The Hopi tribe, both progressive and traditionals, are now entering the most critical period of their long history on this land. It is time now for each village the Hopi people must **recall and reflect on the prophecies** handed down from our elders which are the instructions, guidelines and historical bases for this period of time."

Be Self-sufficient:

"Be Self-sufficient so that you are not dependent upon others for survival. Don't rely on supermarkets for food and don't be entirely dependent upon wages. What will happen to you if some day the White man's world collapses?"

Prepare in advance:

"Take time to review what has happened to you and try to predict what might happen during the coming year. Once you have done this, ask yourself how you will handle each thing that does occur. The ancient Native Americans followed a ritual calendar that forced them to think ahead and prepare in advance, so that they would not be caught unprepared. If you examine the Hopi ceremonial and subsistence cycles, you will see that they follow a progression of steps that help them prepare in advance. While they are doing this, they pray for guidance to the Creator, Maasaw, Mother Earth, and other helper deities."

Use ancient teachings as a guideline:

"We look upon our ancient teachings as a guideline used in order to avoid a downfall for our mistakes. We have learned that through our conduct we can accomplish good and bad deeds. The old ones say that we have gone through at least three world catastrophes and each world was destroyed by the same error in man."

Protect the laws of nature and spirit. Respect all living things.

"We must carry on our purpose to protect the laws of nature and spirit which is our highest priority. Others think that what they're doing is harmless. We think they are destroying the link between Nature and Man. The signs of warning are evident in many parts of the world. We all are to be blamed, for we are abusing our Mother Earth by our mindless actions and by our irresistible urge to better our way through our own inventive thinking. We have forsaken the warnings of our ancient fathers, gradually leading ourselves to ruin. We all should hang our heads in shame. What we say will pain most people, but we hope it will help them to understand themselves and reverse their ways toward better behavior for the good of lesser man and for the survival of our world for coming generations. We have learned and believe that one cannot communicate with Nature unless your existence and behavior are in harmony with the will of the Great Spirit, that he who knows his heart will also find his way in the future.

"Bahannas think everything is wonderful under the name of ecology. They think all things such as earth and heavenly bodies will last forever, but we know we have only one sun, moon and earth. If any of these were destroyed, replacing the balance would be impossible. For years our founding fathers have passed the knowledge of survival from mouth to mouth to respect all living things, for we are all one and created by one. It seems we have forgotten the concept of the right way of survival. Instead we have replaced survival and its way to be gotten with defensiveness. We are going steadily downhill to ruins; we mean all men on earth. We must skid to a stop for a moment and look around. There might be an old dried-up root visible near you; get hold of it for support until you see the light."

By "defensiveness," the Elders mean that the current tactic for survival is to be defensive. That is, to defend whatever is said or done rather than to examine the position. Governments and people alike behave like bulldogs. Once a position is taken, they hold on to it for dear life, defending it rather than evaluating it to see whether or not it ought to be modified or completely changed.

Don't try to control others:

"Trading blame drains our planet of spiritual energy and causes great harm to all land and life. Don't try to control others. The spirit dwells within all of us."

Be satisfied with the Pattern of Life given to us by our Great Creator:

"Be satisfied with the order of our Great Creator, whose light does not blind us and does not lead us into confusion. Instead, His light brightens the road, so that we can absorb its great wisdom and live like humans. . . . Perhaps there is still time for this land to live on under the laws of our Great Spirit and our Great Creator. These are the things we desire. We are very sad for our life of today; it is heading down the direction you have created for us. The tide is gathering, and the high tide which sweeps us away may not be far off."

In connection with the warnings, I want to include an overview of some of the alarming things that are happening in the world today. Doing this bothers me a little, because self-styled "positive" experts are scolding the "negative" environmental and population experts who are sounding the alarm today. These positive people say that where the environment and population explosion are concerned, the negative people are exaggerating their claims and not telling the truth. The fact is, they say, that all of these situations being lamented are either not as bad as is claimed, or are being taken care of by governments and industries, so that they will never become doomsday problems.

So I want to acknowledge both sides, and I think you should do the same, being aware of the positive as well as the negative. Neither Dan nor I would want you to follow the instructions for anything other than the best reasons. You should not do it because you are frightened by the prophecies, or are persuaded unfairly. You should not do it because you think you can gain the Creator's favor by giving the INSTRUCTIONS a try. They will only work for you and for the world when they are followed with conviction and for the right reasons.

At the same time, when problems do exist, I think it is good sense to admit it and deal with them, rather than to act as though there aren't any, especially where the welfare of the planet is concerned. I do not think it is negative to face up to situations and accept truth where it exists. We are, after all, not dealing with insignificant matters here. So why is it negative, or evidence of a doomsday mentality, to face up to them? To do otherwise would be remiss, and has already resulted in terrible harm to the earth and ourselves. I remind you that the Hopi prophecies are not doomsday in nature. The Hopi prophecies are designed to deliver us by pointing us to instructions and warnings that will affect our present and future in the best possible way. Would people prefer to be caught unprepared? They offer people the world over an opportunity to survive.

Nevertheless, while you read my comments about the critical situations that exist in the world today, keep in the back of your mind what the "moderate" people are saying about them. Ultimately, you will need to make your own decision as to what you want to believe and commit your life to.

If you would like a thorough presentation of this "moderate" view, I recommend an up-to-date book edited by Ronald Bailey. It is *The True State of the Planet,* and presents the views of "Ten of the World's Premier Environmental Researchers in a Major Challenge to the Environmental Movement."

In this publication, first-wave environmentalists, those who started the movement in 1970, are labeled "doomsayers." At the opposite extreme are the more recent "cornucopians," who argue that humanity faces no real problems; technological and institutional advances have made, and will continue to make, it possible to address any shortages. The distinguished authors contributing to the book call themselves the "middle-of-the-roaders." I will call them the "moderates." They believe that the statistics used by the doomsayers have not been reliable, and, in consequence, have led to wild exaggerations setting off alarms that are not warranted. They also believe the cornucopians go too far in the opposite direction. Up to a particular point, their arguments are persuasive, although not entirely convincing. That point is the unreliability of human nature where agreement and cooperation are concerned. We might have the capacity to solve many of the planet's problems, but our probability of achieving this with current attitudes is virtually nil. Arriving at solutions on paper is one thing, implementing them is another. The moderates have great faith in technology and institutions, but they offer nothing where total human involvement is concerned. When profits are the primary motivation, the affluent segment of society is not likely to solve everything for everyone.

This is exactly where the INSTRUCTIONS and WARNINGS come in. If the new attitude of one-ness and peace were to spread all over the world, then everyone would work together to accomplish what is otherwise not solvable. Is not the idea of everyone—rich or poor, extraordinary or ordinary, pitching in and

David Monongye

feeling truly worthwhile and good about it—an exceptional one? This, of course, is precisely what the Creator told the Hopi at their Oraibi beginning. He was offering them, along with everyone else in the world, the way to work together to affect the pace, intensity, and violence of the closing down of the Fourth Cycle.

The Elders show us that, where solutions are concerned, the bad side of human nature is the cause of the world's dilemma. How then is this nature likely to be the source of solutions unless it is transformed? Only then will there be hope that environmental and population problems can be ended, or at least blunted to a significant degree.

How do the Elders know when prophesied events are about to happen? The following passages from the newsletters answer this question. They tell us that the Elders watch the behavior of numerous things, but particularly that of human beings:

"We have said that Hopi predictions have no positive set date, but the Hopi have ways of seeing the coming future. That is, by watching the natural balance of the earth, humans, and the behavior and activities of the wild species. We know they have a power of sensibility in detecting dangerous or pleasant surroundings. **The most important factor we were instructed to watch is mankind because he will become the most mindless and heedless foe of earth and nature.** Therefore mankind is our chief source of information for seeing into the future, for seeing that in time he would reach his desired goal through his actions and deeds. Gradually he will decide the future of the world by lowering the important value of the Creator's law. Whether actions in ignoring the Creator's laws will bring prosperity or disaster for mankind, man believes he can solve the world problems to better our way and bring peace.

"Since all men are created as sacred, as humans we were placed upon this earth for a purpose. That is, to take care of the land and protect the earth from harm and to enjoy all the things it offers for a long time to come. On the other hand, if we fail to live up to this law of creation the consequences will be that we lose the land. This is the Universal Planned Structure laid out by our Great Creator.

"As we look on, many things have begun to happen and change rapidly. Through the behavior and attitudes of mankind, old-fashioned ideas the world over are tossed by the wayside as new generations go marching into the future with their technological know-how. We admit it creates many advantages, but, on the other hand, has its effect on our way of life. At this stage our lifestyle and food is not the same as it has been in years past. Farms have declined. Many of our religious ceremonials have vanished. What is left is losing its value and power rapidly as old religious leaders pass on. We trust those with open minds will understand that this means our good ways of life are near the end for our future children to enjoy.

"The present crises of world events is an unfoldment of life cycles which we set in motion through our own behavior. This has caused an imbalance which will bring many problems. We have learned that when people reach great numbers and become highly civilized, soon the people will become a burden upon each other. This creates disharmony, power struggles, conflicts, and wars."

We see here one of the few references in the newsletters to population growth, and to the problems it causes.

"This world is in a terribly confused mess and faces grave danger. Almost all people are now without a genuine moral sense and spiritual discernment. . . . There is almost no limit to hurt people cause each other. . . . Sex and physical expression is their major, fundamental, stumbling block. Along with the pursuit of money, etc. and is the fundamental basis for the varied lying and hypocrisy. . . . **There is very little that can be done at this time to change people. There is very little that can be done to correct the spiritual confusion, or contradictions, in this civilization.** Only through ultimate disaster has the situation of so many errors, seen and unseen, the possibility of being made straight.

"Here in a brief glance is **how Hopi see the coming events**. Although the Hopi do not have a definite day or year when certain extraordinary events will occur, all we can say is, maybe in your life, maybe in your children's lives or their children's. Our views concerning the evidence we see today around the world seems similar to Hopi Land's situation, a world of madness. Hopi have the proud name 'Peaceful' which they seem to forget. What is happening around the world is disturbing. We see immorality flourishing, corruption everywhere. Men in high places promoting mighty still more destructive instruments of war which threaten to wipe out the world and its people. We see the abuse of the earth for its resources, for wealth and power and for destructive purposes. By doing so polluting the air, water, and land, depleting the soil where once all plants grew healthy. Drying up and destroying the forests. The earth's wonderful numbers of life species becoming extinct because of man's carelessness. **The result is the old, original natural order is disturbed causing climate changes to descend upon all parts of the country. We think our ancients are right. Perhaps we are now entering a new phase of life.**"

Does anything that is happening or portended here in the outside world support the Hopi prophecies? Since some of their prophecies are similar to those offered by prophets who are called doomsayers by the moderates, I assume they would call the Hopi doomsayers too. To make this charge, however, would raise an interesting problem. We know that the Hopi claim they are not the originators of the prophecies—the Creator is. Should we then call the Creator a doomsayer? That would present a challenging dilemma, don't you think? Doomsayers are people who aren't supposed to know what they are talking about. Would we want to make the same accusation about the Creator?

Are there things in the works that could propel us into Armageddon? Have you thought about this and seriously examined the world scene?

Factionalism is the mode at Hotevilla Village today. The prophecies predicted another split like that of 1906, and the split has occurred. Throughout the world, national divisions are also prevalent. Twenty-four nations are at war, either internally, or with one another. The Bosnian war threatens to spill over and engulf a good-sized chunk of Europe. Some pundits are saying it might even be the beginning of World War III. Several nations are rattling their sabres. China, the one prophecy points to as the real threat, has turned belligerent. All of us are making book that no nation is going to be so insane as to start a major war. But in truth the catalyst will be what some nation perceives as a threat from some other. Once a minor war begins, it is strange to see the ways in which the attitudes of the combatants change. Day by day, the problem builds until it defies control. Hate and anger work on human psyches in ways we never anticipate.

War speedily gives birth to abnormal and irresponsible behavior. The Bosnian Serbs and the factions of Rowanda are prime examples of this truth. In war, genocide becomes acceptable, even expected, behavior. People don't foresee paying a price for it. Without war, we strive for decency. With war, somewhere a line is crossed that seems to project us like a slingshot pellet into senseless mayhem. We dropped bombs on Hiroshima and Nagasaki, the consequences of which still numb our consciences fifty years later. But the vile treatment the Japanese were meting out to our soldiers and civilians who were prisoners in the regions they controlled, plus more deaths on the battlefield, made continuing the war for even another day absolutely intolerable. During wartime, the folks at home are not really innocents. They have endorsed the war. They know what is going on. They pay for it, and they are supplying the soldiers who are at the front. I found it interesting to hear a beleaguered Serbian woman say on television that she knew about the terrible things Serbian soldiers were doing to Muslims. Yet she never expected that this same thing would happen to her when Croatia ran the Serbs out of their stronghold.

None of this is an argument in favor of using nuclear weapons. Because of what it does to people, it is an argument against war under any circumstances. The Hopi Traditionalists tell us we should solve things through peaceful means. The instructions themselves are peaceful ways to do this. It is something we should think about before the worst of the struggles begin as the prophecies are fulfilled. If we fail to build a brotherhood on the Ark before then, our circumstances will be bitter ones indeed.

WHAT WE NEED TO DO IS CHANGE THE ATTITUDE OF PEOPLE THE WORLD OVER. AND, THIS ATTITUDE HAS TO START SOMEWHERE, SO LET IT BEGIN WITH US AS WE FOLLOW THE INSTRUCTIONS.

To say this is one thing, to accomplish it is another. All of us want to go on and have nothing change, except perhaps where it changes for the better. Even when the fog thickens and we hear the deep-throated warnings coming from the fog horns of other ships, we still don't want to slow down. Governments can excuse anything they do by omission or commission. They no longer face up to situations, they face away from them. With rare exceptions, I haven't seen anything other than a politician's backside since Kennedy faced down the Russians and Fidel Castro. The Gulf War was really a skirmish, and a lop-sided one at that. Look at the difficulties the United Nations has experienced in handling its responsibilities in the Bosnian conflict.

I find it noteworthy that even those whose financial interests are best served by glossing over bad news are being forced to do the opposite today. The Strategic Investment Company of Baltimore, Maryland, just published a thirty-two-page brochure based on the premise that we should use our opportunities to make large amounts of money. We can do this by capitalizing upon the terrible misfortunes that are in the process of overcoming society on a global scale. The authors are not people with environmental interests. They are capitalists who see the handwriting on the wall, and who have made some impressive predictions about world trends in the past. They envision a coming World War which is already in its preliminary stage in Europe. It could continue on from its present 3,000-mile front that already includes Bosnia, Chechnya and Russia. They see this as a worldwide showdown between the Muslim world and the Christian West: "It could turn into a nuclear war."

Beyond this, the Strategic Investment people forecast great changes in leadership, with private armies in control of nations, and a global breakdown in the next few years. Financial chaos is at the top of the list. They tell us that the world has not turned out the way experts expected after the freeing of Europe. It was supposed to become a wonderful place. Instead, these countries have "come unglued." The world is "becoming like Colombia and Sicily—a corrupt, violent no-man's land dominated by gangs and the politicians they've paid off."

The following quoted material fits the Hopi prophecies quite well: "Austria is being plagued by right-wing terrorism."

Bombings are common. The Scripps Howard News Service of January 6, 1996, notes a study by a conservative think tank that says, "Recent drops in serious crime are but the lull before the coming crime storm. . . ." There is a "demographic bulge of young, highly crime-prone males being raised in poverty and neglect. The study calls for immediate changes, or forecasts a nation beset with a worsening crime problem early in the 21st century. . . . Americans face a frightening future in which teenage wolf packs roam the streets, inner-city gangsters spread into the suburbs and hardened criminals waltz out of prisons to prey on innocents."

The proliferation of powerful weapons is sufficient to alarm governments all over the world. Russia admits that her "protective" walls around her nuclear supplies are like a sieve through which nations everywhere are being supplied. We don't even know how many nations have the capability to make nuclear missiles, but we do know there are enough to mount a major threat in the years just ahead. Iran alone can use hers to block the entrance to the gulf that our carriers used to get to Iraq. The unhappy truth is that the kickoff to the final war could come from anywhere at anytime.

Natural and unnatural disasters fit the prophecy picture perfectly. What they predicted would happen before now has happened. In looking at the Hopi prophecies, there is not a single instance where a prophecy that should have been fulfilled by now has not been. But the worst of the prophecies lie ahead of us. If this thought causes you to shudder, I hope I have made it clear that the Creator knows man's nature too well to waste time attempting to frighten us into living as we should. He knows that moderates and cornucopians will always be with us to caution us against going overboard in what we do. He knows a lot of us won't believe these things will happen until they have. But we need to be warned about worrisome things that are taking place in the world today, and I want to mention enough of them to assure you that the Hopi prophecies are not out of line with what is going on.

As the Hopi tribe grows, its troubles grow with it. Is there a population microcosm in this? Some scholars quickly point out to us that social ills have been a problem for as long as records have been kept. They contend that the means of killing and maiming have changed, but that deaths by some means have always been with us. There is, however, a vast difference in the total number of people involved. Arguably, we see more killings in a day now than there were people at some early points in time. Ten percent of 500 is considerably less than ten percent of 5,000,000. And while we could say that there once was a time when civilization could have wiped itself out with clubs, there has never been a period before this when we also had the capability of killing the entire earth. We cannot solve the problems of today and tomorrow by claiming that things are only the way they have always been, hence we can conclude they are just as solvable now as they were then. The numbers of people involved and their perceived needs also complicates what must be done and the amount of time needed to change anything. We are not able to do this as quickly as we once did. Millennia ago humans could subsist on what grew naturally. Today it takes megatons of food to supply Los Angeles alone. We can apply the same factor to every problem that exists. Once people could sit down with their neighbors who lived in the cave next door and thrash out a problem face to face. Now they have to deal with federal and state governments, local boards and regulations, and neighbors in every direction, before the neighbor they want to deal with can even be approached. That is why whole new "attitudes" and not political interests, are our best hope.

"Once a week, that's all we ask," the television commercial goes, and once a week—at least it seems that way—we hear about an earthquake that has hit somewhere on the globe, magnitudes ranging as high as 7.8 on the Richter Scale. Bigger ones are predicted by the experts. The Hopi prophecies say that earthquakes will even come to the midwest. Texas had a pretty good one this year.

What about volcanic eruptions? The Philippine islands have had some huge ones, and Mexico is not far behind. At this moment on the lush Caribbean island of Montserrat, residents are near panic, as a volcano there is threatening its first major eruption in thousands of years. Already shuddering and spewing gas and ash, one small explosion alone blacked out the sky for nearly half an hour. What does a full venting portend for the planet? Byproducts of the impending eruption are constant earthquakes. Ash is also covering a Nicaraguan volcano area. The wells are filled with sand and 6,000 people don't have anything to eat. Leon, a city of 150,000 people fifteen miles away, is also being threatened. Scientists are being brought in to begin tests to determine if and when a full-scale eruption will occur.

What have hurricanes done recently? There is not a person who pays attention to the news who does not know about the wanton burning and logging of forests crucial to the earth's well-being, not to mention the alarming loss of species that is taking place. Acid rain from industry is another problem. *The Los Angeles Times* carried an article about beech trees in New York forests thought restored after acid rain ceased to decimate them, yet now are being assailed by a worse plague. It seems that a certain insect bores holes in the bark into which a fungus enters to plant a disease that kills the tree. Acid rain, it turns out, poisons the tree roots and contaminates the soil. Then, in both cases, the dead trees give off heat that jacks up the already overheating atmosphere.

The bizarre and the unexpected keep happening. In the Florida swamps mutations are appearing that would do justice to a science fiction film. Male alligators are being born with female organs. Mammals and fish are strangely misshapen. In the north country last year, thousands of animals were stricken stone-blind in one night.

Viruses once thought to be a thing of the past are strolling nonchalantly by the antibiotics that until now easily subdued them.

In 1993, a plague called hantavirus began to haunt the southwestern states, and has since spread west from there. It still centers in Navajo and Hopi Land. Contaminated mice are carrying a virus that, when passed on to human beings, kills those who are infected within a few days. Is this a microcosm?

How many of you have read *The Hot Zone* by Richard Preston? It chronicles in a horrifying way how abused forests are striking back at us by releasing rapidly mutating viruses that enter human beings and cause them to decompose in hideous ways in a matter of days. He calls it "the revenge of the Rain Forest." Worst of all is his detailing of how easily these plagues can spread overnight through urban contacts and the miracle of modern travel. This is not fiction. Film makers are obtaining some of their most ghastly ideas by simply watching what is happening in actual life. As the world population increases, the hazards multiply. "If," the World Health officials add, "this had gotten started in Kinshasa instead of Kikwit, it could have caused havoc in the health system there and easily hopped airlines around Africa and even to the U.S. It might not have been contained easily even in American hospitals. In general, industrialized countries have been letting down their guard in public health, even as new threats emerge like the hantavirus, Lyme disease, and HIV. Poor sanitation is a global threat."

Unkillable "super bugs," the most lethal microbes that resist all known drugs, are stirring fears among health care experts. The Associated Press, on September 19, 1995, tells us that this was the No. 1 topic among the 12,000 infectious-disease experts at the Interscience Conference on Antimicrobial Agents and Chemotherapy.

The Scripps Howard News Services of October 17, 1995, reports the World Health Organization as saying that a smaller, less sanitary world is increasingly threatened by a host of new and resurgent diseases. "An outbreak of disease anywhere must now be perceived as a threat to all countries, and despite many warnings we are not yet fully equipped to contain them."

It is unfortunate that we are unable to handle the lethal microbes the way we do plant and animal species. It is custom now to destroy them at will. Latest reports have it that humans are destroying animal and plant species at an alarming rate. The United Nation's first comprehensive report on the world's fading biodiversity says nearly 30,000 species are threatened with extinction. In addition, there is a loss of genes, habitats, and ecosystems that represent the very foundation of human existence: "Yet by our heedless actions we are eroding this biological capital at an alarming rate." In just four centuries, 484 animal and 654 recorded plant species have become extinct.

That a population explosion is underway is a well documented fact. The world population doubled to 2.5 billion between 1850 and 1950. In the next 40 years it grew to 5.6 billion. The moderates think that controls are in place and are effective, that the population will never reach its predicted numbers, and that even if it should statistics prove that there will be enough food. They emphasize that as the population has grown, production has grown, and that health and affluence has improved with it.

Other officials—the doomsayers—say world population will reach 11.9 billion by the year 2050, and argue that we by no means have shown that agricultural expansion can handle it. The Associated Press reports that the world's population grew in 1995 by 100 million people, to 5.75 billion, the largest increase ever.

Earlier, I pointed out that overpopulation is not a factor that is given special treatment in Hopi prophecy, and speculated as to why this might be so. The "ifs" of Hopi prophecy always apply. Depending upon the choices the world nations make, the population explosion could continue, and the expected totals could be reached. It takes very little brilliance to calculate what problems can arise if this happens. We have significant shortages of some things in some places already. What will they be then? How old are you? Will you be around to face the situation that might exist in twenty-five years? thirty-five years? fifty years? If the world does not self-destruct before then, my wife and two sons will be here to experience every potentially ugly stage of it. The thought of that almost numbs me. I don't even want to consider it. The moderates say that even the Third World countries are making remarkable progress in birth control. The ways this is being achieved are not always commendable. China is not Third World anymore, but her human rights and birth control methods still leave something to be desired. Abortions and other birth control methods are coerced by government agencies, and the BBC just reported in a documentary that in government orphanages, "worthless girl children" are being starved to death. Would a country with attitudes like this find global war a problem or an opportunity?

Revolutions are underway in a number of countries. You must have noticed in the Hopi prophecies that world revolution is forecast. Ordinary people are going to rise up against their leaders, and leaders will contest against other leaders. Who, if the previously mentioned financial interests are correct, will actually be doing the leading? The entire picture is a terrifying one. Yet that is precisely where we are either heading, or already are. What do you think will stop it, if indeed it can be stopped? And, how do we adjust to this so as to remain in control of ourselves? How many tons of Dramamine do we want to take? It seems to me that the INSTRUCTIONS and WARNINGS ought to be looking more promising to everyone by the minute.

Planetwise, birth control has made some progress but not nearly enough. Food production methods are being tested on a limited scale by private groups, but where do we find programs in place that will accommodate ten billion people? I search the media for answers and so far I haven't found any. How much lead time do we need to be able to meet the problems when they arrive? The moderates are positive in their projections, but admit that there is no accurate method for forecasting the future rate of population growth anywhere in the world. In other words, they can be no more sure of their position than the doomsayers can. So if we are going to err, which side should it be on?

But the INSTRUCTIONS and WARNINGS are not uncertain. They have worked with the Hopi Traditionalists for a thousand years. If they will work for us, wouldn't we rather use them than face the alternatives?

The *San Francisco Examiner* of September 14, 1995, reveals that the present ozone hole over Antarctica is about the size of Europe and will be the size of the United States within weeks. It is twice as big as it was at this time last year. "Scientists with a climate advisory panel to the Clinton administration announced earlier this month their belief that 'global warming' was at least partly caused by human pollution."

Paul Recer, in the Associated Press of October 25, 1995, says that an International Panel, including scientists from many countries, reported to their governments that as a result of global warming over the next 100 years, "Vast lands will flood, some people may starve, glaciers will melt and deserts could expand and turn more extreme. . . . Scientists from more than 30 nations said that global warming, triggered in part by human activity, will cause a 2-to-6 degree Fahrenheit rise in average surface temperature, melt a third of the Earth's glaciers, and cause a sea level rise of one-half foot to 3 feet by the year 2100. . . . Poor countries already stressed from hot climates, deserts and marginal agricultural production are apt to suffer the most."

Another newspaper features an article that says the ozone layer and ozone hole has reached a maximum point (whatever that is), and that, while the nations of the world have agreed to stop making the chlorofluorocarbons that cause the problem by the end of the century, the danger will continue for at least another fifty years. That is, naturally, *if* all of the nations keep their word.

This last, really, is where the crux of the matter lies. Talk is one thing. Action is another. The *Riverside Press Enterprise* reported that on April 7, 1995, United Nations Climate Conference delegations agreed to share technologies for battling global warming with poor countries. They admitted at the same time that few of the twenty-four nations who, in 1992, voluntarily agreed to limit their emissions of carbon dioxide, and other gases that cause global warming to 1990 levels by 2000, were on target to meet their goals. But some scientists say that if emissions are not cut deeper after the turn of the century, carbon dioxide concentrations will double by 2050: "The atmosphere would then warm up by as much as 8 degrees Fahrenheit, causing sea levels to rise, flooding coastal cities and island nations. Ecosystems would be destroyed and agriculture disrupted." The same article also caught my attention when it said that China, emerging for the first time as a key player, and India—the two most populous nations in the world—rejected calls for meeting the new goals.

The moderates tell us that we can relax about this one. They say the ozone problem is a dubious question. It may not really exist. Economic growth and technological progress will be the solution to environmental degradation. Even though "millions" of people in Third Worlds are being consigned to "squalid and untimely" deaths, the situation will inevitably improve as cleaner environments become more affordable. In light of what the investment analysts are saying, and considering the nature of humankind, do you find this moderate view comforting? If the moderates are correct and there is no ozone problem we need worry about, I wish they would tell us what is happening when all of these chemicals are being pumped into the sky all over the globe every day. Do all of these invasive tons of gases do nothing to the atmosphere?

The flooding in the United States, Europe, and China has certainly gotten everyone's attention this year. The amount of rain has been prodigious in some places. People who have lived for a long time in the areas that have been flooded keep shaking their heads and saying they have never before seen anything like it. Wildfires in areas previously flooded seem to be breaking out in proportions that are frightening too. Here in California, after the fires, come the massive mudslides that scrape houses off of the cliff sides the way a mason trowels his cement. Hotevilla hasn't had any of these problems. Maybe it would be too much to expect the microcosm principle to apply to everything. But we still have some time ahead of us. Who knows what strange things are yet to come up there on the mesa as the cycle closes down?

Is the prophesied melting of polar ice caps a legitimate threat? There is no shortage of ice in the polar regions, and while it is roundly attacked as a groundless theory, the greenhouse effect has not gone away. Rising heat levels cause scientists to shuffle their feet and look askance at one another. If it lasts long enough, they test ice samples to see what precedents there have been for occasions like this. Usually, they come up with something that comforts them. Then, when the globe cools down a little, they sigh deeply and return to solving industry's needs.

Who can say that the warriors who sit on the heads of the giant water serpents have not shifted their positions enough to let the serpents stir to tell us that, where Mother Earth and the environment is concerned, we had better behave ourselves? But like the White Agent Yukiuma would like to have told the secret to, many of us are too intelligent, aren't we, to believe there are actually two water serpents at the poles. Yet something moves the caps. Do we know what that something actually is? And, might that something not, in a changing chemical composition, uncoil like a serpent and stir things up? It would not surprise me in the least if science discovered one day that something in the atmosphere causes built-up ice to stir in a coil-like motion until it explodes. The prophecies of the Hopi may be fable-like in nature, but they contain truths that are surprising in their accuracy.

Water is a popular subject on the forecast list. Even the moderates admit that we have serious problems in this area. Some countries are already experiencing serious shortages of drinkable water. The Elderly Elders see this as another proof of the microcosm Hotevilla and Hopi Land represents. As I have pointed out, it is going dry too. This being the case, we can expect the problem to grow as Hopi Land's does. Whether we recognize it or not, the Peabody Mine and Las Vegas are doing it to all of us. Another foolish thought? Of course it is. We know, don't we, that there must be a more rational and scientific explanation as to why what happens in the world parallels what is happening in Hotevilla? I mean, the termination of the village surely has nothing to do with the termination of Bosnia or wherever else we might mention. Or does it? I am not being snide in asking this question. The microcosm principle is as much a part of Hopi prophecy as anything else is.

Many of the wells in Hopi Land are polluted. Today's *Riverside Press Enterprise*, August 7, 1995, carries an article headlined, "World Bank Warns of Water Crisis." It explains that, unless current trends are reversed, we have a worsening water crisis around the planet. While water is abundant many places in the world, some eighty countries are experiencing shortages serious enough to threaten agriculture. With population increases, the demand will grow rapidly. Meanwhile the supply that does exist is being contaminated by industry, domestic waste, and farm chemicals. "The experts all agree that we need to do something fast," the article warns. But the main problem is the lack of political will to carry out recommendations. Central to this is the projected cost to deal with this problem—$600 billion over the next decade. The World Bank will loan up to $40 billion. After that? Who will come up with the $560 billion?

Might it not be helpful for some persistent newsperson to total up all of the billions needed to repair the various kinds of pollution residues that already exist in the world, let alone those that are yet to come? To my knowledge, all that has been done so far is to treat one problem at a time as though they were isolated from one another. They are not isolated. Their effect is cumulative. The individual circumstances do need investigation, but the sum total is what matters. Should this figure ever be arrived at, I suspect it will amount to more money than anyone in the world will part with, and day after day we are adding to the debt.

Jacques Cousteau makes a pungent comment when he says, "You clean up a polluted river. It makes you feel good. But these are just symptoms of our sickness. We are taking aspirin against pollution. . . . I live day to day, and for the future, not the past. But this is not politics, my friend. I'm not a socialist. I'm not a republican. I'm nothing. I'm only fighting for the future of humankind, whatever it will be."

Are any of the countries affected likely to make trouble when their own is threatened with extinction? Will all of them let their people die of thirst or hunger, while some of us have plenty to eat and drink, and even to waste? Which countries are we referring to where the water shortage and purity is a problem—Northern China, Southern India, western South America, Pakistan, Mexico, the Middle East, North Africa, sub-saharan-Africa, and central Asia? Wouldn't you agree there are some pretty good candidates for troublemakers in the bunch? At least two of them are already known to have nuclear weapons.

All of this is jelling, and, in the face of it, global industry continues to build its dream house of spectacular years to come. They gloss over the damage they have done and are doing to the world and to the atmosphere, and regale us instead with fables of what life will be like in the aeons ahead. Computers will operate everything. We hear boggling words like cyberspace, killer applications, Internet, relationship dynamics, interaction, and virtual reality. We are told that we are going to do our business and our banking with our computers. At regular intervals we are treated to sumptuous descriptions of cities of the future, and of life in space or on some planet millions of miles away. They actually believe all of these things are going to happen big time, and that anyone's prophecies of the contrary are a bunch of rubbish. So too are the cries of the environmentalists and the harbingers of population explosion. Just relax folks, they say. We will take care of you as soon as we have time to get around to it, or at least as soon as it is economically feasible. Have to make a profit you know! Forget all of these unhappy things that are going on in the world. Everything will work out just fine. Seeing themselves as more invincible in real life than Hollywood characters are in robot movies, they cloister around their board room tables and plot the future for all of us. They do not listen to doomsayers. They actually believe all of these things they are working on are going to happen big time, and that prophecies are a bunch of rubbish. Why are they so sure? Do they know something we don't? If so, I wish they would tell us in terms we can understand and rely on. Do you suppose they are working on a way to protect themselves while the rest of us go down?

They could be right in their indifference to the problems and the prophecies. Then again, they also could be wrong. What have they done and what are they doing that gives us reasons to trust them? Do we really want to leave this situation in their hands when we have such a wonderful other way to go?

Where understanding the ecology is concerned, the moderate people are calling for a new middle road to be established. This will be a road that acknowledges that while society must have strict ecological standards, it must also be aware that nature is resilient and has been around for a long time. It will also acknowledge that most environmental trends in the United States and in Western Europe are positive. Air and water are being made cleaner at a spectacular pace. Complacency is a thing of the past.

Don't people who are pointing this out to us think we wish the problem were limited to the U. S. and Western Europe, so that we could indeed relax about it?

The middle-of-the-roaders have some ground to stand on. But they should know better than to imply that industry has done what it has done voluntarily. On the contrary, it stalls for as long as it can before it moves, and only then takes action when government sanctions are threatened or applied. It would also reduce our concerns if items like the following did not appear in the newspapers: "The U.N. food agency is alarmed by a U.S. decision to cut its international food aid by half." Donations to feed the world's hungry have reached their lowest level in a decade. It is estimated that 800 million people are chronically undernourished, and despite technical advances, the figure will only drop to 730 million by 2010. Does this sound like we intend to keep up with world demands?

Add to this sobering truth the point already made about nations who make pledges but fail to reach their goals. There are some experts who suspect that they never intended to reach the goals in the first place. There is little problem in signing a document you intended to forget before you came to the meeting. This is the way it was with the treaties the U.S. Government made with the Native American tribes. The Government officials never intended to keep their word in the first place. A tragic price has been paid for this. Where the environment is concerned, because of double-talk, many scientists feel we have already passed the point of no return, that it is just a matter of time until we pay the ultimate price.

How do the optimists explain those prophecies of the Hopi and Nostradamus that have already been fulfilled? And where is that invisible cut-off point when the optimists think the prophecies will conveniently stop happening, so that we will not need to face the worst of them in the years ahead?

I will answer this last question for you. There is no cut-off point. There are only the possibilities of tempering and delay. We can slow it down—perhaps even for a long time to come—but we cannot stop it. And unless the industrial giants surprise the

Elders and me by coming aboard the Spiritual Ark soon, they will not be the ones who will purchase the time we need to change the pace, intensity, and awesome closing of the Fourth Cycle. Would that they would come aboard. The Creator could use their talents. But history does not indicate that is likely. It will be lesser people who will put first things first and see that the job gets done with no denial, no weaseling, and no self-indulgence. That is why the responsibility has been given to us and not to them, just as it was first given to the Hopi, and not to some prosperous European nation.

Meanwhile, what I tell you in Chapter 11 makes this truth resoundingly clear. The countdown continues, and to get our attention, the Elders tell us a story that relates to our situation:

"The story we are about to tell may seem to be a legendary tale, but one does not have to look very far to find that this story is real. In the past our ancient ones lived at a time when people were at a highly civilized stage. Greed and corruption were at their peak of controlling the so-called 'lesser grade of man.' Leaders and priests were branded with a disgusting evil. It was a time when people disregarded the Great Laws. People did as they pleased. They ignored the advice of their leaders. This was a time of sorrow and frustration, for the leaders loved and cared for the people as children. They warned them of the danger and tried many times to guide them on to the right road and repentance. There were many violent signs in the sky and earth given by nature. This was ignored with laughter, and answered that these things were only seen by lunatics who wanted to create an obstacle of fear for those seeking pleasure and wealth. Immorality and the greed for material gain continued to flourish, disrupting life for those who wished to live in peace according to the laws of the Creator.

"The Great Spirit had been watching the hearts of all Humans.

Failed by His warning to the people, He too was frustrated, sad, and felt betrayed, for His laws and instructions had been forsaken. It hurt Him to think that His own creation had turned against Him. He called together His servants of God, the controllers of the Earth and Universe. 'What will it be?' cried the Creator sadly. 'My children on Earth have betrayed the sacred vows they made with us. They now live beyond all bounds, ignoring all advice from their leader to correct themselves and get on the rightful path.' The gods were grieved, their hearts filled with sorrow and compassion for the wickedness of man, but they could only admit to the wrongs committed by the people.

"'The time has come!' they said. 'We will punish them and re-people the Earth with Humans of good hearts!' They cried and cried. The Great Judgment began. The sky darkened, the great wind began to howl. Birds and animals were first to sense the danger of truth. All creatures fled in search of refuge to the mountains and even to the cities. The people laughed in wonder at the strange behavior of the animals. The Earth and sky grew darker, the wind grew stronger, and the God of lightning lit the sky, sounding a loud thunder call. The twin warrior Gods at each of the Earth's axis released the great water serpents, who cracked the Earth, releasing the fires beneath the crust. Lightning, thunder, wind, and hail struck the people, and in awe they watched the stone of their houses and great temples crumble, falling on top of them. People panicked throughout the ruined streets. Some ran to the priests, begging, 'Oh, great ones, please help save us. We will reform!'

"'We have warned you many times,' they replied loudly. 'Nothing can be done now. The time has come for you to depart, but you all deserve one last thing: take your riches and your wealth with you and go down!'

"The scenes of the catastrophe were full of a frightening terror. The streets were strewn with ruin—corpses killed by falling debris or fear. It was not over. Nature opened up with its full force and the Earth swallowed everything in its wake.

"The catastrophe ended. The Creator's plan had been fulfilled. Spider-Woman, God of Wisdom and Knowledge, had withdrawn all her power. Those still alive had lost all reasoning and senselessly crept on all fours over hills and valleys. Some stumbled into cracks in the Earth, though still alive, their spirit was dead. They attacked each other and ate each other like animals. After many moons, the water cooled and re-seeded the Earth. The brightness returned and the Earth was re-peopled with righteous ones who were saved for the purpose of carrying on the Creator's plan.

"This story is a glimpse into the past. As for the future, what do you think? Do you want to be banished from the Earth by the same patterns as our ancient ones? We hope not, but we are now at that time that is related to the period. . . . Maybe there is a way of correcting our faults. There must be a way!!!"

There is a way. We find it in the INSTRUCTIONS and the WARNINGS. Reading further in what we are told, in the newsletters we learn that:

"Long, long ago, before Bahanna appeared on this land, our Ancient Fathers were the masters of all spiritual knowledge because they dedicated their lives to the laws of our Great Spirit, and our Great Creator. Every part of their bodies and minds was filled with wisdom and truth. They knew and understood the balance of Earth and Nature and Life. They could see into the hearts of people and into the future of humankind. They knew the function of the earthly body and the heavenly body, of the forces controlling the relationship to Life and Nature. They knew human actions are powerful, so powerful that they decide the future of humans and

earth, whether the great cycle of Nature will bring forth prosperity or disaster. So for thousands of years we have lived peaceful lives accordingly, avoiding those things which will destroy our good ways of life.

"Yes, our Ancient Fathers were masters of all spiritual knowledge and judgement for they were ordained by the breath of our Great Creator. Commissioned to bring forth the great orders and teachings in the name of the One superior of all. He from whom the prophecies and instructions were handed down to us as a guideline to live by on earth.

"It is said there is only one Great Spirit, our maker, and that we, as His children, should be one happy family. But instead of equality, we practice cast systems and class struggle, glaring at each other in greed. Most religious groups boost their particular method of attaining perfection, while downgrading and undermining others in order to govern territories and people who wish to live in peace through their own inherent beliefs. We worship one Great Spirit through many different names, and symbols of characters as varied as the lands of the earth. In this way we reach him to get our strength by his blessing.

"We have also said the earth is like a spotted fawn, the spots being areas with a certain power and purpose. We all are provided with a different vibration and frequency which is designed for communicating with the Great Spirit in order to accomplish certain life supporting functions of Natural Laws in accordance with our own customary ways.

"Aware of this Knowledge, we have no intention of forsaking the Great Spirit's words. When the first missionaries came, the Hopi was respectful and did not attempt to interfere with their religion. We trusted they had come armed with knowledge and would show the same respect by not

interfering with Hopi religion. But, as predicted by our elders, this would not be the case. It was said, only those who've made some kind of mistake in their past would forsake their original beliefs. Would join other religions in order to cleanse their spirit and go to heaven, thus escaping the Hopi underworld after death. But this would be in vain, for we have our own original path given to us by the Great Spirit from the beginning. In respect to this, the Hopi do not twist arms of others to join their flocks.

"It was very disheartening because the missionaries did not take the time to understand our culture and spiritual ways. If they had, they would have seen the Hopi believe there is one Great Spirit. Instead they used the time to convert our people from their native ways.

"Conversion can eventually bring destruction to all Humankind. Most of us Hopi have learned from our elders of the prophecy of the end . . . about a sea of water eating us up when we become converted into another religion which is not ours. If any Hopi is doubtful it can be tested, but the consequences cannot bc undone if this is set in motion."

The drawing that follows is the famous Road Plan pictograph drawn on a rock wall near Oraibi, after it was first given to the Hopi circa A.D. 1100. Since that time, it has been consulted at regular intervals by the leaders of Oraibi, and then of Hotevilla. The figure at the lower left is Maasaw, holding his familiar torch in his right hand. With his left hand he holds the reed through which the Hopi emerged onto the surface of the earth thousands of years ago. The circle to the right of the reed represents the Fourth Cycle of the world. The rectangle is the si-pa-pu, through which the emergence was completed, and the opening through which communication is maintained by all generations. The upper straight line emerging from the rectangle is the materialistic path

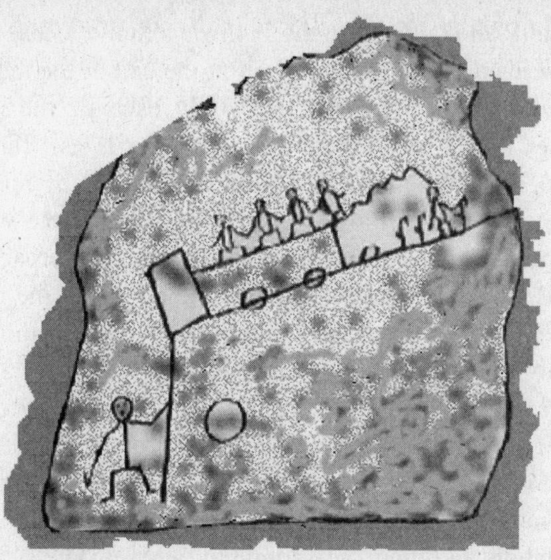

followed by many peoples. Notice that they hold hands to indicate their unified commitment to the materialistic way of life. It ends in the wavy line that indicates chaos. The lower straight line is the path the Hopi are told to follow. It is the narrow beam the Traditionalists walk. It ends at an elderly man standing in a tall cornfield. He symbolizes peace and prosperity awaiting those who remain faithful. Along this line, however, there are three circles and a vertical line. The three circles represent the prophesied major world conflicts. The first two have been fulfilled. The last one is yet to come. After the first two is the vertical line that connects the two horizontal lines. It represents the prophesied exodus of Hopi who give in to temptation, become Progressives, and abandon the ancient faith. Note that it happens before the third circle, which shows the plain fulfillment of another prophecy in its proper historical sequence. The Road Plan is both a warning and a herald of hope. It tells what should be planned for.

The Road Plan is related to the Pathways Stone whose symbols were inscribed by Maasaw himself at the end of the memorable first meeting at Oraibi. As you study each of the symbols, remember that a great deal of information is associated with each one, so that the informed Hopi leaders can, by referring to the symbols, tell their followers a long and complete story. The advantage offered by the symbol is that once this broader information is associated with it and fixed in the mind, the informed student only needs to see the symbol to call up everything that is related to it. Symbols are generally considered to be a form of primitive and limited expression, but they are actually a brilliant means of committing large amounts of information to memory. They are like a key on a computer that can call up an entire document. So Native Americans and other ancient civilizations who used symbols had their own computer system. The stone tablet of the Hopi is a laptop. The Road Plan is read like a stationary monitor.

You will notice that the symbols on the front side of the tablet are addressed to the world situation. They identify the major instigators of the paramount conflagrations that are indicated by the three circles on the Road Plan. The Hopi Traditionalist leaders identify the symbol at the upper left as the Swastika of the Nazi regime, although they also associate it with a particular poisonous plant that grows in Hopi country.

Dan Katchongva has given us the most comprehensive interpretation of the tablet symbols. It is, I think, a terrifying enough view to get everyone's attention, and especially when we know that it was prepared by Maasaw himself almost a thousand years ago. How could all of these things be known then if it were not that the Creator is their author? It is common for Native American prophecies to "get even" with the Whites by letting the natives survive when the final blow comes. The Hopi

Traditionalists are a partial exception here. While in the beginning of the supreme trials they will suffer with the rest of us, they hold open the possibility of being vindicated at the final closing of the cycle.

"We have teachings and prophecies," Katchongva says, "informing us that we must be alert for the signs and omens which will come about to give us courage and strength to stand on our beliefs. Blood will flow! Our hair and our clothing will be scattered upon the earth. Nature will speak to us with its mighty breath of wind. There will be earthquakes and floods causing great disasters, changes in the seasons and in the weather, disappearance of wildlife, and famine in different forms. There will be gradual corruption and confusion among the leaders and the people all over the world, and wars will come about like powerful winds. All of this has been planned from the beginning of creation.

"We will have three people standing behind us, ready to fulfill our prophecies when we get into hopeless difficulties: the *Meha Symbol,* which refers to a plant that has a long root, milky sap, grows back when cut off; and has a flower shaped like a *swastika,* symbolizing the four great forces of nature in motion. The *Sun Symbol.* And the *Red Symbol.* Bahanna's intrusion into the Hopi way of life will set the *Meha Symbol* in motion, so that certain people will work for the four great forces of nature (the four directions: the controlling forces, the original force) which will rock the world into war. When this happens we will know that our prophecies are coming true. We will gather strength and stand firm.

"This great movement will fail, but because its subsistence is milk, and because it is controlled by the four forces of nature, it will rise again to put the world in motion, creating another war, in which both the *Meha* and the *Sun Symbol* will be at work. Then it will rest in order to rise a third time. Our prophecy foretells that the third event will be the decisive one. Our Road Plan foretells the outcome.

"This sacred writing speaks the word of the Great Spirit. It could mean the mysterious *life seed:* two principles of tomorrow, indicating one, inside of which is two. The third and last, which will it bring forth, purification or destruction?

"This third event will depend upon the *Red Symbol,* which will take command, setting the four forces of nature *(Meha)* in motion for the benefit of the *Sun.* When he sets these forces in motion the whole world will shake and turn red and turn against the people who are hindering the Hopi cultural life. To all these people Purification Day will come.

"Humble people will run to him in search of a new world, and the people will cover the Earth like red ants. We must not go outside to watch. We must stay in our houses. He will come and gather the wicked people who are hindering the red people who were here first. He will be looking for someone whom he will recognize by *his way of life,* or by his *head* (the special Hopi haircut), or by the shape of his *village* and his *dwellings.* He is the only one who will purify us.

"The Purifier, commanded by the *Red Symbol,* with the help of the *Sun* and the *Meha,* will weed out the wicked who have disturbed the way of life of the Hopi, the true way of life on Earth. The wicked will be beheaded and will speak no more. This will be the **Purification** for all righteous people, the Earth, and all living things on the Earth. The ills of the Earth will be cured. Mother Earth will bloom again and all people will unite into peace and harmony for a long time to come."

There is little doubt that the flower symbol is related to the swastika symbol of Nazi Germany. While this symbol was not created until the Second World War, it nevertheless clearly indicates Germany as the precipitator of the First World War, out of which Hitler and the Nazis came. The Second War involves both Germany and Japan, whose sun symbol is on the upper right hand corner. Some Hopi have thought that both of these symbols are combined to make the one in the lower right area of the tablet, and believe the angled line signifies it will be the terminal war. But the symbol in the design is a star, and the line is probably part of the entire symbol itself. Have you looked at the flag of Red China lately? Compare its symbols to the Hopi design, and ask yourself whether or not China may be the designated instigator of the Third World War.

As stated earlier, Nostradamus establishes the date of the greatest conflict of all time, the war to end all wars, as July, 1999! Some of those who wonder who might be its instigator have settled upon Red China. She has emerged from slumbering isolation to attain a position of considerable influence in the world. In Hopi prophecy, the nation will come from the West. Her symbolic color is red. The news reports for August 17, 1995, say China was conducting on that date nuclear tests in the ocean. Even though the United States is committed to standing by Taiwan in case of any invasion, China has warned the United States to not officially recognize Taiwan's government. This year, China has conducted unarmed missile tests off the coast of Taiwan.

A Hong Kong source says that China has drawn up a strategy to capture Taiwan in case the Taiwanese president refuses to bow to Beijing. Industries that once planned to remain in Hong Kong when China takes over the British colony in 1997 have changed their minds, and now plan to leave as quickly as possible. China has advised them that she is sending in thousands of soldiers, a new supreme court, that she is changing the business rules, and that textbooks are being rewritten to eliminate an independent Taiwan and anything negative about China. That country has also accused ours of supporting Tibetan independence. It has become the armory for the non-aligned nations of the Third World; in 1993 alone China supplied Iran with twenty-billion dollars worth of conventional weapons and the means to build two nuclear reactors. Diplomats see China as becoming the primary defender of Arab and Islamic rights, and as having great influence over the distribution of oil. Its close relationship with North Korea and Viet Nam cannot be overlooked. China has a population so great its army can easily "fall like rain out of the sky" in an invasion of the United States. I've not heard much about China's air force, but it would be interesting to know what its size and capabilities are, and what plans exist for its future. I suspect they are impressive.

On August 28, 1995, columnist Richard Reeves wrote in the *Riverside Press Enterprise* that "if things go on as they have for the past couple of years" in India and Pakistan, there is "the possibility of a war on a scale the world has not seen for a long time, if ever." His scenario includes the use of nuclear weapons, and of China, Pakistan's weapons supplier, coming in on Pakistan's side with estimated casualties in the millions.

Despite the mass of seeming indictments against China, we cannot say with certainty that it will begin the final great war. But it deserves watching, and when we think in terms of the Hopi Fire Clan tablet, we are led more to China than to anyone else. As for China's favorable attitude regarding the Hopi that is suggested in the prophecies, we need to remember that the Chinese and Japanese think of Hopi and other Pueblo peoples as relatives who are similar in appearance and language. Pueblo Indians who have gone to Japan have found to their amazement that they can converse surprisingly well with the Japanese people without having had any training in their language.

As for some odds and ends in Katchongva's prophecy, the use of "milk" indicates a product that renews itself constantly. Some milky plants are also poisonous, indicating biological and chemical warfare. Regarding the connection between Sun and the Red power, in Hopi lore Sun is the Father of human beings. Hence the picture here is that of Sun disciplining his errant children. The four forces mentioned are fire, water, wind, and earth eruptions, which include both earthquakes and volcanoes. Therefore, these forces will herald and attend the great war, and will make its identity

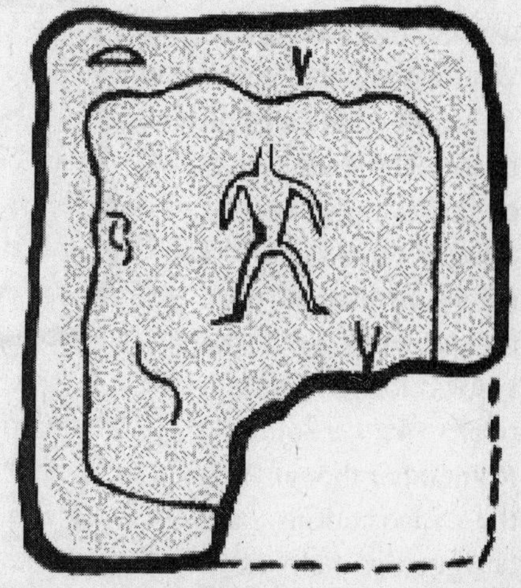

Back

inescapably clear. It is entirely possible that the four forces indicate changes in the environment and in human behavior that cause these powers to react in such ways that they themselves precipitate war.

The bow at the top of the back side of the tablet is the Fire Clan symbol. It identifies them as its caretaker. The line that begins at the bottom of the back side and encircles it is a time line. If the missing corner were in place, any symbols there would probably have to do with Maasaw and Hopi beginnings. As we move along the line, we pass an S-shaped line that symbolizes the meandering days before Bahanna intrusion. Next we pass the interlocking symbol that predicts the three people, or tribes, one of which is a White person or White people, who are supposed to help the Hopi. Then we come to a V-shape that symbolizes the split that took place in 1906. You will recall that another split was predicted, and the next V indicates it. Note that it is positioned to happen when the end is near. Since it has happened, and the Road Plan affirms that it would before the Third World War takes place, we can assume that in historical time the close of the cycle is not far off. By "not far off" I mean we cannot, even by following the instructions, push it back for centuries. Remember though, that the instructions are designed to help us to survive it.

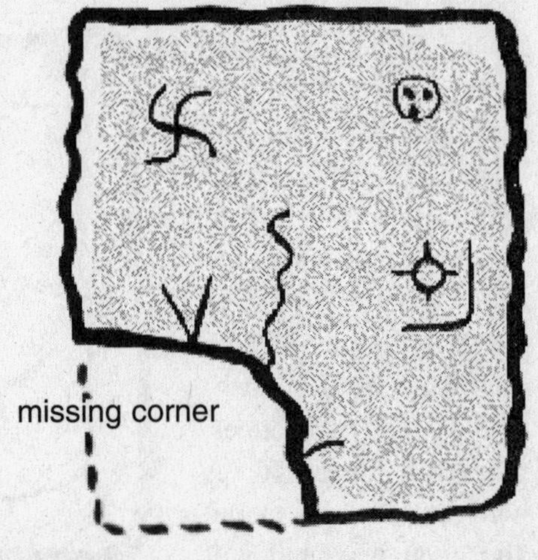

Front

On the front side of the tablet, those portions of symbols that remained after the corner was broken off indicate that the end will involve a great division of peoples and be chaotic. If you look at the upper horizontal line on the Road Plan, you will see that it ends in a line exactly like the one on the tablet. I repeat, a chaotic end of the Fourth Cycle must be assumed. Only when the White Brother returns with this missing corner of the tablet and fits it into place, will we know the exact details of the ending.

We should consider ourselves warned. Once we get aboard the Spiritual Ark, the Creator and Maasaw do not want us to leave it.

CHAPTER 11

The Twist in the Secret

We have seen that in recent years the Tribal Council has been exceedingly busy consolidating its gains, and that it has ambitious plans for the future. Since the perilous water situation could eclipse them too, they are anxious about that. They want the lucrative coal business, but hope the coal can be delivered to Nevada without its having to be floated there in Hopi life-blood. Yet they scorn the idea that the introduction of Bahanna life-ways into the villages diminishes the ancient power and energy created by the rituals, and especially that it has anything to do with the end of the Fourth Cycle. In other words, the Council is so wrapped up in material progress that it does not comprehend what is truly going on. In this way it is acting like the industrial giants that control the outside world. Little matters to them other than what they are pursuing. The rightness or wrongness of what they do to achieve their goals is not what matters. What they earn from their projects is what matters, all of which provides us with another instance of the Hotevilla microcosm to consider.

In cooperation with the U.S. Department of Health and Human Services, the Council has introduced into every village, except Hotevilla, HUD housing, asphalt streets, water lines, sewer lines, electrical lines, and telephones. The residents pay installation, maintenance, and service charges for these, and the paying is never easy. As Traditionalist elder Martin Gashweseoma has said, "Once the utilities go in, the Tribal Council owns you."

What does the prophecy say? "The time will come when one will pay, and one will not."

Despite their economic burdens, the people strive to be Hopi. This means they must do at least some of what Hopi have always done. All but two villages carry on to some extent the cycle of ceremonial life. It appears that there are still an unknown number of Traditionalists in every village, and particularly in Shongopavi on Second Mesa. But the Elders at Hotevilla do not know how many there are, or who they are. Positions are not declared. It is too personal a matter for that, although some indications can be seen in the kinds of lives individuals lead.

As a whole, the number of dances that are held in Hopi Land has been greatly reduced. But the major ceremonies are still held in each active village. For these rituals, every effort is made to be faithful to the ancient rules. If the present Office of Cultural Preservation has its way, you and I will not be able to see any of these ceremonies. What goes on there is already a mystery that the residents keep to themselves. Their excuse is that decades of Bahanna disrespect for Hopi customs has led every village except Hotevilla to close their public dances to outsiders. And, as you are learning, if the Tribal Council and Progressives have their way, Hotevilla is about to be closed too.

When matters of disrespect and theft are considered, it could be argued that the efforts of the Cultural Office to preserve the remnants of the ancient Hopi culture are something we should praise and support. Take, for example, their defense of the *Taalawtumsi* and other thefts. Anyone would agree that these are affairs that ought to be brought to public attention. Furthermore, I do not think they are insincere in what they are doing. But this only makes the problems they create all the more grievous. It exposes the fact that they are so removed from the ancient Pattern of Life and the Covenant that they do not understand what they are doing to Traditionalism. The Cultural Office continually says one thing and does another. If their positions have ever been valid, why have they not once received the praise and support of the Traditionalists?

Were I making these charges on my own, they would easily be refuted. But these have been the unwavering allegations made by the Elderly Elders and the other Traditionalists for two-thirds of a century. Historical evidence is solidly on the Traditionalists' side. And, the worst thing the successive Councils and their followers have done is to impede the Creator and Maasaw. By this they have delayed the proclamation of the great message, and they have upset the balance of the earth. Beyond this they have knowingly cooperated with the enemy in drawing children and young people away from the ancient faith. The cost of these negative acts is beyond calculation.

During this last hundred years, most of the beautiful mesa-top villages of Hopi Land have been abandoned. Magnificent Walpi Village sits like a forgotten golden eagle tethered by age alone to its lofty and precarious perch. Former inhabitants of the ancient villages have moved into drab HUD housing at the foot of the mesas, always close to where the main highway passes by. Some of the villages that did not need to relocate have retained their stone houses, and from a distance appear to be very old. A closer look will reveal that the architecture is of a mixed kind. Newer homes made of milled wood or concrete blocks have replaced deteriorating stone dwellings that do not lend themselves to modernization. It is not cost efficient or decorative to wire or plumb stone walls. Here and there you will find public schools, small markets, a couple of business buildings, traders stores, and a few timeworn mission churches whose membership numbers have for the most part remained static during this century.

Compared to the outside world, Hopi Land is still a private and a quiet place. Unless you are already a friend, or until your intentions are known, intrusion or sight-seeing is not welcomed. The villages follow ancient customs to different extents. They are close enough together to walk from one to the other, yet know surprisingly little about what is going on outside their own village. The Tribal Council speaks of the Hopi as a "tribe." And, it is working overtime in its attempt to pull the villages together so that the Council can function as their legitimate governing body. Perhaps the Council will achieve this. There is no reason why they shouldn't. The opposition is virtually gone. The Progressives stand high in the majority. And, modernization is the watchword. As a whole, the people are still proud to be Hopi, and even those who have turned completely away from the ancient life believe they are satisfactory representatives of the Hopi culture.

Hopi do have an artistic strength and ability that is remarkable. As of today, there are several outstanding painters and sculptors, over fifty renowned potters, and silversmiths whose innovations have changed and enhanced the direction of Indian art. There is a group called The Artists Hopid that perpetuates the best of Hopi cultural art, and there are several excellent young photographers. Carved and painted cottonwood Kachina dolls, so cherished by collectors, continue to provide a major source of income for many of the Hopi people. Bows, arrows, and rattles are made for commercial purposes. Excellent weaving is still produced, and Hotevilla is one of the main sources for this product. As a whole, the Hopi arts are technically and aesthetically better than at any previous time in Hopi history. This is good news for the Tribal Council with its taxation plans. But locking guests outside the Reservation might not be conducive to sales. Any artist can tell you that their inventory builds up impressively if customers aren't there to buy it. What the Council and Office wants to do is make itself the self-appointed agent for every artist. Once the Office has enacted its proposed regulations, and the Council's share of what is earned has been established, individuals who have paid for their written blessings will be able to come in. As Traditionalism fades, though, the artistry and charm will fade with it, and outside buyers may lose interest. For a time at least, the Hopi who work in towns will return home when major ceremonial activities are held. Ironically, it is the ceremonial life that came from Maasaw that has, until now, proven to be the most resilient, resistant, and stabilizing quality of Hopi life.

Despite some of the things I say in the passages ahead about the longevity of Hotevilla Village, it will retain its special mark on the time line of history. Present changes aside, this distinctive Shrine of the Covenant and Microcosm of the World has for a long time stood alone as the fortress of Traditionalism. It has remained more open to outsiders than any other village, while at the same time erecting around itself spiritual walls that have protected the hallowed Covenant. Residents who live here carry with them memories that are not borne by other villages, for no other village has suffered a split so shattering as that which took place at Oraibi in 1906, or the subsequent buffeting that Hotevilla has endured. Perhaps some residents surrendered recently to the Progressives only because they wanted an end to the alienation.

To this day, eighty-nine years after Hotevilla's founding, Dan makes futile gestures when the Oraibi division is discussed. His eyes water, he clasps his hands in his lap, and he grieves quietly. The pain has never gone entirely away. He knows that the Hostiles and the Friendlies did the only thing they could do, but still wishes it could have been different. Bitterness has clung to the hearts of people in both communities like cold, wet cloth, and for decades people who had once shared everything would have nothing to do with one another.

"Why," Dan asks plaintively, "do the Bahannas feel it is all right to separate and to hurt us like this? We do not do anything to them."

Deliberately creating disharmony is not the Hopi way, and Dan is glad that over the past few years the chill between Oraibi and Hotevilla has lessened somewhat. They talk with one another now, and have shared some of the protests made against the Tribal Council. A few relationships have been restored between the two villages. This includes a few intermarriages. Oraibi people often attend Hotevilla dances. For all of the reasons just given, the Hotevilla and Oraibi Elders feel better now. They have another factor to keep in mind. In a sense, Oraibi remains a mother village. The torn marker did not entirely erase that prophesied truth. She still has an important part to play as the fulfillment of prophecy takes place.

Except for Hotevilla, which by the end of August, 1995, will no longer be an exception, village independence, internal vitality, and spiritual energy have been radically reduced at Hopi Land. The pulse of former years is slowing down. Any physician looking for its strength to survive would have difficulty finding a place to measure it. It feels, the Elders of Hotevilla say, different to be at dances in the other villages. Although behavior patterns and the religious cycle appear to be intact, there is almost no facet of Hopi life that has not been grievously affected. An impressive number of ceremonies have been dropped. No one says anything about this. People just don't see certain rituals again. Others have been modified so that important parts are left out, or to fit Bahanna views. The leadership supply in each village has diminished by a significant degree. People mill around a lot more at meetings than they used to. The number of Elderly Elders who hold the precious knowledge of the ancients has, as the *September Song* puts it, dwindled down to "a precious few." Hopi Land's is a fragile situation being played out on the great stage of history, and with nothing more than an egg-like shell left to contain it. The shell could shatter at any moment. Then the world may shatter with it.

The Elders speak to us about these things:

> "Even if we abandon the Great Spirit's path, many of our people may remain on earth for a time. It is said that if the future generations, even our own sons and daughters, find out through books and records that we did nothing to preserve the good ways, they will pull and box our ears and even throw us from our houses into the streets. Our suffering will be of our own making. So we are making our best effort to keep what little we have left.
>
> "Some even mistake the prophecy that one day our children with short hair will become our ears and tongue. The original prophecy is meant to warn us that one day our own children may become our <u>enemies</u>. The meaning has been twisted to cover up the ways of the ones who have done that

very thing. Still there are many among the younger generation who have a true Hopi heart but are forced into a difficult position by the government's influence. We hope the story of Yukiuma will help them retrace their steps.

"Now, to people (the) world over: We have presented our case before you with clear minds of truth and honesty, as one of the last pillars for all Native people of the land, defending our aboriginal Native rights by struggling and resisting the total change of our ways of life. The aboriginal seed must not die in vain. . . ."

As a memorial to Yukiuma, a number of Hopi friends gathered one day in Hotevilla to hear a speech by David Monongye. You will find the full text in the *Hotevilla* book, but I include only a portion of it here:

"So you have come here to help. I hope and pray that your help will come. If you have a way to spread the truth, through the newspapers, radio, books, through meeting with powerful people, *tell the truth!* Tell them what you have seen here, what you have heard us say, what you have seen here with your own eyes. In this way, if we do fall, let it be said that we tried, right up to the end, to hold fast to the Path of Peace as we were originally instructed to do by the Great Spirit.

"And should you really succeed, we will all realize our mistakes of the past and return to the True Path, living in harmony as brothers and sisters, sharing our Mother, the Earth, with all other living things. In this way we could bring about a New World, a world led by the Great Spirit, and our Mother could provide plenty and happiness for us all.

"God bless you, each one. May the Great Spirit guide you

safely home and give you something important to do in this great work which lies ahead of us all."

Considering the unhappy situation the world is in, our need for *The Hopi Survival Kit* is an urgent one. Not long ago a noted Professor of Literature at a midwestern college used a portion of my *Fools Crow* book in an anthology he tacked together for publication. He introduced my material with a short paragraph in which he said it was "bad writing," and that I was too intrusive. Then he quoted fifteen pages from the book—fifteen entire and consecutive pages! It is the most I have ever had quoted in a single publication.

My telling you about the professor will get me to a point that needs to be made about survival. For a man in his position, his ignorance of what is involved in interviewing a Native American who speaks only limited English and requires a translator, is appalling.

For one thing, no direct translation can be made between Lakota and English, or for that matter, between Hopi and English. So the writer is forced to do interpretive writing. In other words, he has to put what the informant says in his own words, and in words that his English audience can understand. For another, if that Professor had ever been invited by some great holy man to do his biography, he would have learned on the first day they sat together that the information would not flow freely out of his informant. The informant might want to do a book, but he wouldn't have the remotest idea about what doing this entails. Informants are not faucets whose handles can be turned to obtain flowing lyrics. They could flow in Lakota or Hopi, but they would not flow in English, even through a capable translator. The writer is forced to ask questions and to make suggestions that will draw the informant out, else all he would get is a pamphlet, and not a book.

Any book done in cooperation with an aged Native American informant is as much the author as it is the person he interviews.

A writer is much more than a pen. That is true of John Niehardt's classic *Black Elk Speaks.* That is true of my work with Fools Crow, and it is true of my work with Dan Evehema. Never get the idea that what I wrote is precisely what they said or what they thought of. It is *approximately* what they said and thought, supplemented with my own thoughts and explanations, and when I read it back to them I modified it until they approved of it. It said about what they hoped it would. Both men believed that if a reader was sincerely reached by the books, God—*Wakan Tanka* in Lakota, *Talowa* in Hopi—would work in the heart of that person to bring everything needed to pass. That, and not they, was what was important.

If people have read the classic *Black Elk Speaks* and deluded themselves into thinking they have heard the real Black Elk, they have a substantial problem. Black Elk was Fools Crow's blood uncle, and the two of them spent a lot of time together. One day when I was with Fools Crow, I read a portion of the book to him. Before long he had a puzzled look on his face, and when I stopped, asked, "Who is that you are reading about?" When I told him, he shook his head back and forth in disbelief and said, "That is not my uncle, Black Elk."

Beyond this, the professor misses entirely the point of my books about Fools Crow and with Dan Evehema. Neither person is telling his story for personal gain or adulation. They deal with critical matters involving the world and its inhabitants, and with expressing the love and concern they have for their readers. Readers need to know that this is part of a pattern followed by the great ones among the Native Americans. They usually begin their prayers by praying for all of the people of the world. They always put others first. They feel a unity of spirit with everyone who exists that is marvelous to behold. And that is why so many people respond to them as warmly as they do—two-hearteds excepted.

You see, neither Dan or I were in the least concerned about creating a literary masterpiece in the *Hotevilla* book or here. We are intensely worried about the state of the world and where we are heading. Specifically, we are worried about you—about how you, and we naturally, are going to make it. And in my writing and my past days in the pulpit, I have found that it is tremendously important to focus everyone's attention on the core of an issue. In other words, to center in what truly matters. Jesus did not come to earth to prattle about the niceties of life. He came to rescue us. He didn't sit in the sun on the beach by the Sea of Galilee, he gave incisive sermons and he performed miracles there.

History is full of stories about people who fiddled while the building they were in burned around them. What the professor did was akin to this, or to a steward on the Titanic who wanted to make certain that proper English was being used on the ship menu while the ship was heading for the bottom of the ocean. Like so many people, he just doesn't get it. He should have been centering his classes upon what Fools Crow said, and not on the way it was said. As young people so commonly say today, the professor should "Get Real." I am not so upset about his criticisms of my writing as I am about his wasting time with things that, at this critical point in history, don't matter a hoot.

The leisurely days when we could do those things are over. The earth and its inhabitants are moving relentlessly into terrible trouble, and far too many of us haven't the sense to stop spinning daydreams while reality waits. Choices and priorities count for everything now. The Creator's message is an urgent one. That is what he needs to be telling his classes, and they ought to be upset with him when he does not do this. You remember, I'm sure, the Elders saying that if future generations find they have not prepared the way for them, they would box their ears. Cover yours professor! The truly agonizing thing is that there are thousands of others out there who are just like you—innocent, well-meaning, caught up in what you are pursuing, but lost in the blinding mist of "life as usual." If what the Elders have told us is correct, there is no time left for such indulgences.

Current information confirms this. However persuasive the moderates mentioned in Chapter 10 may be, the chances that what they suggest will accomplish our rescue are decidedly slim. During the past year, the world experienced the greatest population growth in its history, managing this in the face of laudable decreases in growth rates in places such as China. *The New York Times* reports that the earth's average surface temperature climbed to a record high last year, "bolstering scientists' sense that the burning of fossil fuels is warming the climate." Information also indicates that new global climate records will be reached before 2000. In an article by Anthony Lewis in the *Press Enterprise* edition of January 3, 1996, we learn about a letter from Vaclav Havel, Czech president, sent in October to an international environmental conference. He reports that he comes from a country where forests are dying, where rivers look like sewers and where, in places, it is sometimes recommended that the citizens not open their windows. He goes on to describe the barriers he encounters whenever he seeks to change this. His is a common problem. Lewis adds that "Republican radicals" in our congress have made it a priority to undo the environmental safeguards built up over the past years. In their present budget, the EPA appropriation has been cut back by nearly a fourth. He concludes by saying that "The environmental desolation created by the communist regimes is a warning for the whole of civilization today. . . . [We face] a challenge to defend ourselves against all those who despise the secrets of being, whether they be cynical business people pursuing nothing but the profits of their business or left-wing saviors who have succumbed to the drug of cheap ideological Utopias."

Maasaw knew a thousand years ago, and the Hopi Traditionalists tell us today, that the only thing that will save us is to achieve new attitudes by immersing ourselves in the Spiritual Ark which is the workroom of the Creator. **In this power-filled place we will blend with the land and celebrate life.** We will join with Mother Earth in its regeneration, while at the same time we transform the social ills of the world. Having been exposed to *The Hopi Survival Kit,* we know the secret now, and how it can be done. It is here that we find a one-ness, balance, and harmony that can override any of the negative things cited above, and which will see us through to a new cycle where we can rebuild the world as it ought to be.

The Creator continues in wondrous ways to push us toward this end. Not long ago there was a period when I wondered whether the *Hotevilla* book would ever see the light of day. Certain things that had happened caused me to believe there was a distinct possibility that it might gather dust on a lonely shelf in a darkened room while the world came tumbling down around it. Ironic as that seems, that could have happened, and in some ways it would be to a world that deserves it. As we learn from the newsletters, Dan and the other Elders often had moments of despair. They too wondered whether or not all they had done had come to nothing. Actually, such experiences are a good thing. They teach us an important lesson. Adversity like this tells us that we are onto something. If the damage we can do them didn't have them worried, the forces of evil would not be working so hard as they are to silence us.

The twists in Hopi history are a continuing part of the great play. Just when you assume you have the pattern figured out, you discover you are mistaken. When you think it is turning left, it turns right. As often as he is sacrificed, their Traditionalist Phoenix bird keeps rising from the ashes. But it takes awhile before we see that the Creator knows what he is doing. He is getting it done in the best way possible by making the best use of the situations that develop. Hotevilla has done the job Maasaw intended it to, and we can be grateful for that. But except for the handful of Elder and younger Traditionalists who still live there, the Shrine of the Covenant is close to being finished. My book title appears to praise the village and will give readers the idea that Shrines like Hotevilla never end. This is not true, yet the title is still not out of place. Hotevilla was created to be a ship carrying a precious cargo across the ocean, or to be like the mother who would carry her child until it could be born. Now the child has been delivered. In doing this she has, as many mothers do, put herself in jeopardy. By her sacrifice she has invited continual assaults, and they have finally worn her down. But the two-hearteds did not accomplish this until her job was done.

Though she may struggle on for awhile, Hotevilla Village is going to die both spiritually and materially. And this is how the dying will go: As the utilities are installed and put to use, every aspect of the energy of the village will begin to wane. In fact, the loss of spiritual energy has started already. People who attended the Home Going Dance this year felt it, and heard in what the residents on both sides of the issue were saying, plain indications of factionalism that is tearing the village apart. The decline will happen to Hotevilla in the same way it did to Oraibi after the Hostiles walked away on September 7, 1906. Likewise and in microcosm, the energy of the world will continue to wane too. Those who doubt this and would like an example of what happens should go and look again at the once proud and prospering Mother village, Oraibi. Most of it lies in ruins today, and it is a demise that took only a few years.

But, the secret has been kept alive. The Creator did it. Maasaw did it. The Traditionalists did it. And never in their wildest dreams did the Tribal Council and the Progressives in Hotevilla imagine that Dan could or he would. Sometimes people surprise us by making us look at common assumptions in a new way. One day when I was visiting with a pastor friend at his home in Montana, his young son burst into the room with tears streaming down his cheeks and said, "Daddy, doesn't the Bible tell us that when someone hits you, you are supposed to turn the other cheek? His father's face beamed as he patted his son on the back and proudly answered, "Yes, son, that is what the Bible says." Whereupon the boy testily replied, "Well, I keep hitting Billy, and he keeps hitting me back." I will spare the father by not telling you how exactly his face looked then, but it wasn't beaming.

This is what the Tribal Council and Office of Cultural Preservation have been doing to Dan Evehema. They have counted on their being able to hit him repeatedly in the belief that his peaceful nature would compel him to take it and never strike back. They picture him as a formerly useful but now resolute and stubborn old man who has outlived his time and no longer can influence anyone or anything of consequence. How wrong they are, and how little they know about the resolution of the real Keepers of the Covenant! The forces of evil think believers are really dumb. But neither Jesus nor Maasaw tell us to keep turning the other cheek, and we do not. Where the Covenant is concerned there is a limit, and that limit is reached when the Covenant itself is jeopardized. The two-hearteds should have known better, and they ought to reflect on this fact before they proceed with what they are planning. Even at this juncture, the whole affair will not go down nearly so easily as they think it will.

I see an entirely different picture of Dan. I see him triumphantly waving the newsletters. I see him walking out to the corn fields to sing to his crops. I see him trying to stop the utilities from going in. I see him standing there with Susie and Katherine and me, holding hands and swearing an oath of secrecy. Adding to that cherished memory are the prayer feather, the corn meal, the tobacco, and the ear of blue corn that sit by my side. The lump of coal is still here too, but it seems to be shrinking in size. The Tribal Council and the Office of Cultural Preservation is closing the door, but they haven't done it in time.

The last public letters Dan wrote to protest what was about to happen at Hotevilla were simply laughed off or ignored. But the two-hearteds will not be laughing for long, for the entire story and *The Survival Kit* have been preserved and are spreading around the globe. As the months pass, thousands of outsiders will come to know what has been going on at Hopi Land, and now at Hotevilla, former Shrine of the Covenant, but still Microcosm of the World.

Are any of you Tribal Council members or Office of Cultural Preservation employees reading this today? If you are, you might want to contemplate what is coming.

A steady stream of outsiders will join in to give the Traditionalists a hand. A writer who has already done an article referring to the Hopi situation for *Fate Magazine,* has vowed to pursue this situation to its end, and to enlist other writers in the cause. Mr. Jenkins made his usual mistake in telling the writer that he had no business being there on the Reservation and writing anything about the Hopi. A film on what has been and is being done to the Traditionalists is in the works, and will be on television soon. People with Internet facilities are waiting for materials they can use to pass the word to millions of subscribers the world over.

Obviously, the Tribal Council and the Office of Cultural Preservation, who think that the end of the existing Traditionalists will be the end of their problems, are due for a rude awakening. The revolution is underway. Because of what has happened to them, the newsletters reside in the category of suppressed information. But I would not be surprised if, upon listening to the Traditionalists and having their pride renewed, younger Hopi people who are Traditionalist at heart and want to be proud of their heritage, stand up and ask to be counted. Some of the greatest reversals in history have stemmed from moments just like this one. The prophecies do tell us about a revolution to come when Maasaw's instructions and warnings will be put into service all over the world. The Progressives will not like to hear this and will threaten in every way that they can. Despite the fact that they rejected it themselves while the Elders were writing it, they will tell us the outside world has no right to have this surpassing information. We will be delighted if they do take action, for it will give us the most wonderful excuse we could ask for to publicize and further expose the whole tawdry affair. As for the truth of the charges the Elders make against the Tribal Council and the Government, everything past and present is completely documented. And if any of it is false, we invite them to tell us what it is. And, why, we will ask, didn't they take the Elders to court when the charges were originally made?

While my picture has been colored somewhat by my exposure to true Hopi history, my love for the Hopi and Hopi Land remains. In light of what the Council and Office of Cultural Preservation has done to them, I do not blame the vast majority of the people for what they are doing, and I don't think the Hopi people are happy with what has resulted from some of their choices. There is ample evidence to support this assumption. If a wall is not yet erected, and you can still get in to Hopi Land, go there and look for the serenity that used to be. The only inner peace you will find in Hopi homes today rests in those of the True Traditionalists. Eventually, these dissatisfied Hopi might even decide that the time has come to reverse their position on voting, and go to the polls. Not to vote for individual Council members, but on whether they want a Tribal Council at all. Even aside from the Traditionalists, it appears that not everything is well in the villages. The July 21, 1995 issue of Hopi *Tutuveni,* the newspaper of the Hopi Tribe, reports a man from Mishongnovi as saying that "the Hopi Tribe lacks leadership and needs to revisit the Hopi Constitution, accept their responsibilities to the Hopi people and quit collecting their 'promises' in a sieve." This man also commented that there is a constant struggle and fight for the villages to receive the funds appropriated to them by the Hopi Tribe.

It may bother some readers that the majority of the Hopi have been won over to the Bahanna ways. Their question will be, "If the Traditionalists have failed to convince them, why should we accept and follow what the Elders say? Aren't the Hopi themselves in the best position to know which of the two sides holds water and is right?" But you have seen how Hopi history has gone. Brainwashed and dependent individuals are seldom in a position to make balanced judgments. Materialism is a great seducer, and those who have made it their god have seriously impaired their ability to recognize the truth.

Maasaw said he knew this would happen when he gave his instructions to the people who founded Oraibi. He told them he "saw evil in their hearts." What he meant was there was a potential for evil among them that would manifest itself when temptations came. In prophecy after prophecy it is predicted that the bad side of humanity will become so corrupted that the closing of the Fourth cycle will be necessary. Therefore, our real problem today would be if the situation were any different than it is. How could the Elders say that prophecy is being fulfilled if it isn't? The Hopi have shown their vulnerability to temptation. So have too many of the rest of us. Based upon the nature of man, the defections are as cast in stone as those of the stone tablets, which does not weaken the Elders' case. It strengthens it.

The transformation of Hopi Land only proves the vulnerability of human beings where convenience, consequence and responsibility are concerned. Having been saturated with examples of the Bahanna way of life, having been weaned through orchestrated education away from the simplicity of Maasaw, having been made dependent upon the Tribal Council and the Government for the income needed to sustain their present regard for material things, the Hopi have little choice left to them. Blinded by the dust of possessions that has been constantly thrown in their eyes, they have wandered into the quicksand of materialism. The prophecies have been fulfilled. And the irony of it all is that to keep from sinking entirely, they have only the few remaining gnarled old roots they have rejected to grab hold of and pull them out.

My warm feelings about other Hopi have not changed. They have played important roles in the stage play of life, and will continue to do so in the future. We don't know how exactly the story of the Hopi will read from now on in, but it is in no way closed. Hotevilla could still surprise us. The inner strength that marked them in earlier years cannot be entirely gone. Somewhere down inside them, something of the right stuff remains. Like a smoldering coal fanned by the breeze of hope, it could easily spring to life and come surging back to affect the pace, timing and intensity of prophetic fulfillment. Sometimes we must nearly lose something precious before we realize its actual worth.

I do think the Tribal Council ought to ask itself whether the Director of the Office of Cultural Preservation is an asset or becoming a millstone. For if they do not redirect or terminate his activities soon, the damage he will do to all of Hopi Land can never be repaired. Surely it is going to occur to someone on the Council that when the Whites (the Peabody Mine and exploratory companies excepted) are sufficiently offended, they are going to stop doing business with the Hopi. Is it not fair to ask which of us needs the other most? Having been converted to the materialistic way of life, are the Bahannas dependent upon the Hopi, or are the Hopi dependent upon the Bahannas? Outside of a few possibilities at the Agency or the Peabody Mine, I doubt that Bahannas are going to Hopi Land to look for work.

Earlier in the book, I make reference to a man named Titus Lamson, who made a bold stand against the Tribal Council when they attempted to fence his land. Since he was not able to walk during the last months of his life, a long-time Indonesian friend named Roy Steevensz carried Titus everywhere he needed to go. In gratitude for this favor and a friendship of several years, Titus gave Roy the right to use some of his land, and Rena Murillo, Titus' daughter, endorsed the gift. The sixty-year-old Roy settled down there, and, with the help of some White friends, planted corn and other crops this past spring. In June of 1995, the Tribal Police—called "rangers" now—together with men from the BIA, swept down upon this group and arrested them. They were jailed for twenty-four hours in the nearby town of Holbrook. A State of Arizona judge dismissed all charges and told the Indonesian he could return to his house on Titus's land.

Friends repaired the damage as best they could. According to a report I received, a few days later, the Tribal Rangers defied the court order and forced two of this group out of bed late one night. They searched them and their belongings, and told them to leave the Reservation immediately. Ms. Murillo and Mr. Steevensz say they are "followed and harassed by plain-clothes officers in northern Arizona, while others observe Titus's corn field with binoculars and telescopes. Police surveillance includes a spotlight on her home in Hotevilla."

In an August 7th news release in *Indian Country Today,* the causes cited for Council action are that "Mr. Steevensz was combining various religions to create a cult and advocated eating foods for health, such as seaweed, in an attempt to control people." Other accusations were that "he was acting strangely, basically starting his own religion." This is an unusual charge, since the Tribal Council has included in its membership Mormons and several Christian denominations who for decades, and with Council endorsement, have had mission churches on the Reservation. All of these depreciate the Hopi culture. It is true that Mr. Steevensz and other Whites have made a few threats to do things to stop the utilities invasion of Hotevilla, such as removing pipes or dismantling the water tower. Both Dan and I felt the threats were ill-advised. But the threats were never followed up, and weapons were never employed. Yet when the rangers arrived at Titus's farm with the exclusion order—signed by the Tribal Chairman, who is a Snake Priest at a Second Mesa village—they kicked in the door and handcuffed Mr. Steevensz at gunpoint. After they arrested Roy and his friends, they drove their vehicles back and forth over the newly planted cornfields until they were totally destroyed. Shades of the peaceful Hopi!

Muriel Scott, a recently appointed legal counsel for Hotevilla, said "the exclusion order was the first to be decreed by the Hopi

Tribal Court." And now we get to the core of the problem: "The issue," she said, "was he had been meddling in Hotevilla affairs for over two years. He was trying to get a meeting together to overthrow the tribal government." So, "he was excluded under tribal ordinance 46 which allows for removal of individuals who are a threat to the culture." Aren't the mission churches and the Government a threat to the culture?

The same newspaper, in its August 14th issue, reports that "Hopi rangers confiscated a tipi on the farm of the late Hopi priest and Kiva leader Titus Lamson and delivered a notice of trespassing to his daughter." Despite the fact that Titus and his family had owned and worked this farm since the 1920s, the patrol leader of the rangers declared that Ms. Murillo and all other persons on the land were in trespass and subject to arrest. "The area," he declared, "belongs to the Hopi Tribe. It was Titus Lamson's, and he is deceased. She is in trespass." In other words, despite the usual rights of inheritance that are common in America, the Tribal Council is indicating that it intends to seize the land of every Traditionalist Elder who dies. And, we can expect that an attempt will be made to do this with Dan's property when he goes.

The Tribal Council has no authority save that which they have appropriated for themselves. Even the cited ordinance is their own doing. But in their view and administration there are no longer any private rights at Hopi Land. Is anyone still wondering how it is that the two-hearteds have managed to overcome the Traditionalists?

The affair at Titus's house is getting outside news coverage, and a lot more is coming. Rena Murillo has obtained a Navajo woman attorney who has an excellent reputation and plans to carry the fight all the way to Washington, D.C. In their September 1st issue, the Tribal newspaper carried an extensive article about the situation. They call it the "Hotevilla Conflict," although it is mainly an indictment of Mr. Steevensz and a justification of what the Council is doing. The writer also describes the Oraibi split and Hotevilla's development. If you could read it, you would be amazed at the difference between her history and what the newsletters say. You would, in fact, wonder whether they are even talking about the same people.

Before the Home Going Dance was held at Hotevilla on July 29 of this year, articles appeared in Arizona newspapers requesting that, because of disrespect that had been shown at previous dances, White people not attend the dance. Then White people who either attended because they did not know about the article, or who attended in spite of it, or who were invited to it by Hopi Traditionalist friends, were greeted by Council-sponsored signs posted on village doors that said White visitors were not wanted, and should no longer attend dances at Hotevilla. My information is that approximately fifty Whites were in attendance in the afternoon, compared to several hundred in 1993.

When my son Ryan and I went to the Home Going Dance in 1993, the Traditionalists were still in charge. There were no "keep out" signs on the doors. Whites were welcomed, and if there was any disrespect I did not see it. The Kachinas even brought gifts to both of us. Mr. Jenkins was not present at that dance, but he was present at this recent one. With the number of Elderly Elders decreasing, and dozens of Council-employed or otherwise supported Progressives lodged in Hotevilla village, he is bold enough to go anywhere he pleases. A White friend of mine who was there reported that several of the younger people treated her rudely, and that the atmosphere was surprisingly tense. They also snapped at White people, were often hostile, and gave brusque orders as to where visitors should park their cars and stand to watch.

There was even a Hopi man wearing military fatigues who carried a rifle. Can you believe that—a Council guard dressed like that at a sacred dance and carrying a rifle in the stronghold of a people who have practiced peace for almost a thousand years? What was he going to do with it, I wonder? Would he have shot disrespectful Whites, and since Whites were not supposed to be there, was he present to shoot disrespectful Traditionalist Hopi? Mind you now, the Director of the Office of Cultural Preservation was present while this was going on, and surely knew it was happening. He probably arranged it. What Hopi tradition do you suppose he was teaching and preserving?

Considering all of this, it appears that if there is disrespect at future dances, it will be the Progressive Hopi who are showing it, and not the Whites.

The dance itself seemed to be done well enough, but there were twenty fewer Kachinas dancing than the seventy who danced in 1993. As usual, the older people were gracious and kind.

With the Hotevilla dances closed down, there will no longer be dances at which Whites will be welcomed. The feeling of universal love expressed by the Traditionalists at Hotevilla Village over the past century is gone. We can, of course, lament this for many reasons, but we must remember that from now on the dances will no longer be what they were. Perhaps there is no reason we should want to go to them until or unless the situation changes. When the Progressives have performed theirs without proper instructions and in splendid isolation for awhile, they might wish things were different, and want to change their minds.

Prophecy is right again. The second split has come to pass, and the evidences are everywhere to be seen. There is open friction at Hotevilla. Even without the utilities being installed, the spiritual energy of the village is already waning. Traditionalists were upset with Progressives—some from the Tribal Council—who without proper instruction joined in the dance. One elderly Traditionalist said that the wrong-colored feathers were worn on the masks.

Traditionalist parents say that they and their families are being taunted and otherwise harassed. On the other side, a Hopi woman said she "thought the elders are trying to flush out the Progressives until they show all of their cards, and then will kick the worst offenders out of the village." If there were enough Traditionalists left to do that, the utilities would not be put in. The report given at the dance was that the Tribal Council had announced that the utilities would be installed at Hotevilla at the end of August. The Traditionalists were trying to get enough people together to form a human barrier to prevent the installation, and were even preparing their children to join in.

When August 31 came, there was an interesting shift in tactics. The Council and Department of Health employees were at work at the north end of the village and no longer attempting to enter from the east side and water tower. Dan, Martin, and Emery, along with a few other Traditionalists, asked the Hopi workers to stop until after the Butterfly Dance was over, and a meeting with the Council representatives was held. A policeman who was at the site did stop the work, but it has resumed. The reason for the shift to the northern entrance was not explained to the Traditionalists. With the enormous budget cuts now being experienced by the BIA, it would be wonderful if there is not enough money available to complete the Hotevilla utilities project! That would give the Fourth Cycle of the world a whole new lease on life.

The most eloquent statement made at the Home Going Dance this year was issued by someone who was not present

at the public performance on July 29, 1995. To show his displeasure with what is going on, my co-author, Dan Evehema, did not attend. It was the first Home Going Dance he had missed in over a hundred years.

For his entire life Dan has been a central part of every Home Going Dance that has been held at Oraibi and Hotevilla. Nothing has been closer to his heart. It takes little imagination to share the anguish he experienced there at his little house. I have learned that he felt ill, and I don't know how he could have felt otherwise. Perhaps he spent some of the time out in his fields reliving in his mind and heart the history he has been an inseparable part of. Surely he contemplated, too, what he has done and what there is left to do. I can see him there sprinkling white corn meal on the earth and offering a prayer to Maasaw for the success of the dance, for Dan would want that, even though he would not be there.

Now though, the final gauntlet had to be flung. The gritty little root would not go down easily. While so many others capitulated, he could not, for any reason, pretend that all was well. He must, as he has promised Maasaw he would do, take a stand against what the Tribal Council, the BIA, and the Department of Health and Human Services are in the midst of doing to the Hopi and the entire world as they force the utilities into Hotevilla. Dan is echoing the words and the concern of Yukiuma who said he was taking his stand as much for us as he was for himself. As you will recall from Chapter 1, Yukiuma said that if he did not do this, the great water serpents at the poles would turn over, and cause such tidal waves that huge parts of the continents would be flooded with water.

Is it not fascinating that the film "Waterworld," which portrays the aftermath of a scene very much like this, has recently made its debut in theaters? The inundation shown in the movie comes from a melted ice cap, which you will find is also predicted in the Hopi prophecies. The film is probably not an accurate picture of how things will be if this actually does happen. Perhaps, though, the film hits closer to home in its message than anyone imagines or hopes it will. If even a fraction of it proves true, I wonder what it will do to all of those grand dreams industry has about the immediate future. Will we have to reinvent and rebuild Internet, cyberspace, and all of the rest? Where will the cities of the future be, and even the coastal cities of the present? Can you imagine what it would be like to be so preoccupied with a situation like this that the world would no longer waste time on things that would be of no comparable consequence!

Even if any of this happens, the INSTRUCTIONS will work, you know. The Spiritual Ark will still be afloat, just as Noah's ark was. One way or another, however, we are heading for a different kind of world the next time around.

On September 2 and 3, 1995, a Butterfly Dance was held at Hotevilla. As is usual for this particular dance, the performance was beautiful. The tablita headdresses the dancers wear are probably the most spectacular the Hopi make. But the Progressives and the Council members were out in force again and displaying the same sour attitudes they did at the Home Going Dance. Traditionalists said that they expected their dances would soon be closed to outsiders. The harassment has grown steadily worse, and a Traditionalist girl who was performing became ill, fainted, and was not able to finish the dance. Another Traditionalist girl was so afraid of what the Progressives would say or do to her that she became sick from it and refused to join in the dancing.

The wretched 1906 story is repeating itself. Hotevilla is being torn apart just as Oraibi was, and even to the point where curious, perhaps even supernatural, things are happening in the village. During the dance a woman wearing a full-length white robe and a white hood that shielded her face appeared suddenly on a roof top and stood there looking down on the performers for two hours before she quickly disappeared. In the middle of the night on Friday and Saturday, all of the dogs in the village barked so furiously that a visitor was awakened. On Saturday morning she asked her hosts what had caused the unusual barking. They told her that for the past several nights a mysterious woman had walked through the village. She didn't make a sound, and yet each time she appeared the dogs barked like this.

"She is warning the people," the hosts said.

"About what?" the visitor asked.

"About the terrible things that are going to happen to the village," they replied.

Having passed on the great and urgent message, when Dan laments the situation at Hotevilla today, it is mainly because he has found the Traditionalist life to be a wonderful one, and doesn't want it to end without as many people as possible having shared in it. To this end, he wants the Traditionalist chain to remain unbroken. Even if they lack the training he has had, others must step in to continue the work. The world must be kept in enough balance and harmony to give as many of us as is possible the opportunity to live the satisfying life Dan has known.

What are our chances really?

For survival? If we are willing to make immediate and drastic changes by following the INSTRUCTIONS, the chances are very good. For entirely avoiding the fulfillment of the worst of the prophecies, the chances are not so good. Our problem is that we keep playing Russian roulette with destiny, and we need to change our thoughts and actions toward one another and the planet in a decisive way. "Too lates" hold a prominent place among the great agonies of life. We are always getting ourselves into situations where we let the things we ought to do or say go to waste while we pursue something else that has fleeting rewards. During my years as an active pastor, the laments I heard most often at funerals were: "I wish we had spent more time together," or, "I wish I had told him I loved him," or, "I wish we hadn't spent so many days doing things that didn't matter a whit."

Maasaw's way, the Pattern of Life that he gives us, takes all of this into consideration. And, by following his instructions and his warnings, we—you and I—can slip so easily into becoming what deep down inside we really want to be, that we will hardly know it is happening until it already has.

In the meantime, it would not surprise me if Mr. Jenkins and his friends called for checkpoints to be set up at the Reservation borders. In his mind, he is placing imagined barriers there already. Hopi should consider this, and remember that the Berlin Wall was erected to keep people in, not out. The remarkable thing is that he is jousting with people who no longer have any reason to come to Hopi Land and contest with him. No one is astride his supposed opponent's horse. The scientists have gone to Africa and Middle America. Almost a century ago they learned and published virtually everything they wanted to know about the Hopi. It was wrong for them to do this without Hopi permission, and, because of the intimate details that were revealed, until recently, I had assumed they had. The books and articles are in libraries all over the world for anyone who wishes to see them. Of course, no outsider could perform the rituals anyway, because the intruders could not photograph or tape record what was going on in the Hopi mind. Artists still love to portray the Kachinas, but to my knowledge, outside of trying to decipher petroglyphs, no anthropologist has sought to delve into Hopi religious secrets for a long time. The Office of Cultural

Preservation is shutting out a ghost they have conjured up on their own, but the pay is good, better than that of any other job on the Reservation, so making the job seem necessary is a plus. The threatened Government budget cuts pose a problem. If, however, the tax program the Council is implementing can take over when Peabody peters out, the Council might be able to hang on for some time.

They might point to Dan and me as another example of the problems they face. But neither of us have ever plotted or attempted to overthrow the Tribal Council. Dan does believe that the Council is illegitimate and has rendered numerous disservices to the Hopi. On this basis he and the other Elders have often disagreed with the Council and its offices, and believe that by their own free choice the people should return rule to the Traditional leaders of each village, and have the Council serve them. In any event, that option appears to have become a moot point now. The Council dominates the scene, and the Elderly Elder Traditionalists are virtually gone. Not to worry though. In just a few more pages, you will see what it has all come down to, and you will be astonished by the twist it has taken.

As for other things the Council could charge either Dan or me with, there are no ritual secrets in what I am writing. Except for feelings and attitudes, there is not a word here about what goes on in a Kiva, and there is not a single photograph or drawing of religious paraphernalia. What Dan and I reveal has not been secret for some time, and was in fact published by Hopi in Hopi Land decades ago. Had it not been for the wanton conduct of the Tribal Council, the newsletters probably would not have been published then. Now though, everything is signed, documented, and attested to, and the most eminent of the living Elderly Elders, the epitome of the Traditionalist world and a high priest, is its co-author.

At this point in time, I cannot say exactly what course the play will follow at Hopi Land and Hotevilla. For the moment, having grown fat on Peabody Mine and other exploration money, and filling their pot even higher with Hopi taxes and permit fees, the Tribal Council and the Office of Cultural Preservation think they have succeeded to where they can lock up the Reservation and let in only those they wish to. Then no one, Hopi or outsider, will know what is going on there, and no Hopi will dare hold them to account.

But this very page is proof in itself that the horse is already out of the barn. It is too late to close the door. The Traditionalists already have a host of friends. And when other outsiders learn why the security measures are being installed, they will be clamoring to get in. That's the way human nature works. In fact, people who are reading this and believe in human rights are at this very moment saying to themselves, "Hm-m-m, we fight such restrictions of freedom in foreign countries and here at home. Why don't we just go and see what the Tribal Council and its police Rangers can really do to us up there at Hopi Land?"

So, the Tribal Council and Office of Cultural Preservation can if they wish proceed with the water and sewer pipes in Hotevilla. They can obtain the garbage trucks and for a monthly fee send them in to collect the trash. They can make Hopi and other people purchase permits to do everything, even ceremonial performances. We can appreciate that it will cost money to police the dances while they are going on, and someone will need to pay the individuals who are carrying rifles. The keep-out posters needed for the dances and the camping sites will be expensive too. The Council can tax every craftsperson on the Reservation. They can enact their rules and regulations, stifle every voice of dissent, set up their barriers, and confiscate Traditionalist properties. The Tribal Council can show the world what the people who have been peace incarnate until the Traditionalists were overrun have truly become under Council rule today.

Finally, the Council can bring in the tarred telephone poles and the drooping telephone lines that clash so openly with ancient stone buildings. Have they, I wonder, been to Zuni Pueblo to see how unsightly they look there? They had better pray though that as the trenches and post holes are dug the workers do not strike the hidden "object," for if they do, the worst imaginable curse will be fully let loose. The wrath of Maasaw is going to come thundering down upon the heads of everyone involved. Dan did not tell us where this object is buried. But if Council members do some thinking about it, I believe he has given them a clue. Even being as displeased with them as he is, I think he wants to spare them the awesome punishment I just mentioned.

Unfortunately, by microcosm there is more. Should it happen, the striking of the "object" will reach out to guarantee and to speed up a cataclysmic closing of the Fourth Cycle. No matter what anyone does of a positive nature, the worst of the prophecies that are yet to be fulfilled will be fulfilled. But the exact details of that coin are unknown. We can only focus on the known side.

What we know is that when Maasaw gave a small group of Hopi his Pattern of Life to follow, it included prophecies, instructions, warnings, the challenges of keeping the earth and the universe in balance, and the carrying of an incredibly important message to the world. The people covenanted with him to do as he asked. To commemorate this historic agreement, he then inscribed this Pattern of Life in symbols on small stone tablets that immediately became the most sacred objects possessed by the Hopi. The people also inscribed on a mesa wall His Road Plan to be followed. All of these, and particularly the Pathway Stone, were icons to be reviewed frequently as the years passed by.

From that time on we can picture the people as marching forward, walking a narrow beam into what would be their future—the leader in front with the tablet in his hands, and the people following. As they march, two-hearted forces attempt to draw or to force them away from their group and their promises. For a time, the Traditionalists resist, but the temptations are slyly presented and unrelenting. With every passing mile there are fewer loyalists left. Maasaw bows his head in sorrow. Finally, there is only a single unified group remaining. To his joy it becomes a stronghold standing firm in its commitment. Still, the Traditionalists decrease in number until, like the defenders at the Alamo in Texas, they are standing back to back to guard the tablet and to keep the vow they have honored for nine memorable centuries. When at last they are reduced to five or six who are very old, they seek without success to get the message out to the world, and begin to call for the White Brother to return to Hopi Land. They know that unless things change drastically, the time has come for the great Purification.

Today, the number of living Elderly Elders still holding fast to the Covenant vow has been reduced to three. Of these ,just one is able to carry on the required work. He is Dan Evehema. I shake my head in awe as I write this, for I find it hard to believe that the Creator led me to Covenant Land and to the last man in the line of servants that began at Oraibi so long ago.

There are a few older Traditionalists who can be counted on to adhere to the Covenant vow in the future, and no one should sell them short. The fact that I don't say more about them does not mean that they haven't been an integral part of what has been going on at Hotevilla. On the contrary they have been and are standing up to be counted, and as I have said, together with Dan and Susie met the Tribal Council and the Government employees when they came at the end of August to lay the utility pipes. As for the rest, it is just that I don't know them personally, or how many there actually are. But they include Martin Gashweseoma, Yukiuma's nephew; Emory Holmes and his wife, Mildred, who is Martin's daughter; Manuel Hoyungowa; Thomas Banyacya; Rena Murillo, and Dorman Kootsvayouma. There is evidence that more Traditionalists exist at Hotevilla and in other villages. Which of those will stand up and make their position known will not be clear until the continuing confrontations take place. In future writings, I will tell you what this microcosm at Hotevilla is doing, and what that portends.

But Dan Evehema will remain in a category by himself, for he fulfills perfectly a prophecy given by Dan Katchongva. This is what I was referring to in Chapter 1 when I said that a certain prophecy was aimed at Dan, and that a time came when Dan knew it, and knew that it was his responsibility to pass the secret on through me.

I have described Dan Evehema as irreplaceable, and said that when he moves on to join the Kachinas on the San Francisco Peaks the loss to everyone will be immense, especially to the Hopi, who will no longer have him as a resource. Whenever I think about the situation at Hotevilla, it has been good to know that he is still there to carry on the fight against the two-hearteds. Now he has a copy of the *Hotevilla* book in his hands, and knows that the urgent message and the story of Hotevilla has been preserved, and that it is being passed on to the world. Having accomplished this, and having lived a faithful life, he will have fulfilled his entire responsibility to Maasaw, the Creator, and his ancestors, and he can continue to live in peace.

When he has moved on, if I am ever again at a dance in Hotevilla, and the puffy white clouds are passing lazily overhead, I will look up at them and try to guess which cloud he is in. Then I will do what the masked Kachinas are doing while they are dancing, which is to now and then leave their bodies for a moment to carry up to the Kachinas in the clouds the prayers that are being generated in the plaza. This happens so quickly that none of the spectators see it. I will carry my prayers of thanksgiving up to the cloud that I think Dan is in. If he is not in the cloud I select, whatever spirit is there will pass it on to him when all of the Kachinas have returned home. And Dan's spirit will smile, just as I will be smiling here.

What a godsend it is that we came together to do the Hotevilla book when we did! That first trip to his house was no accident. As I said previously, if we had waited until now, the book could not be done.

Before he moved on to the San Francisco Peaks in February of 1972, Dan Katchongva told some of his life story, which included this poignant memory: "I have lived to journey to Washington, D.C. at least two times, and to the 'house of glass,' and on all occasions I found eyes and ears closed. Mouths were too tight to let out anything positive. I have lived to see and ride on the 'road in the sky,' the 'moving house of iron,' and the horseless carriage. I was fortunate enough to speak to many people through the 'cobwebs,' and through space as well, as our old leaders had predicted, to reach people with my message. I have lived to wear, and wear out, many pieces of white man's clothing, and eat many of his fine foods. I am getting old and will pass on someday. It makes me sad to think I may not get to meet our True White Brother in person, but it is prophesied that just two or three righteous persons will be plenty to fulfill his mission. *Even one truly righteous would be able to do it.*"

This is another prophecy fulfilled. The carriers of the vow have not fallen short in any way. From its inception at Oraibi, the Keeping of the Covenant was scheduled to expire in conjunction with the closing of the Fourth Cycle of the world. Although the play may have followed a somewhat different course than the Creator preferred, what he intended to happen has happened. Dan stands at the crest of a promise that is both fearsome and filled with joy. Lonely as he may be there at the edge of the mesa and looking up at the invisible Creator, he knows in his heart exactly what he has become, and he is ready to move on to the San Francisco Peaks where the great Kachinas dwell.

Dan Evehema is that "one truly righteous" person Dan Katchongva wrote about. He is the last Elderly Elder gladiator in an unbroken line that has, like a relay team, passed the Pathway Stone on for nine consecutive centuries. Over this course of time, it has become a full-blown and amazing story.

On this very day, whenever you read this, he is finishing his own century-long run and knocking at your door. And when you come to see who it is, he will hold out to you in wrinkled mahogany-colored hands *the wonderful secret*. It is his gift to you, so that in the days ahead you can prepare and safeguard yourself and those you love. When you take it from him and put it to work you will help the whole world survive. As soon as possible, be sure to pass on to others what you have learned. I could use some jubilant music in the background now to accompany what I am about to say: Forces of evil, two-hearteds, be damned. Through Dan Evehema, the Traditionalists have run their course and turned over to us the great challenge and responsibility for fulfilling the way everything will turn out.

The Creator and Maasaw would not be doing this if they didn't believe we can do it. They make good choices. They entrusted the Hopi at Oraibi with the great message, and the Traditionalists did not fail them. With this in mind, those of us who board the Spiritual Ark can turn *our Survival Kit* into works of radiant magic, works that come alive to do for all of us and for the earth what Maasaw promised they would when he gave his prophecies, instructions and warnings to the Hopi 895 or more years ago. The remaining Traditionalists will help us. How exciting then it is to know that the Creator and he were thinking of us way back there at Oraibi, and that his plans included turning some of us Bahanna usurpers into survivors who will enhance the survival of the world!

Some final thoughts from the Elderly Elders: "Don't let the burden of worries trouble you into sickness," the Elderly Elders say. "Let your hearts be filled with happiness, enjoy your lives to the fullest, for this is the best medicine for sickness. Live long, for there are great and exciting adventures awaiting you. So time passes on, and the prophecies handed down by our ancient people begin to unfold. Many great events lie before us, and we are witnessing with astonishment today the fact that our ancients' words were right.

"Often we are sad and discouraged that our voices are not being heard,we try not to grieve, instead we gather strength from the teaching we learned: that we must neither lose sight of our prayers or the Divine Laws of our Creator, Laws which never change or break down, that often bring miracles when one meets obstacles which seem impossible to pass. For better or worse we must struggle on until our prophecies are fulfilled.

"The wisdom accumulated by anyone who is willing to stand up and be counted is respected. Anyone with a strong spirit and strength who is unafraid of reaching our goal of destiny, which is for the good of the earth and all life, can understand the tasks involved, and can count on support from others. There is a saying, 'If one or two be strong, three or four will be greater under the banner of the Great Creator.'"

This entire struggle is a miracle! Hotevilla Village itself is a miracle! It even started out that way. When the Hostiles left

Oraibi in 1906, they took a handful of sand from the major wash that fed Oraibi fields. That wash never ran again. But when they put the sand in a wash near Hotevilla Village that had never run before, the water came into it and nourished their crops every year. Depending on how the word "miracle" is defined, many have taken place in the lives of the Traditionalists as they have struggled over this past century to keep their vows. In fact, one of profound significance is taking place at this very moment. You will recall that the Hopi Traditionalists made, as they were directed to, four trips to the "House of Mica"—the United Nations Headquarters in New York City. They did this in an effort to share with the delegates the Creator-given prophetic message of warning, peace and harmony. Since little came of these attempts, the Traditionalists concluded that the missions were a failure, and wondered why they were told to do something that appeared to be useless.

But we have seen that the Creator accomplishes his purposes in marvelous ways. As I write these closing lines, it is wonderful to report to you that the United Nations connection is proving itself after all. I mentioned in Chapter 1 how fortunate it was that John Weber of Marlowe & Company became our publisher. This serendipitous gift continues to bear fruit. In October of 1995, he attended a book convention in Frankfurt, Germany, where he showed an unbound copy of the *Hotevilla* book to a publicist he works with in the European market. She was so excited about it that she immediately took it to UNESCO representatives. They were equally enthusiastic, and offered to underwrite its immediate translation into French. From this French edition translations can be made into the other languages of the world. Thus the prophecies, instructions and warnings will soon be available everywhere.

Although it often happens in the most unexpected of ways,

consider now how faithfully the promises of the Creator are worked out. However saddened the Hopi Elders were when nothing of consequence materialized at the United Nations, they nevertheless were led to preserve the message in the newsletters, whose copies were subsequently kept for this propitious time when they could be set forth in our books. It is entirely possible that someone in UNESCO who saw the book in Frankfurt remembered the Hopi and their visits to the United Nations headquarters, recognizing this as an opportunity to do even more than the Covenant keepers originally hoped for. Our gratitude to them is endless, and Dan Evehema was overjoyed when he learned what UNESCO is doing.

In this surprising development it is implicit that the rest of the teachings received at Oraibi will one way or another be fulfilled also, and it is important to remember that this very day you can become one of those who will unite in this transforming miracle. The water of purification and survival can run in your life in a way it has never run before.

It is time now for the formation of a global family that is blending with the land and celebrating life, for people who will be environmentalists by nature, and a universal family by choice.

When you take up the banner of the Creator and board the Spiritual Ark, you are going to blend in a wonderful way. By expressing your new feelings toward others, Earth Mother, and the rest of creation, you are about to develop a new attitude that will bring superb things to pass. In dealing with life in general on the Ark, and with specific life in the instance of plants and other created things, you will be living each day in the midst of a transformation that will assure survival. Everything will be softer, quieter, and more gentle. Peace and beauty will be your guiding stars. When this feeling reaches Mother Earth, she will quiet down too, and all of us can rest easier while we prepare for the future.

For example, the point in developing a new attitude toward your plants is not only beneficial in terms of what it does for the plant, it is beneficial in what it does for you and for others. What you send out in every instance comes back to you a thousand-fold. Changing what you think about yourself will change the whole of you. Other people will see and feel this, and it will stimulate and change them. The Elderly Elders' attitude promotes this kind of ripple effect. It fills you up, overflows, and then ripples out to touch and change the rest of the world. The direction of the Great Play will be influenced, the prophecies will soften, and the severity of the ending will be reduced. The pace will slow, and the intensity will be diminished. Even the form will change. Every threat will be pushed back, so that we will have the time we need to shape the closing down of this cycle, and to determine how the next cycle will begin.

You will have noted that on some years the Hopi ceremonial cycle begins with the initiation of family and friends who are ready to come on board. These are individuals who will join you in the carrying-out of the ceremonial and subsistence cycles. When you have achieved your own place in the Spiritual Ark, it is time to initiate others, to welcome them into the Ark, and then to teach them what you have learned. Begin with your own children. Then reach out to others. Do the initiation on the day of the winter solstice, December 21. What will the initiation consist in? Well, you won't try to duplicate what the Hopi do. You should make it your own personal moment, and keep it simple. Tell the initiates about the Hopi Elders and the ongoing Traditionalists, and then tell them your own story of how you emerged from an underworld of what you were and into a whole new opportunity for life. Add that you did this at this critical time when the world is edging closer to the closing of its Fourth Cycle. Then tell them everything you can about the Spiritual Ark, and what you are doing as you live there. End with a prayer for one-ness, for hope, and of thanksgiving.

Perhaps the greatest pity in all of this is what the two-hearteds and Government have cost everyone in the world where the carrying out of the Covenant is concerned. As the instance with Yukiuma shows us, the delivery of the secret could have been made earlier, and could have helped the world avoid most of the consequences it suffers today. Yukiuma knew this when we observed him in his jail cell, but he also knew it would be a waste of time to try to tell the Colonel and the Agent the secret.They needed to know it. Everyone needed to know it. But they just weren't listening. Can you imagine how painful if was for the Hopi to live with that knowledge? Perhaps, though, this painfulness is a common experience for the Creator's servants. We recall that the beginning was difficult for Maasaw, too. Yet you have seen in the case of Hotevilla that the vessel destined to carry the great message has completed its voyage. Its crew has been pounded. Its sails are in shreds. There are hundreds of holes in its sides. But it is afloat and tied up at the dock. Hotevilla has done its job. It has brought its cargo to us, and placed it in our hands. Of the different ways that might have been, this is the way it has worked out. **For while those Traditionalists who remain still have their assignments, the task of saving ourselves and the earth has been for the most part turned over to us, and we have been given the tools to do it.**

Contrary to what I thought when I started to write the Hotevilla book, the Creator and Maasaw never intended that the Hopi should do it all for us. One way or another, the secret was to be delivered into our hands. And it was not good news that said everything is fine, so relax and go on about your business. It said everything is not fine, so we have to finish the job. Rationalizing the whys and wherefores of this truth is one thing. The greater question is, now that the ball is in our hands, what are WE going to do with it?

Let me be clear in what I am saying about Hotevilla as the Shrine of the Covenant. I see now that its role was always compassed by a time frame. And, the length of that frame was at best a hundred years. Contrary to my wish and to what the Traditionalists once thought, their work was never intended to go on "forever." Even then, the Pattern of Life followed by the Traditionalists probably lengthened the period for awhile. My guess is that the fire that extended the term was rekindled the day the first issue of *Techqua Ikachi* was published. That bought Hotevilla another twenty years. But as it will with the Fourth Cycle, the moment of closing down has still come to the village. I just didn't see this coming at first. I don't think the Traditionalists saw it either. They assumed the natural thing, and believed that because right was on their side, they would win the struggle. They have won it, but not the way they thought they would. The way it had to be was always on the stone. From the beginning, Maasaw knew that the time would come when the Traditionalist Hopi will have done their job, and needed to turn the rest of what has to be done over to us.

"For years," the Elderly Elders say, "our founding fathers have passed the knowledge of survival from mouth to mouth, which is to respect all living things, for we are all one and created by One. It seems like now people have forgotten this concept of the right way of survival. They have replaced it with defensive tactics, and as a result are always running behind. They are racing steadily downhill to ruins. We mean that all nations on

earth are doing this. People must skid to a stop and look around. There might be an old dried-up root visible near you; get hold of it for support until you see the light."

There was a brief time when I dreamed that for years to come I could go alone, or with family or friends, to visit my Traditionalist companions up on the Reservation. I lived in the mental romance of now and then walking across the mesas and down the quiet streets of the ancient villages, where I could stop to rest and to live again in memory the history of this splendid people. There is so much there that cannot be experienced anywhere else. Perhaps you are having such dreams too. But until things change drastically, this will not happen. We are being shut out.

Here again, the Creator and Maasaw foresaw this complication. In their kindness they provided us with this survival kit. Along with the other things it will accomplish, it is our way to have something of this experience within the privacy of our own lives. As we follow the INSTRUCTIONS we will feel the connection. The spirits of Dan and the others will come to be with us and urge us on. The Tribal Council can slam the doors to Hopi Land. But no one can ever take these jewels of understanding away from us.

Katchongva twice points out that the fulfillment of the prophecies has given the Traditionalists strength. Their fulfillment tells the Hopi that they follow a reliable path. The Creator has done, is doing, and will do what he has promised. They have not been wrong or wasted their time. That is the good news that keeps the bad news in its proper place.

Something else needs to be said here about good news, and I do this now so that you will not forget it. The prophecies and warnings are sobering things to consider. And if they are not kept in proper perspective might leave us wondering whether there is any point in trying to change things now.

We see in the lives of the indomitable Elderly Elders that there is always a reason to continue on and to do battle. They knew the odds were against them, but they have never given up. No one understands the forces of evil better than they do. So they speak from experience when they tell us how we can, by following the INSTRUCTIONS and WARNINGS, alter the pace, intensity, and force of the closing of the Fourth Cycle. They show us in the lives they have led how we can, by our actions, purchase the time we need to work and the time we need to play. They also tell us about the happiness in their lives and how they want the good things to continue. They share with us the thought that it is disheartening to even imagine the enjoyable things of life might end. The citizens of most countries still enjoy friendships, music, art, literature, nature, good food, travel, recreation, sports and more. It is, therefore, very important for us to understand that the INSTRUCTIONS and WARNINGS are not only a way to solve our problems, they are ways the Creator Himself has given us to continue to experience these cherished things. As we work with the surviving Traditionalist Hopi to keep ourselves and the planet in balance and harmony, we will assure ourselves that the good things will remain with us. Even while the Fourth Cycle closes down in the tumultuous way that is predicted, and even while segments of the world self-destruct, we will have with us the ingredients for serenity, and good things to balance the bad. As Hopi prophecy indicates, no one can plot the exact course of the future. But the Creator and Maasaw promised that if we follow their instructions it will work out acceptably, and their word is sufficient for all of us.

ADDENDA

Copies of *Hotevilla, Hopi Shrine of the Covenant, Microcosm of the World,* co-authored by Thomas E. Mails and Dan Evenhema, can be obtained from your local bookstore, or from the publisher: Marlowe & Company, 632 Broadway, 7th Floor, New York, NY 10012 Telephone: 1-800-788-3123, credit cards are accepted.

Hotevilla Village will continue to be a microcosm of the world, and the remaining Traditionalists will continue to do their part in keeping the world in balance. Readers who wish to keep in touch with what is happening at the village and who want further guidance in putting *The Hopi Survival Kit* to work in their daily lives, can write to the author in care of:

The Pathways Foundation, 30491 Longhorn Drive, Canyon Lake, CA, 92587. The telephone number is 909-244-2737, but please be aware that Mr. Mails has a busy schedule. Social calls are not encouraged.

A global network of individuals who are boarding *The Hopi Spiritual Ark* is forming. To assist in this, Mr. Mails is completing a workbook entitled *Blending with the Land and Celebrating Life.* It is a detailed and illustrated manual that will assist those who are looking for an analysis of the prophecies and what to expect, a simplified schedule to follow, specific survival information needed to prepare for personal situations, and help in preparing for natural or man-made disasters. The workbook is intended for individual or group use and discussion, and will be available either in the Fall of 1996 or the Spring of 1997.

The Traditionalist Hopi desperately need our help. Their letter that follows will tell you how you can do this. It is a way you can thank them personally for what they have given you:

How You Can Help

- Prayer

To cover expenses for removing all intrusions in Hotvela created by the Hopi Tribal Council we need:

- Legal funds to pay for lawyers, court costs and technical experts
- Legal and technical assistance and research
- Telephone bills, xeroxing bills or lease or xerox machine
- Travel expenses and gas to attend meetings, court hearings
- Trailers for an office

We have a 501 (c) (3) through Don't Waste Arizona, Inc. Please send TAX DEDUCTIBLE contributions for our Legal Fund to:

Stephen M. Brittle, President
Don't Waste Arizona, Inc.
6205 S. 12th Street
Phoenix, AZ 85040
Phone # 602/268-6110

Please put in memo portion of check: for Caretakers of Hotvela in Hopi Legal Fund